Baedeker's

ALGARVE

D1392492

Hints for using the Guide

Following the tradition established by Karl Baedeker in 1846, buildings, places of natural beauty and sights of particular interest are distinguished by one ★ or two ★★ stars.

To make it easier to locate the various places listed in the Sights from A to Z section of the guide, their coordinates on the large map included with the guide are shown in red at the head of each entry.

Coloured strips down the outside edge of the right-hand pages are an aid to finding the different sections of the guide. Blue indicates the introductory material, red the descriptions of sights, and yellow the practical information at the end of the book.

Only a selection of hotels and restaurants can be given: no reflection is implied, therefore, on establishments not included.

In a time of rapid change it is difficult to ensure that all the information given is entirely accurate and up to date, and the possibility of error can never be entirely eliminated. Although the publishers can accept no responsibility for inaccuracies and omissions, they are always grateful for corrections and suggestions for improvement.

Preface

This guide to the Algarve is one of the new generation of Baedeker guides. These guides, illustrated throughout in colour, are designed to meet the needs of the modern traveller. They are quick and easy to consult, with the principal places of interest described in alphabetical order, and the information is presented in a format that is both attractive and easy to follow.

This guide covers the Portuguese coastal region of the Algarve as well as interesting places in the hinterland, i.e. the historical province of the Algarve which is today identical with the district of Faro. The guide is in three parts. The first part presents a general survey of the Algarve,

its topography, climate, flora and fauna, population, economy, history, culture and famous people who have played a part in its history. A selection of quotations leads on to the second part, in which, after some suggested itineraries, the individual sights and features of interest are described. The third part contains a variety of practical information. Both the Sights and the Practical Information sections are in alphabetical order.

Idyllic spots in the hinterland of the Algarve coast: Monchique and Alcoutim on the Guadiana

Baedeker guides are noted for their concentration on essentials and their convenience of use. They contain numerous colour illustrations and specially drawn plans, and at the end of the book is a fold-out map, making it easy to locate the various places described in the Sights from A to Z section with the help of the coordinates given at the head of each entry.

Contents

Baedeker Specials

The Faces of

Azulejos
on the Palácio de Estói

Extensive slopes clad with cork groves, fig and carob trees, yellow-flowered mimosa, lush almond and peach orchards, meadows red with poppies, and everywhere the trilling of cicadas and the sweet fragrance of orange blossom – spring in the Algarve must surely be one of the loveliest things of which those wearied by winter in less favoured climes might dream. But it isn't just in spring that the Algarve proves itself one of Europe's most-popular holiday destinations. With 3,000 hours of sunshine a year this delightful region, famous for its enticing beaches and sandy bays encircled by picturesque rocks, attracts visitors throughout the year.

In recent decades, though, the people of the Algarve have had to confront the all too obvious disadvantages such blessings of nature can bring. All along the coast tourist centres have sprung up to accommodate visitors hungry for the sun. In many places development has run riot.

But amazingly, only a few kilometres from the ugly concrete dormitories, another magic survives, scarcely receiving a mention in travel brochures. Even today along the coast there are long sandy beaches and idyllic coves with not a soul in sight. And a completely different Algarve lies waiting to be discovered in the hinterland, a peaceful, undulating, garden-like countryside, a world away from the glitzy hustle and bustle of the seaside resorts.

Rock landscape
Impressive coastal scenery near Lagos

Serra de Monchique
Woodland scenery in the hinterland

the Algarve

As well as beaches and a frequently still-enchanting rural atmosphere, the Algarve has delightful little towns, each with its own unique character – beautiful Tavira, its hipped-roofed houses reflected in its waters; the royal frontier town of Vila Real de Santo António, laid out with elegant symmetry on the banks of the Rio Guadiana; Olhão with its sugar-cube houses and whimsical atmosphere; the cosmopolitan Faro, happily preserving its charming historic centre; the old Arab capital Silves; Lagos, city of noble past and agreeable present; and last but not least, the cluster of houses at Sagres, seeing which it is hard to believe that, in the 15th and 16th c., this south-westerly tip of continental Europe was the hub of epoch-making events when Portuguese seafarers traversed the oceans on ambitious voyages and colonised new continents. Virtually every one of these little towns grew out of ancient settlements. Phoenicians, Celtiberians, Romans and Arabs all appreciated the Algarve's fortunate location, and left behind traces of their highly developed cultures.

And finally a word about the people. The Portuguese are renowned for their friendliness and warmth of welcome. They accept with good grace the unending foreign invasion, treating each individual tourist with traditional courtesy. Holidaying in the Algarve guarantees not just a sunny climate, but a stay among people of sunny disposition too!

Ceramic chimney pot
– *symbol of the Algarve*

Fishermen in Olhão
There is always time for a chat

Albufeira
One of the largest tourist centres of the Algarve

Nature, Culture History

Facts and Figures

General

The Algarve, the most southerly of Portugal's 11 historic provinces, extends east–west between latitudes 36°58' and 37°35'N and longitudes 7°25' and 9°30'W. It thus lies in the extreme south-west corner of the Iberian peninsula and of Europe.

Area

At 4,960 sq km, the historic Algarve region, identical with the Faro district of today, represents less than one twentieth of Portugal's total land area. In shape it is a trapezium, about 135 km wide, stretching from the Atlantic in the west to the Rio Guadiana forming the frontier with Spain in the east. The distance from the southern coast to the northern border with the Alentejo is 27 km at the narrowest point and over 50 km at the widest.

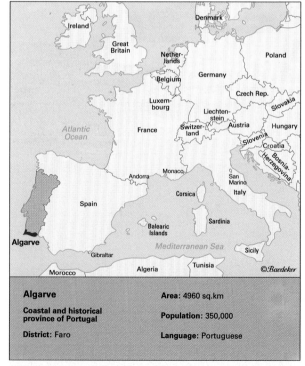

Algarve	Area: 4960 sq.km
Coastal and historical province of Portugal	Population: 350,000
District: Faro	Language: Portuguese

◄ *The picturesque fishing village of Ferragudo, near Portimão*

Its situation, isolated and exposed in the far south-west corner of the Continent, has had a determining influence on the Algarve's history. For centuries it enjoyed close links with North Africa. Friendly trade relations, an influx of North African peoples into this part of Europe, and periods of occupation by one side or the other, have left an indelible mark on the cultural identity of the region. The ambitious ocean voyages of discovery and conquest by the Portuguese in later times, in which the western Algarve in particular played a crucial role, were born of the area's harsh economic realities. Even the Algarve's present popularity with tourists is due chiefly to its geographical location and the mild, already North African, climate.

Importance

The name Algarve goes back to the time of Moorish rule. The Algarve was then part of the emirate of Córdoba and, lying on the very western edge of their empire, was called by the Arabs Al-Gharb (the West). Under the Portuguese this became O Algarve, *o* being the Portuguese masculine article "the".

Name

The boundaries of the historic Algarve coincide with those of the administrative district of Faro today, of which the town of Faro is the chief administrative and regional centre. The district (*distrito*) is further divided into 16 sub-districts or councils (*concelhos*) and 77 parishes (*freguesias*).

Administrative divisions

Topography

The Algarve is bounded on three sides by water: in the west and south by the Atlantic and in the east by the Rio Guadiana which forms the border with Spain. To the north it is sheltered by two substantial mountain ranges, the Serra de Monchique (north-west) and the Serra do Caldeirão (north and north-east). The region can loosely be divided into three: a narrow coastal strip (*litoral*), the foothills (*baroccal*) and the sparsely inhabited mountains (*serra*). Some parts of the former two areas have been highly developed for tourism, while most of the latter lies off the tourist track.

The landscape of the Algarve is exceedingly varied, something the ordinary travel brochure scarcely hints at. Even the coastline shows tremendous variation, with steep rocky shores contrasting with flat, sandy beaches. North of the coastal strip a swift transition occurs to the more hilly hinterland, which in winter and spring in particular is clothed in green and ablaze with flowers. In the central and eastern sections stretches a gentle, fertile horticultural landscape with plantations of almond, fig and olive trees. Westwards, as the influence of the Atlantic makes itself increasingly felt, the hinterland becomes more and more barren until, in the very far west, scrub and Mediterranean-type *macchia* take over the landscape. The mountains are dominated by forests of eucalyptus, chestnut and holm oak, while higher up hardy cistus shrubs are to be seen almost everywhere.

A submerged mountain range, a continuation of the coastal mountains, exerts a critical influence on mainland Portugal. Just 65 km south of the Algarve coastline the sea floor plummets to depths of about 4,000 m, while 250 km or so south-west lies the Gorgine Bank, a submarine ridge the height of which varies as much as 5,000 m. Here, under the Atlantic Ocean, the Eurasian and African continental plates collide, causing frequent tectonic movement. The Gorgine Bank was the epicentre of the catastrophic earthquake which struck the Algarve coast in 1755 wreaking dreadful havoc.

Tectonic movement

Among its many attractions the Algarve boasts one very special geographical feature, the spectacular, legendary Cabo de São Vicente, the

Cabo de São Vicente

Topography

Impressive rock and caves along the coast near Lagos

extreme south-westerly point of the European mainland where the Continent ends in a rock plateau some 60 m high, dropping abruptly into the Atlantic.

West coast/
Costa Vicentina

The Costa Vicentina, taking its name from Cabo de São Vicente, extends north of the cape and eastwards nearly as far as Lagos. The whole west coast northwards of the cape comprises rugged cliffs rising to heights of 150 m above the sea and interspersed with large and small sandy bays. Along this stretch of coastline the waves come rolling in with all the force of the Atlantic, pounding against the rocks and breaking into surf on the beaches in the bays. Conditions are generally similar, though somewhat ameliorated, along the southern part of the Costa Vicentina, east of Cabo de São Vicente. Beyond Lagos the might of the Atlantic perceptibly diminishes, with the consequence that many of the more-sheltered bays harbour picturesque villages and small coastal towns.

In 1988 a 90 km stretch of coastline on the Costa Vicentina, extending northwards far into the Alentejo, became a conservation area, the Parque Natural do Sudoeste Alentejo e Costa Vicentina. One of the most unspoilt coastal regions in Europe, the 74,788 ha Parque provides an important habitat for a range of flora and fauna of a kind otherwise found in only one or two places in the world, including some 200 species of bird. Many migratory birds, some very rare, also find an excellent breeding ground here. Additionally some 60 per cent of Portugal's reptiles and 65 per cent of its amphibians are found in the Costa Vicentina area. Over a hundred species of fish have been identified in the waters of the Costa Vicentina.

Rocky Algarve

The western section of the southern coast of the Algarve, extending from Cabo de São Vicente eastwards almost to Faro, is known as the Rocky Algarve or Barlavento (the windward side). Here are steep cliffs and sandy coves interspersed with longer sandy beaches dotted with picturesque rocky outcrops. Countless caves, solitary stacks and intriguing rock formations give this region its scenic charm.

The eastern section of the coast, the Sandy Algarve or Sotavento (lee side), extends roughly from Vale do Lobo, west of Faro, to the Guadiana estuary. Much less exposed to the Atlantic than further west, it comprises on the one hand long stretches of wide sandy beaches and on the other an extensive network of lagoons. Reminiscent of tidal shallows, the large lagoon system to the west and east of Faro is protected by low, elongated island dunes lying close offshore.

Sandy Algarve

The Parque Natural da Ria Formosa, which incorporates the lagoon to the west and east of Faro, covers a total area of about 18,400 ha, roughly 4,000 ha of which are saline, with little channels and watercourses, salt pans, shellfish beds and fish ponds. The lagoon is separated from the sea by a chain of islands some 60 km long, stretching from Praia de Faro to Manta Rota west of Tavira, and broken in places by shallow natural, and in one or two cases artificial, channels such as those connecting Tavira, Faro and Olhão with the Atlantic. Continuous deposition of sediments means that, in the course of time, the lagoon is becoming increasingly closed off, its natural outlets to the sea gradually silting up or shifting eastwards. With only a small influx of freshwater from the hinterland and continual replenishment by the tides, the saline content of the lagoon is very high. The combination of relatively warm shallow water, soft clay bottom, and high salt and oxygen content produced by the regular exchange of water, creates an extraordinary habitat for an immensely rich and varied fauna and flora. The Ria Formosa was made a conservation area in 1987.

Parque Natural da Ria Formosa

The mountains of the northern Algarve form a protective barrier separating the region from central Portugal and keeping at bay any incursions of cold air from the north. In consequence the foothills and southern coast enjoy climatic conditions that are already distinctly North African. The extensive Serra do Caldeirão rises to 589 m. The highest summits though, Fóia (902 m) and Picota (773 m), are both in the Serra de Monchique. The most-common rocks are argillaceous slate and sandstone, the latter widely used as a building stone in the Algarve. In the Serra de Monchique there are hot springs of volcanic origin, exploited for, among other things, therapeutic purposes. Numerous small rivers rise in the mountains of the Algarve hinterland, flowing southwards towards the coast. Replenished by rain in winter and spring, they only just ensure sufficient water supply. Towards the end of the 1950s several reservoirs were constructed in the foothills.

Serra

The Rio Guadiana (from the Arabic *Uadi-Ana*, Ana's river), forming the eastern border with neighbouring Andalusia, is the Algarve's principal river. Some 830 km long, it rises in the La Mancha region of Spain. Navigable in Roman times to beyond Mértola, only the lowest 48 km between Pomarão and Vila Real de Santo António are navigable today and then only by small vessels. Here the river is anything from 100 to 500 m wide with an average depth of barely 5 m.

Guadiana

Climate

The Algarve boasts one of the most dependable climates in the world, with some 3,000 hours of sunshine a year. Protected by the mountains from the influence of cool northern air, conditions on the

Climate

Spring in the Algarve hinterland

coast are similar to those on the coast of North Africa. High sunshine values are complemented by a warm, dry Mediterranean-type regime on which the Atlantic exerts a moderating effect, producing pleasant mild temperatures even in winter.

Temperatures

The warmest months are June, July, August and September. During this period the mean daily temperature climbs to 28°C, but with an ever-present light sea breeze it is not unbearably hot. In winter on the other hand it is never really cold, temperatures rarely dropping below 10°C, an exception being Cabo de São Vicente where values are the lowest in the Iberian peninsula (6.2°C).

Nevertheless holidaymakers should pack something warm to wear. The breeze can give a fresh feel to even the warmest summer evening, and with winters never very cold, rooms often have no heating, so it can be distinctly cool indoors at this time of year.

Water temperatures

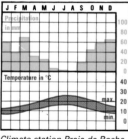

Climate station Praia da Rocha

Atlantic sea temperatures are generally below those in the Mediterranean; in summer the water heats up to about 22°C, dropping in winter to only 15°C. Sea temperatures along the western Algarve tend to be somewhat lower than further east where the influence of the Atlantic becomes progressively weaker and that of the Mediterranean begins to make itself felt.

Rainfall averages range between 350 and 600 mm a year, being generally higher in the mountains of the hinterland than on the coast. November as a rule is the wettest month. In recent years, however, rainfall has been considerably below average, leading to acute water shortages.

Nature

Flora

Plant lovers should visit the Algarve in early spring. Even as early as December the brown, sunburnt landscape is beginning to turn green again. Then in January and February the almond trees are the first to burst into blossom.

The Algarve hinterland, the Serra de Monchique in particular, harbours a huge variety of species, but on the undeveloped stretches of coast too there are many different kinds of plants to be discovered. Of special interest here are the Ria Formosa and Costa Vicentina conservation areas. Across this whole region an unusually varied flora and fauna has been able not only to develop but also sustain itself, relatively undisturbed, in a succession of extensive interconnecting areas.

Additionally, many exotic plants from different parts of the world thrive in the Algarve. The age of discovery in the 15th and 16th c. saw many species of plant brought back from overseas, since when they have taken root and spread. For centuries even before that, plants were brought to southern Portugal from all over the Mediterranean by the Romans and Moors.

The gnarled, slow-growing olive is a common sight in the Algarve, as throughout the Mediterranean region. Brought to Portugal by the Moors, olive trees can live as long as 2,000 years. Known to have been cultivated since the earliest times, the olive was considered a symbol of wealth. The tree comes into blossom in May and June. For the fruit to ripen a long dry summer is needed; the maturing olives change colour from green to black. The harvest begins in November and continues until March. Presses are used to extract the oil.

Olive

Also a familiar feature in the Algarve landscape is the carob tree, which for some time growers have been attempting to cultivate systematically. The region's high sunshine values make for ideal conditions. The carob tree develops large brown pods which are very nourishing and make good animal fodder.

Carob

Strawberry trees, another common species in the Algarve, often seen growing on the roadside, are a kind of erica. Only 2–3 m tall, they have leathery leaves. They take their name from their fruit, which looks a bit like a strawberry and from which *medronho*, a clear schnapps with a high alcohol content, is made.

Strawberry tree

Orange trees are special in that they blossom and bear fruit simultaneously. Blossom time is between February and June, in which months too the fruit starts to grow. The small white flowers emit an incredibly aromatic fragrance, which in the right weather conditions wafts across the whole of the eastern Algarve where most of the orange groves are found.

Orange

Lemon trees are less often cultivated in plantations than orange trees are. They have larger leaves than the orange tree, and their blossom is slightly pink at the tips.

Lemon

The fig tree is distinguished by its attractively shaped leaves with their

Fig

five symmetrical "fingers". The green or dark mauve fruits with a soft pulpy inside are produced in spring and autumn.

Pomegranate

The thorny pomegranate tree is a native of the eastern Mediterranean. It bears red blossom between May and September. Pomegranates have a very hard, leathery skin enclosing a mass of seeds, each in a fruit-like casing. Because of its numerous seeds the pomegranate is a symbol of fertility.

Japanese medlar

The Japanese medlar was introduced to Portugal about 200 years ago. The cherry-size yellow fruit (*nêsperas*) with large brown stones is sold in every market.

Cork oak

The cork oak plays an important role in the Portuguese economy, Portugal being the world's largest cork producer. Cork trees develop a layer of dead cells around the trunk as a way of reducing water loss and counteracting fluctuations of temperature. This layer of cork, approximately 3 cm thick, can be peeled off for processing. The tree must be 20 years old before cork stripping begins. The cork layer grows back and stripping can be repeated every six years on average.

Holm-oak

Like the cork oak the holm-oak is also an evergreen. It can be recognised by its dark green leathery leaves with whitish felt-like undersides. Holm-oaks are still sometimes found growing in large stands. When solitary they can form very lush crowns.

Eucalyptus

In Portugal the eucalyptus, frequently seen in the more mountainous areas, encounters an ecosystem very different from that in which it thrives in its native Australia. Able with its long roots to extract water from great depths, this newcomer is a significant factor in the devasta-

The mimosa ...   *... and jacaranda in blossom*

The Legend of the Almond Blossom

Try and imagine the Algarve without almonds. No snow-white sea of blossom in January or February. No fallen petals whirling in the breeze. On the markets no almonds for sale. No sweet, no salted, no roasted, no burnt almonds. And to crown it all, no marzipan delicacies.

Yet at one time the Algarve was just such a place, hardly an almond to be seen. That was before a certain Arab emir fell in love with a Swedish girl called Gilda. She packed her belongings and came to him in the warm sunshine of the Al-Gharb, where they married and should have been happy ever after — so at least a fairy story would claim.

But something depressed the Swedish girl even in the first winter. In the second winter too she was silent and withdrawn. And in the third she became very sad, staring for hours at the castle's luxuriant green surroundings and never uttering a word. The emir was at his wits' end. Head in hands, he pondered long and hard. Every passer-by was asked for advice. At last he took his wife's maid into his confidence. She of course had known all along what the trouble was. Her young Swedish mistress, she said, was simply homesick, her longing for northern climes worsening by the year; it scarcely bore thinking about how things would be the following winter.

The love-torn emir at first despaired but quickly showed himself a man of resource. Another day and night spent brooding – and then inspiration. Sparing no trouble and no expense he had thousands of almond trees brought secretly from his homeland to the Al-Gharb. Ship after ship arrived and unloaded the little *Prunus amygdalus* trees. They were planted in next to no time without the unhappy Gilda noticing as she was much too busy feeling homesick for her homeland.

Almond blossom comes early in the Algarve

So it was a complete surprise when, the following year, the many thousands of almond trees bloomed and the emir, taking his young bride by the hand, led her onto the castle wall from where they gazed out over an endless expanse of white almond blossom. "Look: the snow of the Al-Gharb!" said the proud and generous-hearted emir. And the astonished girl? She is said to have been made truly happy by the sight of the snow-white blossom and the wilting petals drifting gently down.

tion of large parts of the Portuguese countryside. Growing extraordinarily quickly and requiring substantial quantities of moisture, its systematic cultivation for the paper industry has caused great tracts of land to dry out. Even after the trees are felled it takes about 60 years for an area made desert by the eucalyptus to recover its ecological balance.

Judas tree

In gardens or on verges Judas trees are often seen, their branches clad in April with pretty pink blossom; only afterwards do the distinctive, heart-shaped leaves form. Later in the year the trees can be recognised by their long pods. Judas is said to have hanged himself on one such tree.

Mimosa

The *Acacia dealbata*, widely known as mimosa (➤ picture, p. 16), is also very attractive, blossoming into a myriad yellow bobbles in February and March. It has unusual, very fine, pinnate leaves that curl up when touched.

Jacaranda

From May to early July the jacaranda or palisander tree is covered in wonderful violet-blue blossom, only a very few leaves forming thus in early spring. The Portuguese often plant jacarandas by the roadside or in car parks.

Umbrella pine

The distinctly decorative umbrella pine is noted for its widely spreading crown. It grows in small pine groves or more often standing alone, when its luxuriant umbrella top offers welcome shade. The large cones contain edible seeds tasting like hazelnuts.

Araucaria

The araucaria or Norfolk Island pine comes from New Caledonia. In Portugal it is often planted in parks. It is immediately recognisable by its distinctive shape, its brush-like needles growing in echelons one on top of the other.

Canary date palm

Native to the Canary Islands from where it has spread throughout the Mediterranean, the Canary date palm is one of the most-common palms seen in the Algarve. It can be recognised by its small orange-yellow fruit (non-edible) hanging in long clusters between the palm fronds.

Agave

While today it is almost impossible to imagine Portugal or the Mediterranean countries without the agave, it was only brought to Europe from America at the time of the voyages of discovery. Agaves produce a distinctive flower cluster on a tall stalk growing as high as a tree. After flowering the leaves die off, but the root survives to generate again.

Cistus

Cistuses are among the more-common shrubs found in the Algarve. At higher altitudes these low bushes form a sea of yellowy-white flowers from the end of March to June. The petals look slightly crumpled and the leaves have a sticky appearance.

Fauna

While uncontrolled development has caused widespread destruction of coastal habitats, the still relatively unaffected *serra* and nature reserves ensure the survival of many different species of wildlife, some quite rare.

Birds

Particularly in the more sheltered parts, herons, ospreys, snipe, oyster-catchers, kingfishers and plovers are seen. Storks come right into the towns to find nesting sites. The marshland near Castro Marim is renowned for its many flamingos. The woodlands are home to the azure-winged magpie, and orchards to the rufous warbler. The cliffs provide breeding places for rollers and bee-eaters.

Of the 200,000 species of butterfly identified worldwide, some 1,600 are found in Portugal. Only about 300 of these inhabit the Algarve, among them the emperor moth, egger moth, death's head hawkmoth, red admiral, hummingbird moth, swallowtail, large blue and brimstone. Conditions on the whole tend to be inimical to butterflies: many parts of the region are densely populated and the more sheltered areas are near the sea where the vegetation is generally unsuitable. Though an abundance of species are found further north, few butterflies succeed in crossing the barrier formed by the mountains of the Alentejo and northern Algarve.

Butterflies

Domestic species account for most of the mammals found in the Algarve, donkeys, goats and sheep being the most common. A few animals do survive in the wild, almost all of them in the mountains (wild boar, deer, foxes).

Mammals

Lizards are very prolific and can often be seen sitting on walls basking in the sun. They disappear as quick as lightning when they sense movement around them. Moorish geckos have suction pads on the ends of their strange toes, enabling them to scale smooth vertical walls. In sheltered parts there are chameleons, which protect themselves from predators by changing the colour of their skin to blend in with the light and background conditions. There are also snakes in the Algarve, some of them poisonous.

Reptiles

Some parts of the Algarve coast support a greater variety of molluscs than others, the sandy beaches of the eastern section being poorly endowed compared with the chalky cliffs and rock strewn beaches further west, which offer a wider range of habitats. The most common shells are venus and razor shells, mussels, cockles, oysters and murexes.

Shells

Environment

Tourism, with its far-reaching consequences, bush and forest fires every year, and a worsening water shortage seriously threaten the Algarve today.

In recent years the expected rainfall has failed to materialise even in winter and spring, so that throughout the Algarve as well as in the Alentejo adjoining to the north, an acute shortage of water is evident. Already by spring the water level in the reservoirs falls substantially. During the summer and autumn months a dearth of water is noticeable throughout the plant world. The cultivation of eucalyptus for the paper industry exacerbates the problem because the eucalyptus, introduced from Australia, draws great quantities of moisture from deep down in the ground. Since this is one of the most profitable branches of the Portuguese economy, the country faces an acute dilemma.

Lack of water

In tourist centres the water shortage is not yet too apparent: the fountains continue to bubble, the many golf course greens are kept copiously watered, and supplies to holiday accommodation are guaranteed. For many months of the year, however, the local population lives in daily expectation of interruptions to their supply.

Throughout the summer and autumn months every part of Portugal has a risk of woodland or forest fires, often burning completely out of control. The foothill region of the Algarve's Serra de Monchique is particularly prone. In addition to the general dryness due to lack of rainfall, and

Forest fires

the fire risk posed by refuse burning, monoculture, especially of eucalyptus and pine, is a further factor in the increased incidence of fires.
European Union subsidies encourage these forms of reafforestation at
the expense of mixed woodland. Often whole areas are set alight deliberately, clearing the ground for eucalyptus plantations. Some fires burn
for several weeks. Firefighting planes, most of them brought in from
Spain, are used to try and stem the flames, water being drawn, in the
case of this particular region, from the broad Rio Arade estuary. Because
this is very salty, the land remains uncultivatable for many years afterwards. It is normally about two years before any shrubs take root following a fire – trees take even longer.

Tourism

Tourism and its effects represent a massive problem for the Algarve.
Over 50 years ago the *litoral* was still largely undeveloped. Then great
sections of the coastline were built on, destroying the habitats of countless plant and animal species and transforming the landscape almost
overnight.
 The annual invasion of holidaymakers puts an enormous seasonal
strain on the environment. In the peak season, refuse, sewage and water
consumption soar and traffic is swollen by great numbers of rental cars.
In 1986 this prompted publication of a National Plan for the Development of Tourism which, though mainly concerned with promoting the
tourist industry, also lays down guidelines for environmental and nature
conservation.

Environmental
awareness

For a long time environmental awareness in Portugal remained at a low
level. Large areas of the country were or appeared unspoilt, and there was
little to prompt public concern. Tourism among other things has changed
all that, demonstrating clearly the perils of taking the environment for
granted. Portugal's entry into the EU in 1986 was also a turning point: suddenly funds were available for industrial development and road building,
while at the same time a series of EU environmental directives came into
force. In 1987 a legal framework for the protection of the environment was
introduced, the first in Portuguese history. This was followed in 1989 by the
creation of a Department for the Environment, and in 1990 of a full
Ministry. The Portuguese media, however, are as reticent as ever in report-
ing environmental problems and scandals. The task of raising public
awareness thus falls mainly on independent environmental protection
agencies, the best known and most powerful of which are Amigos da Terra,
APEA (Associação Portuguesa dos Engenheiros do Ambiente), GEOTA
(Grupo de Estudos de Ordenamento do Território e Ambiente), QUERCUS
("oak" – Associação Nacional de Conservação da Natureza) and the LPN
(Liga para a Protecção da Natureza), the latter already founded in 1948. In
the Quinta de Marim near Olhão a nature conservation centre has been set
up bringing schoolchildren face to face with environmental issues.

Conservation
areas

A total of 16 areas of various sizes have been declared nature reserves,
of which the Costa Vicentina in the west, the lagoons of the Ria Formosa
west and east of Faro, the banks of the Guadiana north of Castro Marim,
the marshland south of Castro Marim and the banks of the Rio Arade
north of Portimão are the largest. Then there are the Ponta da Piedade
near Lagos, the lagoons in the estuary of several rivers at Alvor, parts of
the Serra de Monchique, the Rocha da Pena mountains between Alte
and Salir, one or two places with hot springs in the hinterland, and the
dunes near Monte Gordo.

Society

Population

Portugal has a population of some 10 million. Of these roughly 350,000
live in the Algarve, which in area comprises about one twentieth of the

Albufeira: the Portuguese find time to relax

country; by comparison, more than 2 million live in Greater Lisbon. The average density in the Algarve is 70 per sq km (excluding the tourist influx in the summer months). The most sparsely populated regions (fewer than 20 inhabitants per sq km) are in the north-eastern Algarve between Salir and Alcoutim, in the west between Aljezur and Vila do Bispo and in the mountains east of Monchique. In contrast the entire coast east of Luz (near Lagos) is very densely populated (more than 100 inhabitants per sq km) with the exception of pockets west of Faro and east of Tavira.

The Algarve is experiencing a population explosion, reversing past trends when the only places in Portugal deemed attractive for living and working were Lisbon and the industrial area of Setúbal. The population of the *serra* has dropped steadily since 1930. On the coast there was a notable influx about 1940; thereafter numbers fell, only rising again after 1960.

Language

The official language is Portuguese. There are no recognised dialects, though the Portuguese spoken in the Algarve does differ slightly in pronunciation. Algarvios tend to colour their vowels a little differently and swallow their end syllables more than is the case elsewhere. In Portuguese generally, a relatively large number of Arab words have been preserved, and these can be recognised in some Algarve place-names. Almost all words beginning with "al-" are of Arab origin, including, of course, the word Algarve itself; also names of towns and villages such as Albufeira, Aljezur, Almansil, Alvor, Alcantarilha and Algoz, and words like *almoço* (lunch) and *almofada* (pillow).

Religion

More than 95 per cent of Portuguese are Roman Catholic, the other 5 per cent being Protestant, Muslim or Jewish. Constitutionally there is no

21

established church in Portugal and no tithes are levied. The extent to which Catholicism is practised varies widely in different parts of the country; in the Algarve observance is limited in comparison with further north. But even in the Algarve, feast days in honour of the local patron saint are major events in the calendar. Here, as throughout Portugal, celebrations are noticeably more in the style of folk festivals. Though generally commencing with mass and a procession, they soon dissolve into very worldly forms of entertainment – dancing, folk music, eating and drinking. A well-known and popular pilgrimage or *romaria*, attracting people from far and wide, takes place annually, two weeks after Easter, in Loulé. The patron saint's statue is carried in procession through the steep streets, after which there is a mammoth folk festival.

Education

Since 1974 great emphasis has been placed on providing a sound basic education nationwide. Throughout the period of Salazar's dictatorship, illiteracy remained quite high (in 1970, 29 per cent of all Portuguese over the age of 15 were unable to read or write). By 1994 the figure, though down, was still 13 per cent, including a large proportion of older men and women. Even now signatures are often made with a thumb mark.

Compulsory schooling in Portugal lasts nine years from the year in which the child reaches the age of six. There is then the option of a further three years secondary education in a comprehensive school augmented by a range of additional courses. Students now have the opportunity to go to university in the Algarve, at Faro.

Family structure

In recent years the Algarve has witnessed accelerating disintegration of the old family-based social structure that, until not so long ago, saw large families of several generations living together under one roof. Now young men and women become independent much earlier, thanks largely to tourism and the job opportunities it brings. There is an increasing number of small families. Women often have to shoulder the responsibility for housework as well as a career, and in this respect, as elsewhere in the world, the equal-rights movement appears no stronger in Portugal today than before.

Social problems

Within Portugal the Algarve is a special case, deriving its income chiefly from tourism. The growth of tourism brought about a general restructuring. Large numbers of people live and work on the coast, while rural areas, especially the remote mountain regions, are deserted or have very ageing populations. In such places poverty and unemployment are widespread. The poorest part of the Algarve is the Alcoutim district in the north-east.

Tourism has also resulted in a two-tier population with disparate standards of living. Many younger people find work in one or the other branch of the tourist industry, achieving a degree of prosperity as a result. Meanwhile older Algarvios, or those in traditional occupations such as farming and fishing, have seen their already low standard of living reduced even further. In this respect the Algarve is not alone, the same phenomenon becoming increasingly apparent throughout Portugal. A younger generation with good urban jobs enjoy standards of living comparable with those in central or western Europe; in contrast, older rural folk in particular often exist below subsistence level.

Political system

When in 1974 Portugal's dictatorship was swept away in the Carnation Revolution, a socialist constitution was introduced under which the country became a republic and a parliamentary democracy. In 1982 the constitution was amended, watering down the more radical socialist measures; in 1990 legislation restoring private ownership came into force, removing them completely. The head of state is the president, who is elected for a five-year term. A new parliament is elected every four years. The president appoints the prime minister, guided by the polls.

The two largest parties are the Partido Social Democrático (PSD),
founded in 1974, and the Partido Socialista (PS). In spite of its name the
PSD is broadly liberal-conservative in outlook. The PS, founded in 1973
by Mário Soares while in exile in Germany, is social-democratic. Among
the more influential smaller parties are the Partido Popular (PP), which
developed from the Christian-Democratic CDS, and the Partido
Comunista Português (PCP), founded in 1921 following the Russian
October Revolution and later banned by Salazar. The abbreviation CDU
sometimes seen blazoned on walls stands for a communist coalition.
The Green Party (Os Verdes or Partido Verde), established in 1982, is pol-
itically marginal, as is the Partido Popular Monárquico (PPM) which,
while also green, favours restoration of the monarchy.

There is no regional daily paper published in the Algarve. As elsewhere
in Portugal, people read the *Diário de Notícias* or the *Público*. Popular
weekly publications are the *Visão*, the *Expresso* and the *Independente*.
Portuguese television currently has four channels: the state RTP 1 and
RTP 2, the private company SIC and the religious channel TVI. The state
radio station is the RDP.

Economy

Tourism is the mainstay of the Algarve's economy and the great
majority of the population is employed in the hotel, holiday or building
trade. A minority of Algarvios continue to make a living from farming,
fishing and fish processing. Until the late 1960s these were the region's
primary sources of income; since then their importance has markedly
declined.

The last few trawlers of the former fishing fleet of Portimão

Economy

Algarve industry, chiefly small-scale fish and cork processing, has never been of great significance nationally. Portugal's main industrial zones are located further north. Even building materials, the profitability of which owes much to the building boom in the Algarve, are manufactured in central and northern Portugal.

Joining the EC

Portugal became a member of the EC (now the European Union) in 1986, hoping with financial aid gradually to improve the country's economic performance and bring it closer to the EU average. Ten years later, however, Portugal still ranks alongside Greece, Spain and Ireland as one of the poorest member countries. EU funds are targeted on modernising Portuguese industry, developing an infrastructure, improving the internal transport system and building warehouses. Today new roads are under construction all over Portugal, including the Algarve. Entry into Europe has also brought new problems, especially for agriculture. Because Portuguese fruit and vegetables do not meet EU standards, there is no real market for them in Europe. Indeed large quantities of foodstuffs are imported into Portugal from other member states.

Fishing

Fishing, together with farming, was long the leading industry of the Algarve. The tuna and sardine harvests in particular have long been vitally important to the economy of this coast. Today the Algarve still accounts for about 20 per cent of the total Portuguese catch. The main fishing ports are Olhão (19,000 tonnes per year) and Portimão (17,000 tonnes per year); among the smaller ports is Vila Real de Santo António (4,400 tonnes per year). Vessels leave Olhão for ocean fishing grounds off the African coast and the cod banks of Newfoundland. In the lagoons around Faro and Alvor and in the vicinity of the Rio Arade estuary near Portimão, considerable quantities of mussels are harvested. In the 1950s measures were taken to modernise the fishing industry, including the introduction of trawlers for sardine fishing. Now, however, Portugal's fishing fleet is out of date and unable to compete with its European rivals, especially the Spanish. Poorly equipped boats restrict Algarve fishermen to coastal waters, where sardines are the principal catch. While enough of these are netted to meet local demand, some other types of fish have to be imported and are expensive.

Fish processing

Fish processing too is in sharp decline. Since 1974 this branch of the industry, centred mainly on Portimão and Olhão, has received virtually no subsidies, forcing many plants to close. The situation in Portimão tells the story: until 1974 there were 61 canning factories in business, now there is only one.

Farming

In the *barrocal* and *serra*, where the normally favourable climate allows as many as four crops a year, a high proportion of the population used to be employed in farming. But since the late 1980s agriculture throughout Portugal has been severely affected by the EU entry, in addition to which southern Portugal has experienced a catastrophic shortage of rain. Drought (and in some places poor soil), antiquated methods of cultivation and uneconomic use of labour result in produce below EU standards and relatively high in cost. EU agricultural subsidies are currently targeted on "set aside" (non-use of land) and early retirement, the preconditions for which many small farmers in the Algarve cannot meet. Consequently farmers in areas near the coast often find it more profitable to sell their land for development. Another problem, likely to become apparent only some years hence, is that only 25 per cent of those currently engaged in agriculture are under 35, while a similar proportion are over 65. This suggests that in future agricultural production could be threatened by a shortage of labour.

Fruit

Statistics for the fig harvest illustrate the decline in farming. Between

Orange trees on the sides of the Serra de Monchique

1953 and 1962 annual fig production was 16,000 tonnes, now it is only 1,000 tonnes. One reason is that fig trees are being felled to create larger farm units or room for citrus plantations. Citrus production has risen accordingly from 16,000 tonnes between 1953 and 1962 to 150,000 tonnes today. In general, output of figs, almonds, olives and carob has sharply declined. Existing trees are neglected or crops remain unpicked, there being too few people left in rural areas to do the work. Virtually no new trees are being planted. Olive oil production is down by 75 per cent today compared with the 1950s. Only carob production has held up relatively well, new research having shown how the pods can be utilised commercially. But even here output, which in the 1950s was 40,000 tonnes, is down to 30,000 tonnes today.

Wine production is also in decline in the Algarve. At one time many Algarve farmers produced wine, but small vineyards are nowadays barely profitable and not always able to satisfy quality controls. Good table wine, though, is still regarded as having a future. Well-known labels are Algar Seco from the Lagoa region, Moscatel from Lagos, and Dom Paio from Tavira.

Vegetables

Sweet potatoes, tomatoes, beans, cucumbers, peppers, lettuce and herbs are all grown. Greenhouse cultivation is common, providing protection from the sun's burning rays and, in the winter months, from storm and rain damage.

Forestry

The eucalyptus is of major importance to the Portuguese economy: in the Algarve whole hilltops are seen planted with young trees. The wood is processed to produce cellulose. Because of the comparatively lax regulatory regime, the ecologically problematic cellulose industry is firmly established in Portugal, mainly on the Tejo. Both the industry and its raw material, the eucalyptus, are environmentally damaging. The

Cork oaks: Portugal is the largest producer of cork in the world

fast-growing trees extract large quantities of moisture from the soil, causing it to dry out.

The growing of cork is becoming less and less important. Though Portugal is still the world's largest producer, the cork industry has been badly hit by competition from man-made alternatives.

Tourism

Tourism is without question the pillar of the region's economy. About 50 per cent of all visitors to Portugal spend their holiday in the Algarve; in contrast only 25 per cent head for Lisbon and its surroundings, while the rest make for the northern Atlantic coast and Portuguese islands. No other part of the country experiences mass tourism on anything like the same scale. In the 1980s alone tourism in the Algarve grew by 15 per cent a year. In 1983 there were 75,000 hotel beds; today the figure is nearer 250,000. Over the years the coast of the Algarve has proved especially popular with the British. The majority of visitors, however, are Spaniards, many of whom come just for the day and mainly to shop. Towns such as Vila Real de Santo António and Tavira in the eastern Algarve are the chief beneficiaries of this Spanish invasion.

Building has escalated to such an extent in the Algarve in recent years that it has attracted considerable adverse criticism. In future, quality not quantity is to be the watchword, the hope being that this will limit further damage to the landscape, wildlife and nature reserves.

Transport

Roads

At the beginning of 1994 Portugal introduced a vehicle test. Lorries, taxis and ambulances are required to be checked annually by IPO (Inspecçoes Periódicas Obrigatórias), private cars every two years.

As part of a general scheme to improve transport links with Spain, the motorway-style EO1 or IP 1 (Via do Infante de Sagres) through the Algarve has been recently upgraded. This is the fastest route between Lisbon and southern Spain. From Albufeira to the Spanish border the IP 1 runs parallel to the much frequented N 125, but because it is further away from towns the IP 1 is only used by non-resident traffic. In the near future the western part of the Algarve will also be further developed for traffic. The link from Albufeira to Alcantarilha is now open for traffic, but the improved urban motorway to Lagos is still under construction.

The international airport at Faro opened in 1965; in 1989 a new terminal   Air
was completed. Passenger traffic reached about 2.5 million in 1989 and increased to 4.1 million in 1998. Soon the 6 million passenger mark will be passed. Faro airport will be hardly capable of meeting this dramatic increase in passenger numbers and the related increase in takeoffs and landings. Therefore modernisation and an extensive enlargement of the airport area are planned.

History

Stone Age	Cave paintings and rock drawings are created by a Stone Age culture (from 20,000 BC) in Portugal.
Copper Age	A considerable number of remains survive from the Copper Age (from 5000 BC). Burial sites dating from the period have been discovered particularly in the Alentejo, neighbouring the Algarve to the north, but also in the Algarve itself.
From 2200 BC	Iberians arrive in the peninsula probably from North Africa, settling in the Algarve.
From 1000 BC	Phoenicians trading amber and copper on the Portuguese coast set up trading posts.
From 700 BC	Celtic peoples coming from the north and settling in Portugal mingle in subsequent centuries with the Iberians to become Celtiberians. Some 30 to 40 Celtiberian tribes, the Lusitanians, form the largest ethnic majority on the Iberian peninsula. Fortified settlements (*castros* or *citânias*) are built on easily defended hilltops.
From 500 BC	Greek merchants set out for the Portuguese coast where they establish trading posts.
Ca 450 BC	Carthage extends its sphere of influence beyond North Africa to include the Iberian peninsula too.
218–206 BC	During the Second Punic War Roman strategy in the Iberian peninsula is directed mainly against the Carthaginians; the Romans are also concerned to defend their frontiers against the Celtiberians in the north and Lusitanians in the west.
197–179 BC	War between the Romans and Lusitanians results in Lusitania being incorporated into the Roman province of Hispania Ulterior.
147–139 BC	The Roman occupation is strongly resisted by the Lusitanians whose leader, Viriatus, "the man with the bangle", is later lauded in literature and art as a national hero. Resistance peters out following Viriatus's murder in 139.
61–45 BC	The province of Hispania Ulterior is finally subdued by Caesar during his campaigns.
27–15 BC	Augustus divides Hispania Ulterior into the two Roman provinces of Baetica, roughly covering the area of present-day Andalusia, and Lusitania. Lusitania extends along the Algarve coast to the Duoro in present-day northern Portugal and east into present-day Spain. Vulgar Latin, spoken throughout Roman territory, later evolves into Portuguese. In the Algarve the Romans build bridges in Tavira and Silves, and north of Faro large baths and a spa are constructed. Cabo de São Vicente, the most southwesterly cape on the European continent, becomes a sacred

site called Promontorium Sacrum on account of its exposed position. The Romans are also already extracting salt from sea water for preserving fish. Finally they establish a network of roads, the course of many of which still survives in places: the present N 125 highway running east–west along the coast of the Algarve was originally built by the Romans; also the road from Faro through Tavira and Mértola to Beja was a major Roman highway.

The Christianisation of Lusitania is thought to have begun at an early date; the existence of Christian communities is attested in the 3rd c. AD.

From AD 200

During the great movement of the Germanic peoples, Vandals and Alans migrate as far as southern Portugal.

From 410

The Visigoths advance into the Algarve. They occupy Faro and establish a bishopric there. They erect the first Christian church and practise a form of Mariolatry (idolatrous worship of the Virgin Mary).

418

Following their victory over Roderick, the last of the Visigoth kings, the Moors overrun (713–18) the whole of the Iberian peninsula except the mountainous regions in the north – Asturias, for instance, remains in Visigoth hands. The area of present-day Portugal becomes part of the Moorish emirate (later caliphate) of Córdoba. Xelb, today Silves, is the capital of the Moorish province of Al-Gharb. The Moors bring a highly developed culture to the Iberian peninsula. They possess a wealth of scientific knowledge, especially in the fields of medicine, geography, navigation and astronomy. They establish a system of irrigation that largely remains unchanged and Algarve land is successfully cultivated. Citrus, fig, almond and olive trees are introduced. Trade with Arab North Africa flourishes. The Algarve prospers: Xelb is a rich and much admired city of 40,000 inhabitants. Under Moorish rule peoples of different religions live peacefully side by side and in the towns there are Arab, Jewish and Christian quarters. In the south of the Iberian peninsula Arab rule lasts for 500 years.

From 711

Vikings launch an incursion north up the Rio Arade intending to attack the wealthy provincial capital of Xelb; they are encircled and halted only a short distance up the estuary.

922

Under King Ferdinand I the Great of Castile and León the Christian reconquest of Portugal truly begins, with the Christians retaking territory from the Moors.

1035–65

Starting with León-Castile, control of the peninsula is gradually wrested from the Moors. A Portuguese state is established. Now as before, Portugal is required to resist Castilian claims.

1112–1385

Afonso Henriques, having secured Portugal's independence from León-Castile, is crowned king. With the help of German, Anglo-Norman and Flemish crusaders he is able to seize Lisbon. His successors extend their territory by further conquests in the south.

1139

Under Sancho I, some noted crusaders, among them Frederick Barbarossa and Richard the Lion-Heart, assist in recovering parts of the west Algarve including Silves and Albufeira. A bishopric is established in Silves and a Flemish priest appointed bishop.

1189

With reinforcements from Seville and Córdoba, the Moors succeed in recapturing towns they have lost in the Algarve.

1191

During the reigns of Sancho II and Afonso III the Moors are finally

1240–9

defeated, losing control of all the Algarve towns. The *reconquista* is complete. Disputes continually erupt with neighbouring Castile. Under Portuguese rule trade between the Algarve and North Africa ceases. An economic, cultural and religious restructuring occurs throughout the region. Jews and Arabs are either driven out or forced into slavery. Only a few *mudéjars*, Arab artists and craftsmen, are permitted to stay and work in the country. The Moorish agricultural system is taken over. The Portuguese also benefit from the Arabs' scientific knowledge.

1250   The Algarve towns are annexed to the kingdom of Portugal with the result that Portugal becomes the first European nation state to attain its full territorial limits, which have remained unchanged.

1319   Diniz I establishes the Order of Christ at Castro Marim.

1385–1580

Magellan's ship Victoria

João I founds the Avis dynasty. In the 200 years of its existence Portugal becomes the leading maritime and colonial power in Europe. The country amasses enormous riches. The major voyages of discovery and conquest occur at this time. Though the spirit of adventure is one reason for journeying across the world's oceans, the explorers are motivated more by economic considerations. Among other things they seek an alternative to the Arab-controlled overland route to the spice-rich countries of Asia. Together with Lisbon the Algarve is a centre of expansionist activity. Lagos becomes one of the premier Algarve ports.

1444   Following the discovery of the Senegal estuary in the reign of Afonso V the first slaves are auctioned in Lagos. The slave trade, like the spice trade, becomes a major generator of wealth. It is not abolished by law until the 18th c.

1485–1521   Manuel I lays the foundations of Portugal's commercial power, establishing trading posts in the East Indies, east Asia, South Africa and Brazil. Lisbon becomes a focal point of world trade. The crown, nobility and merchants enjoy undreamed-of riches; but the unparalleled colonial expansion imposes such a strain on the Portuguese people that the population declines rapidly in a very short time.

1497–8   Vasco da Gama, setting out from the Lisbon port of Belém, sails round the Cape of Good Hope and becomes the first European to reach India by sea. Belém has replaced the ports of the Algarve as the principal departure and arrival point for ocean voyages.

1527   The Algarve has 54,000 inhabitants.

1540   Establishment of the Inquisition. Jews, Judaeo-Christians, atheists and witches are persecuted, as are any Christians whose ways of life, attitudes or convictions the Inquisition finds inimical. The Inquisition is not abolished until 1820.

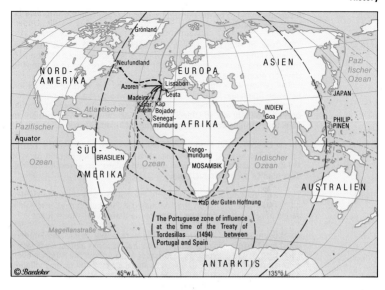

Portuguese Voyages of Discovery

→ Henry the Navigator (1394–1460) founds a court and centre of learning at Sagres, which leads to the conquest of Ceuta (1415), the discovery of Madeira in 1419 and the Azores in 1427, and the rounding of Cape Bojador by Gil Eanes in 1434.

···▶ The sea routes to India. In 1444 Álvaro Fernandez and Diniz Diaz discover the mouth of the Senegal river. In 1482 Diogo Cão reaches the mouth of the Congo. The circumnavigation of the Cape of Good Hope in southern Africa by Bartolomeu Dias in 1488. (In a Spanish expedition, Christopher Columbus reaches the West Indies in 1492.) Pedro Álvares Cabral reaches Brazil in 1500. In 1497 Vasco de Gama sails from Belem near Lisbon, lands the following year in Mozambique and continues to Calicut in India.

···▶ Gaspar Corte Real sails to Newfoundland in 1501.

···▶ Fernão de Magelhães (Magellan) sets out from Sanlúcar de Barrameda in 1519 in the service of the Spanish. He crosses the southern Atlantic, rounds what was to become known as the straights of Magellan at the tip of South America, and in 1521 reaches the Pacific island of Mactan in the Philippines, where he is killed by the natives. One of his ships crosses the Indian Ocean and the southern Atlantic, thus completing the first circumnavigation of the world in 1522.

→ David Melgueiro travels north from Japan in a Dutch ship in 1660 and reaches Europe by the northern route.

Lagos becomes the provincial capital of the Algarve. The bishopric is transferred from Silves to Faro.	1577
The young King Sebastião sets out from Lagos on a crusade against Morocco, only to be killed, together with most of the Portuguese army, at the battle of Alcácer Quibir.	1578
With no successor to the throne the Avis dynasty ends. Philip II of Spain, a grandson of Manuel I, claims the Portuguese throne, occupying the whole of Portugal by force. During the interregnum Portugal loses some of its colonies in southern Asia and South America. Spain finances its colonial wars in part by taxes levied on the Portuguese people. In 1640	1580–1640

a successful rising by the Portuguese nobility results in Portugal regaining its independence.

1640–1701   The Duke of Bragança, one of the nobles involved in the rising, is crowned king as João IV, the first of the Bragança dynasty. Throughout this time the country becomes ever poorer on account of a failure to develop economically.

   The period after 1640 is overshadowed by the wars of restoration between Spain and Portugal. The frontier towns on the Guadiana are the scene of numerous armed conflicts between the two countries. Britain provides military aid, so consolidating British influence over Portugal. In 1688 Spain finally acknowledges Portugal's independence.

1706–50   Under its spendthrift King João V, who sides with Austria in the War of Spanish Succession, Portugal becomes impoverished despite its vast holdings of Brazilian gold and diamond mines; as a result financial dependence on Britain increases.

1750–77   The reign of King José I represents the heyday of enlightened absolutism. His chief minister, the Marquês de Pombal, carries through a series of reforms inspired by Enlightenment and Mercantilist ideas.

1755   On November 1st 1755 a devastating earthquake strikes the Algarve coast and Portuguese mainland. The capital Lisbon is almost completely destroyed. There is likewise great damage throughout the Algarve, even extending to Monchique in the mountains. Coastal towns and villages are hit by a 20 m high tidal wave. Several ports and river estuaries are blocked by sand. Further tremors are experienced the following year, the last on August 20th 1756.

1756   Faro replaces Lagos as provincial capital of the Algarve. At this time 85,000 people inhabit the province.

1774   The Marquês de Pombal rebuilds the flood-destroyed town of Vila Real de Santo António on the Guadiana, using the reconstruction of Lisbon as his model.

1777   After the death of José I, most of the Marquês de Pombal's reforms are reversed during the reign of Maria I; Enlightenment thinking is stifled with the aid of the Inquisition.

1807   Napoleon's troops occupy Portugal. The royal family flees to Brazil. In the Algarve opposition to the occupation is widespread.

1820   Liberal revolution, starting in north Portugal. It marks the beginning of conflicts between liberals and absolutists throughout Portugal, culminating in the Miguelite Wars.

1832–4   Miguelite Wars: adherents of the liberal Pedro IV oppose the reactionary monarchists, who support the regime of Pedro's absolutist brother Miguel. In the Algarve the notorious Remexido and his pro-monarchist guerrillas create a reign of terror. Albufeira is besieged in 1833 and then torched. The Miguelites are defeated in 1834. Miguel leaves Portugal.

Mid-19th c. Industrialisation begins in Portugal, starting relatively late and proceeding only slowly. In the Algarve fish processing and the cork industry play a leading role.

1889   Opening of the Lisbon–Faro railway line. The population of the Algarve reaches 230,000.

1910   After several abortive uprisings a civilian and military revolution succeeds in Lisbon. Manuel II, last king of the Bragança dynasty, flees to Britain. On October 5th the republic is proclaimed. Subsequent years are characterised by internal political strife and numerous changes of government.

The democratic system, which has just begun to stabilise, is abruptly terminated by a military putsch.	1926

The Estado Novo era begins. President António de Oliviera Salazar, previously finance minister and founder of the Fascist União Nacional, establishes a dictatorship. — 1933

In the second world war Portugal remains neutral though on May 6th 1943 diplomatic relations with Germany are severed. — 1939–45

During an earthquake in the Algarve a large number of houses are destroyed. — 1969

Popular resistance to the dictatorship increases. The restrictive nature of the regime and the senselessness and cost of the colonial wars in Africa become ever more evident. On April 25th the dictatorship is overthrown in the Carnation Revolution in Lisbon, a military coup supported by a majority of the population. A socialist constitution is declared. Frequent changes of government and the formation of numerous coalitions result. The basic political orientation is pro-West. — 1974

Portugal becomes a full member of the EC (now the European Union). — 1986

The Algarve now has a population of 340,100. — 1991

Following the parliamentary elections of October 1st, António Guterres of the Socialist Party (PS) becomes prime minister, taking over from the liberal-conservative Anibal Cavaco Silva. — 1995

The election of the socialist Jorge Sampaio as the new Portuguese president consolidates the noticeable swing to the left evident in recent years. — 1996

From January 1st the Euro is the common currency in 11 European countries including Portugal. At present only used at the stock exchanges and in cashless transfers, the Euro will be the official currency from January 1st 2002. — 1999

Famous People

The following famous people all had connections of one sort or another
with the Algarve, whether as the place of their birth or death, or because
they lived or worked there.

Martin Behaim
(1459–1507)

Martin Behaim was one of only a few Germans known to have been
associated with the Portuguese voyages of discovery, for which the
Algarve was an important centre. He was influential in the scientific work
preparatory to the circumnavigation of the globe.

Behaim, son of a rich cloth merchant, was born in Nuremberg on
October 6th 1459. At the age of 17 he went to Flanders where he set up
in business selling textiles. Evidently not a born businessman, the young
libertine soon encountered financial difficulties that caused him to aban-
don his ventures. Back in Nuremberg he crossed swords with the authorities and, threatened with arrest, set off for Portugal where, in Lisbon,
in 1484, he passed himself off as a pupil of the mathematician and sci-
entist Regiomontanus. Regiomontanus, whose real name was Johannes
Müller, was an astronomer working in Nuremberg and engaged at the
time in calculating the precise positions of the planets; he produced
tables of the constellations for every day of the year as an aid to
mariners in determining their position at sea. On the strength of his
fraudulent claims the Portuguese court of João II admitted Behaim to the
Junta of Astronomers and Mathematicians, a body established
expressly to equip Portuguese seafarers with the best available theoretical knowledge. In 1486 Behaim was in all probability a member of an
expedition led by Diogo Cão, which sailed along the African coast as far
as Namibia. Behaim acquired real authority as a geographer in Portugal,
though his actual accomplishments are uncertain. He corresponded with
Magellan and had contacts with Christopher Columbus and is thought to
have carried out important preparatory work for their pioneering voyages of discovery. Little is known about his status. Some historians
claim he was made a knight of the Portuguese Order of Christ.

In the late 1480s Behaim arrived in the Azores, where he married
Joana de Macedo. Returning to Nuremberg in 1491, he produced a
globe, the earliest of any to survive; it can be seen today in the German
National Museum in Nuremberg. It shows the Indian Ocean as an inland
sea and Japan considerably further to the east than in reality. America,
which Christopher Columbus had only just reached, does not appear at
all. In 1493 Behaim returned to Portugal. He died of the plague in Lisbon
on August 8th 1507.

João de Deus
(1830–96)

The well-known writer and educationalist João de Deus was born in the
little town of São Bartolomeu de Messines. Son of a shopkeeper, he
grew up in modest circumstances in the Algarve. At the age of 19 he
went to Coimbra, enrolling at the faculty of law where he studied for ten
years. He was 30 when he found temporary work as a journalist in Beja
and Evora in the Alentejo. In 1868 he became elected representative for
the Silves district in which his home village was situated; feeling
unequal to the task and claiming he could achieve nothing through his
political work, he soon resigned his seat.

His first book of poems, *Flores de campo*, was published in 1869. By
then resident in Lisbon, he joined the literary circle in the celebrated
Café Martinho. He was valued as a poet whose lyrics are characterised

by unaffected emotion. His best poems are contained in the last of his anthologies, *Campo de flores*, which appeared in 1893. His satirical poems are less well known.

From 1877 he became increasingly interested in education, developing a method similar to that of Montessori; his theories inspired the building of 29 nursery schools in Portugal. Though lauded by some his ideas also met with considerable hostility.

As a knight of the Order of Christ, Bartolomeu Dias had a decisive role in the Portuguese voyages of discovery and conquest in the 15th c. He achieved worldwide fame as the first modern European to navigate the southern tip of Africa.

Bartolomeu Dias
(ca 1450–1500)

Commissioned by the Portuguese king to find a sea route to India, Dias set sail from Portimão in 1487. He rounded the Cape in 1488 without at first realising it, being engaged at the time in battling a fierce storm. It was only on the return journey that it became clear he had rounded the southern tip of the African continent. He called the cape Cabo Tormentoso (Cape of Storms). It was João II who more optimistically christened it Cabo da Boa Esperança (Cape of Good Hope), an expression almost certainly of his confidence that, with the reconnaissance of this southernmost point of Africa, a significant milestone had been set for the discovery of a sea passage to India.

In subsequent years Bartolomeu Dias was involved in other important sea voyages. When Vasco da Gama set sail in July 1497 for India, Dias accompanied the expedition as far as Cabo Verde in West Africa. In 1500, aboard his own vessel, Dias participated in the voyage of his fellow countryman Pedro Alvares Cabral which led to the discovery of Brazil. While sailing around the southern tip of Africa a storm broke near the Cape of Good Hope. Dias's ship got into difficulties and he died within sight of the cape he had reconnoitred.

Gil Eanes, who came from Lagos and whose dates are not known with any exactitude, made a name for himself in 1434 by sailing round Cape Bojador. It was widely believed in the Middle Ages that beyond this West African promontory lay a bubbling, boiling sea that swallowed up any ships venturing there. Henry the Navigator, however, became convinced on the basis of his explorations that the ocean beyond Cape Bojador was no different from the waters off the Portuguese coast. Gil Eanes let himself be similarly persuaded and set sail into the unknown, his faith being rewarded with success. Returning safely from this exploratory voyage, he then set sail again, landing some 300 km further south on the West African coast. There he encountered signs of human habitation though not the inhabitants of the region themselves. In 1444 he took part in an armed expedition to Lanzarote.

Gil Eanes
(born ca 1400)

Because of his ground-breaking exploits Gil Eanes is considered the pioneer of Portuguese exploration and conquest on the west coast of Africa and especially of the first circumnavigation of the African continent.

Henry (in Portuguese, Henrique), born third son of João I on March 4th 1394, has gone down in history as Henry the Navigator, though he himself never went on any long voyages.

Henry the
Navigator
(1394–1460)

The young Infante (➤ Baedeker Special, p. 118) distinguished himself at the conquest of Ceuta (1415), as a consequence of which his fame soon spread throughout Europe. The king granted him the titles of Duke of Viseu and Lord of Covilhã, at the same time entrusting him with the

35

defence and governance of Ceuta. It was then, if not before, that Henry began to take an interest in seafaring, poring over charts and documents and eliciting information from mariners. A man of deep piety and asceticism, he otherwise lived, according to Zurara, the court biographer, a very secluded life, dressing with extreme simplicity.

Henry's appointment in 1418 as Grand Master of the Order of the Knights of Christ gave him access to almost limitless financial resources and thenceforth he was able to turn his seafaring dreams into reality. He is thought to have founded at Sagres a scientific centre for the advancement of geographical and nautical knowledge. In the shipyards of nearby Lagos a new type of vessel, the caravel, was built, far superior to conventional sailing ships in terms of manoeuvrability and seaworthiness.

Since Sagres was ill-suited for a port because it lacked a hinterland, the voyages of exploration that Henry financed and organised set out from neighbouring Lagos, in the first instance discovering (or rediscovering) the islands of Madeira (colonised by 1423) and afterwards the Azores (1427). Later, Henry the Navigator's ships pressed further down the west coast of Africa, reaching Cape Verde, Gambia and finally Guinea. Henry's seafaring enterprises, which laid the foundation for Portugal's development as a colonial power, were motivated as much by the struggle against Islam as by the desire to set up trading networks and the lure of gold, spices and slaves.

Henry the Navigator died of a fever in his palace at Sagres on November 13th 1460.

João II (1455–95)

João II earned himself a place in history as John the Perfect, having guided his country's development with a sure touch at the time of the voyages of discovery and conquest, and having prepared Portugal for its role as one of the foremost maritime and trading powers. The Avis king died in 1495 in the Algarve.

João was born on May 3rd 1455, the son of Afonso V and Isabel. A marriage was arranged for him with his cousin Leonor, a sister of Manuel I. Whereas his father, whom he succeeded in 1481, remained deeply rooted in the Middle Ages both in thought and style of rule, João II proved open to Renaissance ideas. The young king governed the country strictly, bending the nobility and clergy to the will of the Crown. He purposefully fostered the voyages of discovery, and during his reign Portugal began to develop into one the leading sea powers. He established the Junta of Mathematicians and Astronomers specifically to advance theoretical knowledge of seafaring use. Both the discovery of the mouth of the Congo and the rounding of the Cape of Good Hope were achieved with his financial support. It was also during his reign, however, that Christopher Columbus discovered America, his voyage funded by the Spanish Crown – which even today in Portugal is clearly remembered with bitterness. It arose from the Portuguese obsession at that time with discovering a sea route to India. Columbus repeatedly urged João II to consider his suggestion of an alternative route to the spice islands. When the king referred the Genoese's plans to his scientific advisers for their opinion, they concluded variously that the westward passage proposed by Columbus could not lead to India and "Cipango" (Japan), or that it would prove substantially longer than the eastward one. While the Portuguese accepted that unknown lands probably existed to the west, they did not consider financial backing for Columbus's enterprise justified. So when in 1492 Columbus finally made his chance discovery of the American continent, Portugal could claim no share of the glory. To this day Portuguese historians persist in attempts to establish some family connection or even to show Columbus is of Portuguese descent, so that their country may claim a part in the discovery of the New World.

Another painful episode in the life of João the Perfect was the premature death of his son and successor, killed in a riding accident on the banks of the Tejo near Santarém.

In 1495 João, who was gravely ill, travelled to the Monchique spa in the Algarve. He died shortly afterwards in Alvor near Portimão and was buried in Silves Cathedral. His remains were later transferred to Batalha.

Lídia Jorge, a native of the Algarve, is one of Portugal's best-known writers. An only child, she was born near Albufeira in the small town of Boliqueime, where she spent her childhood and youth. At nine she went to secondary school in Faro where she was confronted for the first time with life in a small city. On leaving school she went to Lisbon to study Romance languages and literature. During the colonial wars she spent some years in the former Portuguese colonies of Mozambique and Angola. She now teaches in a secondary school in Lisbon.

Lídia Jorge
(born 1946)

With the appearance in the 1980s of her novels *O Dia dos Prodígios*, *O Cais das Merendas*, *Notícia da Cidade* and *A Costa dos Murmúrios*, Lídia Jorge has achieved a lasting place in contemporary Portuguese literature. She takes as her recurrent theme the political and social situation in Portugal following the Carnation Revolution, the changes and absence of change experienced by the country since 1974. In *O Dia dos Prodígios* (*The Day of the Miracle*) she describes life in sleepy Vilamaninhos, an imaginary village in the Algarve where the people hope for better things in the wake of the revolution. Many of the characters and events have their roots in the writer's childhood.

The Marquês de Pombal, chief minister and proponent of enlightened absolutism, left the mark of his philosophy on the Algarve when he completely rebuilt the town of Vila Real de Santo António near the mouth of the Guadiana.

Sebastião José de Carvalho e Mello, Marquês de Pombal (1699–1782)

Born into Lisbon's minor aristocracy, his first experience was in the diplomatic service as an envoy to London and Vienna where his brief also included economic matters. In 1750 José I appointed him minister for foreign affairs, and in 1756 chief minister.

Pombal proved adept at using his powers in office singlemindedly to promote his own ideas, showing few qualms about the means employed to achieve his long-term aims. He saw his most important tasks as reorganising the state finances, reforming education, promoting trade and industry (to free Portugal from the economic hegemony of Britain) and the abolition of slavery. He passionately opposed the Jesuits and the minor nobility whose inherited privileges stood in the way of his reforms.

He also had an outstanding role in the reconstruction of Lisbon following the devastating earthquake of 1755. And when some years later Santo António da Avenilha in the Algarve was destroyed in a catastrophic flood, he masterminded its replacement, completing a whole new town, Vila Real de Santo António, chequerboard in plan, in just five months, drawing on the very latest models of town planning that he had employed in rebuilding Lisbon's Lower Town.

After the death of José I the Marquês fell from favour; in 1781 pressure from his many enemies brought about his banishment to Pombal where he died the following year.

Famous People

Dom Sebastião
(ca 1554–78)

The reputation and importance of this Portuguese king owe more to myth than to the man.

Dom Sebastião was born in 1554, shortly after his father died in an accident. As a result, on the death of his grandfather João III, Dom Sebastião succeeded to the throne. A brother of João III acted as regent until the boy, known since birth as The Longed For, reached the age of 14; thereafter the young king ruled in his own right. Described as arrogant and a religious fanatic, one of his main ambitions was to bring North Africa under Christian rule. In 1578 he set out from Lagos to fulfil his mission. Before leaving he attended a mass held in the open near the harbour, afterwards boarding ship. Shortly thereafter he marched into Morocco. At Alcácer Quibir there was a disastrous battle which cost the lives of 80,000 men. Back in Portugal people refused to believe that the young king was among the fallen, retaining for some time a hope for his return. But The Longed For never did reappear; instead a succession of pretenders emerged claiming to be the missing king.

Since that time a legend has grown up around Sebastião, elevating him to a knightly figure whose homecoming is still awaited, especially when times are bad. Were he but to appear, everything would be all right. A new term – Sebastianism – has even been coined to denote not only the passive fatalism and laissez-faire attitude allegedly widespread in Portugal but also the typically Portuguese *saudade* (nostalgia); both reflect a backward-looking element in Portuguese dreams and hopes, and a deep-lying sense of resignation, recurrent themes in Portuguese literature, art and music.

José Joaquim de
Sousa Reis
(1747–1838)

José Joaquim de Sousa Reis, leader of a guerrilla group active in the Algarve in the 19th c., is known in Portuguese history by the name Remexido.

Born in the village of Estômbar near Portimão, de Sousa Reis lived for many years in São Bartolomeu de Messines. During the absolutist reign of Miguel I, under whom every liberal reform introduced by his brother and predecessor Pedro IV was reversed, de Sousa Reis commanded a Miguelite force in the Algarve. This was a period when the political climate of the entire country was dominated by the struggle between liberal elements and Miguel's supporters. In 1833 liberalist forces landed at Cacela in the eastern Algarve, seizing control of large parts of the region. In the civil wars that followed, Remexido directed operations against them in the western Algarve. Algarve towns were fiercely fought over with control passing back and forth. On May 26th 1834 the so-called Miguelite Wars were ended by the Treaty of Évoramonte, though friction continued beneath the surface for some time.

In 1836 Remexido took up arms again, gathering about him members of his former band; he carried out attacks on Algarve towns and villages in defiance of the liberalist regime. On August 23rd 1836 he was responsible for an appalling massacre in the infantry barracks at São Bartolomeu de Messines where a number of soldiers were murdered. Remexido's guerrillas hid out in inaccessible parts of the Algarve hill country; even special military units sent by Maria II at the request of the town of Silves proved impotent at first.

Eventually, in May 1838, well-equipped government troops were despatched into the Algarve uplands. José Joaquim de Sousa Reis was tracked down east of São Marcos da Serra and taken prisoner. He was sentenced to death in Faro and summarily shot on August 2nd 1838.

São Vicente
(died 304)

Cape St Vincent (Cabo de São Vicente), the south-western tip of Portugal and of contin-ental Europe, takes its name from São Vicente.

Little is recorded about the life of the saint. It is not known when he was born though sources refer to Zaragossa as his birthplace. As deacon there he worked in close cooperation with Bishop Valerius. During the reign of Diocletian he was brought before the governor Decius, taken to

Valencia and incarcerated. In 304 he was sentenced to death, allegedly being laid, while still alive, on a red-hot grill. During his martyrdom the room is said to have suddenly become filled with light, a carpet of flowers appeared and angels' voices were heard. He was buried in Valencia.

Subsequently canonised, a hundred or so years later a cult became associated with his name. Portuguese tradition has it that in the 8th c. an unmanned skiff bearing the saint's corpse was washed up on the headland that now bears his name. His only companions, it is said, were two crows. A more credible account is that Christians fleeing Valencia during the Moorish invasion took the saint's body with them. Having landing at the cape the Romans called Promontorium Sacrum, marking the most southwesterly point of the European mainland, a chapel was erected there in the saint's honour. Arab writings mention a "crow chapel", and the headland itself is referred to as "crow cape" (from whence also derives the Portuguese name for the high point of the promontory, Monte Corvo, crow mountain).

In the 12th c., having retaken Lisbon from the Arabs in 1147, Afonso Henriques had the saint's bones removed there. At first they were preserved in the forerunner of the present Igreja de São Vicente, later being transferred, in a shrine inlaid with mother-of-pearl, to Lisbon's cathedral, the Sé.

Today São Vicente is venerated in Portugal as the patron saint of seafarers and vintners. He is also the patron saint of Lisbon, depicted on the city's arms together with a boat and two crows. The Portuguese are not alone, however, in their devotion to the saint. The Spanish too venerate him and, in a Romanesque church dedicated to St Vincent in Avila, in Spain, there is what is said to be his grave.

Culture

Art History

The Algarve has relatively few historical art treasures of note, having been decimated, as was Lisbon, by the 1755 earthquake. A great many buildings were either completely destroyed or so badly damaged that little from previous centuries survived, often just fragments.

Until the mid-13th c. the Algarve's development mirrored that of neighbouring Andalusia. In 1250, though, the Algarve was incorporated into the kingdom of Portugal, after which its culture and the culture of Andalusia diverged. As a result, the 500 years of Moorish rule have left few enduring marks on the landscape, their legacy being seen more in various aspects of daily life and work, such as language and agriculture, than in architectural heritage.

However, the Algarve also differs in important respects from much of the rest of Portugal. The Moors having been driven from the north that much sooner, most of the early churches in northern Portugal date from the Romanesque period. In the Algarve on the other hand, Moorish rule continued into the 13th c. and the earliest Christian churches are early Gothic. The building stone used shows interesting variations, in some

The Roman fish mosaics at Milreu

cases red sandstone from the Serra de Monchique, in others yellow sandstone from the coast.

The most important relics of the Roman period are found at Milreu near Faro. They include the remains of a Roman patrician villa, thermal baths and shrines. Roman mosaics have been uncovered at Vilamoura, and Roman salination plants on the Quinta de Marim reserve near Olhão. The bridges at Tavira and Silves are of Roman origin but rebuilt.

Roman

Though virtually all the castles in the Algarve were built originally by the Moors, a courtyard in the Castelo dos Mouros at Silves is the only substantial reminder left today. Fragments of wall forming parts of fortifications at Salir, and a few items in the archaeological museum at Silves (a cistern and one or two small finds) complete the scant Moorish legacy.

Moorish

The earliest Christian church, a well-preserved early Gothic chapel (13th c.), can be seen near the village of Raposeira. The 1755 earthquake almost completely destroyed the cathedrals in Silves and Faro, leaving little of the Gothic fabric standing. In Silves the main doorway, former choir and crossing are still clearly discernible; in Faro the bell tower has stood the test of time.

Medieval

Manueline, so called after Manuel I, is a distinctive Portuguese ornamental style that developed in the early 16th c. The prosperity flowing from Portugal's overseas conquests brought a cultural flowering, which found expression in architecture as well as other ways. This being the period of transition between the Gothic age and the Renaissance, Manueline buildings incorporated both late Gothic and early Renaissance elements while simultaneously drawing on contemporary events of national importance in their ornamentation. Specific recurrent motifs were used: the cross of the Order of the Knights of Christ, the crown and "M" for Manuel, the king whose hand guided Portuguese conquests; ropes and hawsers in stone, miniature caravels (ships), anchors, and the armillary sphere (a nautical instrument), symbolising the sea and seafaring; and stylised corals, shells, tropical plants, leaves and flowers denoting new links with distant tropical lands. Very occasionally architecture took inspiration from foreign cultures, the Torre de Belém in Lisbon being a good example. The leading architects of this period were Diogo de Boytaca, Diogo de Arruda, Francisco de Arruda and João de Castilho.

Manueline

Grand buildings representing the pinnacle of the style grace Lisbon, Batalha and Tomar rather than the Algarve. But its close association with the voyages of discovery means that many, albeit more modest, examples are found in the districts, towns and villages directly involved in Portugal's maritime exploits and overseas conquests. Accordingly, a comparatively large number of the Algarve's small churches have Manueline stylistic elements. Typically, entrance doorways, and less commonly the arches between nave and choir, display Manueline decoration. Splendid examples of Manueline ornamentation can be seen in the churches at Alvor, Alte, Monchique, Luz de Tavira, Estômbar and Odiáxere. Silves still boasts a Manueline wayside cross.

Generally speaking the Renaissance style never really became established in Portugal. This was partly because of Manueline, which had a retarding effect on new developments, and partly because, by the mid-16th c., not only was money for ambitious architectural projects noticeably scarce, but also, with the passing of the Golden Age (1385–1580), there was no longer cause to erect magnificent buildings. Isolated Renaissance features, mostly entrance doorways, survive in a handful of Algarve churches, such as the Igreja da Misericórdia in Tavira, the Igreja de São Pedro in Faro, the Igreja Matriz in Mexilhoeira Grande and the Igreja da Misericórdia in the castle courtyard at Castro Marim.

Renaissance

Towards the end of the 17th c. the gold mines for which the Portuguese had long searched in Brazil were finally discovered and money once again flowed into the country. Under the extravagant King João V, numerous churches and palaces were built in Portugal in the first half of the 18th c.; at the same time existing churches acquired baroque altars and chapels. Churches in the Algarve are rich in baroque furnishings. The Igreja do Carmo in Faro is pure baroque. The Igreja de São Lourenço in Almansil is renowned for its *azulejo* walls, and the Igreja de Santo António in Lagos for its sumptuous *talha dourada* decoration.

Ceramic tiles, **azulejos**, adorn the walls of chapels, churches, palaces and railway stations throughout Portugal, sometimes covering entire house façades. Moorish in origin, the name derives from the Arabic *azzuleycha* meaning mosaic pieces. They were first imported from southern Spain at the beginning of the 16th c. At that time, to keep the various different colours separate before firing, the Moors relied on indentations in the surface of the tile. Green, blue, black, rust and white are the dominant colours on *azulejos* of this period.

After the Moors were driven out of southern Spain, the first *azulejo* factories were established in Portugal. Thanks to the majolica technique taken over from the Italians, tiles could now be produced with a flat surface instead of relief. They were given a white tin glaze on which designs were painted using metaloxide pigments. In the 17th c. a distinctive Portuguese style evolved, influenced by porcelain painting of the Ming dynasty and by Delft tile-makers. Whole floors were carpeted with tiles in shades of blue, white and yellow. Clearly defined patterns such as the *ponta de diamante* with its stylised cut diamonds also began to appear. Then, in the 18th c., the large tile pictures typical of the baroque period came more and more into fashion. The walls of churches, the interior and exterior walls of palaces, staircases, fountains and banks, were all decorated with tile pictures. The Igreja de São Lourenço in Almansil is an outstanding example of a church interior completely tiled in the baroque manner.

In the early 19th c. when Portugal was convulsed by civil war, the production of *azulejos* virtually ceased. By the middle of the century, however, they enjoyed a revival. Following the Brazilian model, tiles were used, both externally and internally, for the decoration of middle-class houses and commercial, municipal and other public buildings. The practical advantages of tile façades were widely appreciated, and the use of paint on large expanses of wall became less common. Tile making flourished once again during the art-nouveau period, after which enthusiasm noticeably waned. In recent decades new interest has been shown in the tradition surrounding Portuguese *azulejos;* decorated with contemporary as well as old established motifs, they are used again in the decoration of public buildings.

Equally distinctive of Portuguese baroque are the wood sculptures, gilded in fine gold leaf, known as **talhas douradas**, predominantly seen in church interiors. The wood was usually oak and the gold came from Brazil. *Talhas douradas* served, in essence, to display the wealth that flowed into the country after the discovery of Brazilian gold. Initially confined mainly to picture frames, they were later also incorporated into pulpits, high altars and even walls. In the Algarve the Igreja do Carmo in Faro has *talha dourada* decoration; but the best example of this style of church furnishing is the Igreja de Santo António in Lagos.

Almost every building in the Algarve, whether private house, public building or church, dates from after the 1755 earthquake. Some of those destroyed were rebuilt, others replaced by something completely new. At the end of the 18th c. the then bishop of the Algarve, Francisco

◄ *The interior of the baroque church of São Lourenço at Almansil*

Lagos: squares and streets surfaced with black and white mosaics

Gomes do Avelar, committed himself to rebuilding much of the ecclesi-astical stock. The Italian architect Francisco Xavier Fabri, responsible for many buildings in Lisbon, was invited to the Algarve where his contri-bution to the work was substantial. Of new buildings constructed after the earthquake, the Palácio de Estói deserves special mention.

Portugal in the second half of the 18th c. represents something of a special case in the history of **town planning**. The 1755 earthquake caused widespread devastation and complete towns were destroyed. Lisbon's Lower Town was rebuilt from scratch. Those responsible fol-lowed a blueprint laid down by chief minister, the Marquês de Pombal (▶ Famous People). At his instigation the Lower Town was reconstructed to a rational, supremely orderly and functional chequerboard plan. The Marquês applied the same principles in designing the new town of Vila Real de Santo António in the Algarve, built on what was to all intents and purposes a virgin site.

20th c.

The face of the Algarve has fundamentally changed during the 20th c. Tourism began in the 1960s, and by the late 1970s high-rise blocks had mushroomed. The road bridge built over the Rio Arade near Portimão in the early 1990s is one of the more impressive modern structures.

Throughout Portugal there are squares and pavements laid with attrac-tive black and white **mosaics**. After the 1755 earthquake people hit upon the idea of turning the rubble from houses, palaces and churches into small rectangular stones and setting them in the pavements. Motifs and patterns are often painstakingly worked in. The craftsmen who lay them are called *calceteiros*. Mosaic laying used to be a common trade in Portugal; today the work is very poorly paid and there are very few *calceteiros* left. The pavement mosaics in the centre of Faro, Lagos,

Albufeira and Portimão are a delight to the eye. The finest designs of all are on the Praça do Marquês de Pombal in Vila Real de Santo António; the radial pattern was laid out in 1879.

In the Algarve as elsewhere, working **windmills** are a thing of the past. Whitewashed, slightly conical mills were once a common sight in the landscape. They had small triangular sails, often with clay vessels attached that made a whistling sound as the sails turned and told the miller the strength of the wind. Of the few remaining windmills, the two finest are at São Brás de Alportel and Odiáxere.

In Olhão and neighbouring Fuzeta in particular, distinctive cubical fishermen's houses are found; all have the flat roofs or roof-terraces known as *açoteias*, used traditionally for drying fish, fruit, laundry, fishing gear or simply for taking the air. Many of the *açoteias* have look-out towers called *mirantes*, from where the fishermen's wives are said to have kept a look out for their men returning from the sea.

Chimneys, **chaminés**, are a real feature of the Algarve, works of art rather than just smoke outlets (➤ picture, p. 7). They come in many different shapes and sizes, some round, some square, some with little hipped roofs, some with spires, some looking like tall birdcages, others like squat minarets. The vents in their sides make very varied patterns too. Once *chaminés* were handmade: today they are mass-produced.

Few **paintings** or **sculptures** of historical interest are to be seen in the Algarve. The collection of the former diplomat and connoisseur Ferreira d'Almeida, now attached to the archaeological museum in Faro, has one or two pleasing 19th and 20th c. Portuguese paintings but nothing of great worth.

The most notable modern sculpture is the statue of Dom Sebastião in the Praça Gil Eanes in Lagos. Erected in the early 1960s, it is the work of João Cutileiro, one of Portugal's most-celebrated 20th c. sculptors.

Literature

Portuguese literature is not widely known elsewhere in Europe, though more is now being translated into other languages. Among the more-familiar modern writers are Fernando Pessoa, José Saramago and Luís Vaz de Camóes. Literature from the Algarve or about the Algarve is extremely rare.

A number of Portuguese writers chronicled the age of discovery and conquest, their work being best known in that context. One or two voiced criticism of Portugal's adventurism overseas and the "conquistador" mentality, but always in veiled terms or minor works (the Inquisition threatened any writer adopting a too openly subversive stance). Among the greatest historians of the 15th and 16th c. are Fernão Lopes (1384–1460), Gomes Eanes de Zurara (ca 1410–73), João de Barros (ca 1496–1570) and Diogo de Couto (ca 1542–1616). — 15th and 16th c.

Best known of all Portuguese works and a source of fascination to many foreign writers especially in the 19th c. is *Os Lusíadas* by Luís Vaz de Camões (ca 1524–80). To this national poet the age of discovery was a glorious era in almost every respect, a viewpoint not shared by Fernão Mendes Pinto (ca 1510–83) whose *Peregrinação* cast a more-jaundiced eye over Portuguese exploits. More importantly, Pinto's work, unusually for that period, includes valuable descriptions of the countries about which he writes. Another very well-known 15th–16th c. author was Gil Vicente (ca 1465–1540), famous as the founder of

Portuguese theatre. A critical observer of his times, his so-called *autos*, one-act dramas with music and dancing, brought him into conflict with the Inquisition.

18th c.

In the early 18th c. Portuguese writers began to concern themselves with the ideas of the Enlightenment. A number of literary circles emerged seeking a revival of literature and the theatre. One author to make a name for himself was Manuel Maria Barbosa do Bocage (1765–1805), persecuted by the authorities on account of his emotive works and eccentric lifestyle.

19th c.

The 19th c. produced a considerable number of writers, many of whom remain popular with modern readers and some of whose works have been translated from Portuguese. Their books are mainly about Portugal, its people, and the various regions of the country. Among the most famous are Almeida Garrett (1799–1854), Camilo Castelo Branco (1825–90) and José Maria Eça de Queiróz (1845–1900), of whom the latter, with his *The Maias*, *Cousin Basílio* and *The Illustrious House of Ramires*, is the leading Portuguese exponent of the social novel.

The Algarve writer João de Deus (➤ Famous People) established a reputation throughout Portugal with his poems, distinguished by their unaffected emotion.

20th c.

The most-celebrated 20th c. Portuguese writer is undoubtedly Fernando Pessoa who, together with Almada Negreiros and Mário de Sá-Carneiro, inspired an avant-garde circle whose activities threw middle-class Lisbon into a state of turmoil; they also used to meet in Faro in the Algarve (➤ Baedeker Special, p. 133).

José Saramago (b 1922) has written numerous novels on themes from Portuguese history. His *Hope in the Alentejo* chronicles events in the Alentejo from the turn of the century until the Carnation Revolution in 1974. His novel *The Gospel according to Jesus Christ* was initially banned by the authorities as offensive to religious sensibilities. Lídia Jorge (➤ Famous People) is a native of the Algarve; her novel *The Day of the Miracle* describes life in an Algarve village against the background of the Carnation Revolution.

Music

Rock, pop and jazz

While Portuguese rock and pop music have much in common with these same genres in other Western countries, they also incorporate elements from Portuguese folk music. Among the most-successful artists are the singers Fausto, Sérgio Godinho, Vitorino and José Afonso and groups such as Trovante, GNR, Delfins and Peste e Sida. Helped by Wim Wenders' film *Lisbon Story*, the Madredeus have become one of Europe's most-popular groups. Dulce Pontes is another vocalist to win international acclaim, as is jazz singer Maria João.

Classical music

Despite the royal patronage bestowed on Portuguese music by kings, many of whom were keen musicians themselves, practically no work by Portuguese composers is ever performed outside their native country. From the 12th c. when Christianity was finally restored, music in Portugal mirrored developments in the rest of Europe. Some composers have given Portuguese music a national flavour by introducing elements from folk music or by reinterpreting themes from Portuguese history. The most acclaimed composers are João Domingos Bontempo and Alfredo Keil (19th c.), and Fernando Lopes-Graça and Jorge Peixinho (20th c.). The pianist Maria João Pires has gained a universal reputation for her performances of classical music.

Fado is unique to Portugal. No one is quite sure of its origins. It is thought to have evolved either from the *lundum*, an African slave dance brought to Portugal by way of Brazil, or from the Brazilian *modinha*, a form of sentimental song that, when it became popular in Portugal, acquired a more lyrical, yearning quality. Since the Portuguese like to attribute almost everything to the age of discoveries (1385–1580), some have also claimed on account of the "wave-like" melodies and deep sense of longing, that fado actually developed among the seafarers of the 15th c.

One thing is certain, namely that fado first made its appearance at the beginning of the 19th c. in the port area of Lisbon, where it was sung or, more accurately, performed (because fado is acted not just sung) in simple bars or *casas de fado*. Accompanied by one ordinary and one special twelve-stringed fado guitar (*guitarra portuguesa*), the *fadista*, who can be male or female, evokes the mood of the song not only by voice but also by posture and gestures. Women normally dress all in black and always wear a black stole, which they wrap tightly round themselves as if for protection, especially when singing fados of a serious, melancholic nature.

Sometimes these are the purest laments, with more than a hint of the music of the Arab world. Their themes are lost or unrequited love, homesickness, a longing for distant places or a general malaise resonant with every conceivable human sorrow. Thus the fado is a setting to music of the supposedly widespread, typically Portuguese *saudade*, that passive fatalism reflecting an insatiable, boundless yearning – for a better past, a better future, something distant and unattainable like a lover in a far off land. It is captured in the gaze from the harbour wall across the restless waters of the Atlantic to the horizon and beyond. And this is indeed the dominant mood of fado, at least for the most part. But there is also, in sharp contrast, a very popular type of song that is witty, amusing and not infrequently bawdy. These songs often take the form of a coquettish duet and the audience, infused one moment with life's sorrows, is convulsed with laughter the next.

Great *fadistas* have always been very special to the Portuguese, celebrated and revered. In the 19th c. there was the legendary female singer A. Severa, who died when she was only 26. Today it is Amália Rodrigues. Born in 1920, hers was a fairytale rise from simple flower girl to renowned fado singer appearing on the world's great stages. Other famous 20th c. *fadistas* include Alfredo Marceneiro and Carlos Ramos.

Most performances of fado in the Algarve are laid on specially for the tourists. In the holiday resorts there are no true casas de fado where authentic fado can be heard.

Folk Music

The many *festas* that take place in Portugal throughout the year offer the best opportunity for getting to know the country's folk music and dance. Virtually every public festival, especially religious ones, feature troupes of musicians and dancers who, decked out in traditional costume, perform the music and dances of that particular region or area. Much of what passes for folk music and dance in the Algarve is actually contrived for the tourist trade; it is a lucky visitor who happens upon a festival where the authentic music and dance of the Algarve are performed. Typical of the instruments used in Portuguese folk music are the guitar, sometimes the *viola de arame* strung with metal strings, pipes (*pipas*), bagpipes (*gaitas de foles*) and, in particular, a square, double-sided tambourine (*adufe*).

There are two kinds of dances: the *danças*, intended for particular occasions, and the *bailes*, specific to this or that area. Very popular in the Algarve is the *corridinho*, a fast polka danced to the accompaniment of guitar, accordion and sometimes also flute, mandolin and castanets.

Quotations

The quotations are arranged in chronological order.

Luís Vaz de Camões

These lines on Cabo de São Vicente by Portugal's national poet Luís Vaz de Camões are from his epic poem Os Lusíadas (1572).

Most westerly point of Europe,
Where the land ends and the sea begins,
And where the spirit of belief
And adventure lives,
Which sent Portugal's caravels
To new worlds for the world.

Reinhold Schneider

Reinhold Schneider made several visits to Portugal, a country for which he felt a great affinity. This description of Cabo de São Vicente, the most south-westerly point of Portugal and of Europe, was written in 1960 (Portugal. Ein Reisetagebuch, 1984).

And now we drove straight towards the sea, as though wanting to throw ourselves into it. A lighthouse keeps watch over decaying walls: Cape St Vincent. The corpse of the saint is said to have been worshipped here in early Christian times. A little dog lies asleep on the stones. He lives out his life at the extremity of Europe, keeping company with a fisherman below on the last pinnacle of rock throwing out a line into the eerie, foaming depths. A rock tower fights a losing battle against the surf. A large rock lies beneath the cliff like a wreck; the light beams out, and the foam breaks ceaselessly over the blue. From here Henry the Navigator, son of King João I, founder of Portugal's second and most important dynasty, despatched his ships to the coasts of Africa; and here, guided by ancient tradition, he conned their reports – the navigator of the spirit who, with typical European eyes, saw above all Europe beyond Europe.

Hans Obergethmann

Not half a century ago the Algarve was yet to feel the impact of mass tourism, as this extract by the German author Hans Obergethmann shows (Portugal. Ein Bildwerk, 1960).

Fewer foreigners visit the south of Portugal – most unfairly because it too has scenic charm, particularly the province of Algarve where a breath of the tropics can already be felt ... Its name is of Arabic derivation and means "west land". This is where southern Europe meets West Africa. A damp warm coastal climate with frequently tropical temperatures characterises the flora of the area. In January the countryside is shrouded in a white mantle of luxuriant almond blossom. Palms, prickly pears and agaves grow. The wine from the vineyards of the Algarve is heavy and full of the glow of the hot sun ... True, here in the extreme south there are nothing like as many sights to be found as in the northern cities and towns. But there is instead a little carefree paradise to be discovered, a flavour of the East, a touch enchanted, and Europe, as we think of it, already far, very far removed. It is, for all that, a region long cultivated by man and – as mentioned at the beginning – a worthwhile destination for anyone who does not want the route he travels to be determined by current fashion or the dictates of mass tourism.

Hugo Loetscher

For the Swiss writer Hugo Loetscher, Portugal and Portuguese history were a recurring theme (Portugal und die portugiesische Welt – Geschichte und Aktualität, *1984*).

O mundo portugues, the Portuguese world; a concept so meaningful for the Portuguese but hardly known elsewhere, here included ... The Portuguese world is in the first place a world of mere relics. Reminders of it are to be found on the map. In a multitude of names. Like Lagos, for example, capital of Nigeria. The name echoes Lagos on the south coast of Portugal; a town at one time important for shipbuilding and where the first slave market in Europe was held. Or Portuguesa, a state and river in Venezuela, so called just because a Portuguese woman made her home there.

Reminders are not just found on the map but also in chronicles. A Ceylonese one, for example. It records the arrival of the Portuguese in Ceylon – they drank blood (wine of course), ate stones (unleavened bread) and walked restlessly to and fro in their armour. On one of the first encounters between West and East, the Asians noticed that Europeans had a different, rather jittery attitude to time.

Lídia Jorge grew up in Boliqueime. Her novel The Day of the Miracles *is the diary of an Algarve village. Forgotten by central government, life carries on in its own way, illiteracy, an increasingly ageing population and loneliness dominating everyday happenings (*Der Tag der Wunder, *1989).*

Lídia Jorge

One day they trimmed the roadsides, and the next day they spread gravel. And later the tar stuck to our shoes. Drat. That was the start of a new century, they said, which was very late arriving here. A period of crazily fast things, made completely of wheels and levers, urgent panting and speed. But many people felt sick. And many came back again from Faro green in the face and dizzy, as if they had set off to get some shopping and bits and pieces and ended up making a journey round the world. At the beginning the bus was green and grey, and everyone who could read said it was called "Eva". The windows were clean, and if they wanted the passengers could draw the curtains up and down with a boat-hook. Then gradually it lost its splendour. The upholstery tore, the floor was dirty and the windows grimy. The curtains came off their rails and leapt about during the journey and made a dull noise. All the supports broken. And so on. People looked at these new things of a new century and thought that, when it came down to it, even the tools, children of this century of the future, wear out quicker than our iron and wooden ones. And so when we went to Faro, instead of taking the bus, which virtually always drove past at the same time and never waited for anyone, we started to saddle our donkeys again. I even got up at four o'clock in the morning, neighbours, to be able to leave before the sun rose. Everybody did the same. And I did so too. I preferred to buy fodder of oats and beans for five escudos than pay for a bus ticket for a drive, which only made a person dizzy, no conversation, and didn't stop where it was most convenient. But the worst, neighbours, and the reason why I never went by bus again, was because later, when the curtains no longer gave any protection from the sun, it was forbidden to open an umbrella on the bus. The heat burnt down on the window panes, and the people in their Sunday best felt as though they were in a greenhouse. During the journey the fruit even fermented on their laps. When they arrived home everything smelled sour. Now it makes the return trip every day. But takes no one there and brings no one back. Only people who go from one place to another and stare as if they were asking. Who lives in those houses buried there?

**Sights
from A to Z**

Suggested Routes

These routes focus deliberately on the less familiar Algarve hinterland with its varied scenery and often picturesque little country towns and villages. The coast, on the other hand, hardly features at all. The coastal towns are of course worth visiting, but this is better done at greater leisure.

Faro is the starting point for the tour of the eastern Algarve, Albufeira for the circuit of the central Algarve, and Portimão for the route through the western Algarve. All three can be reached quite easily on the N 125 or IP 1 from any of the popular holiday resorts. Alternatively, since all the tours described are circular, they can be followed easily enough starting at any convenient point along the way. Headings in the margin and the map below give an overview of the routes. Locations with a main heading in the Sights from A to Z section of the guide appear in bold. Others are listed in the index.

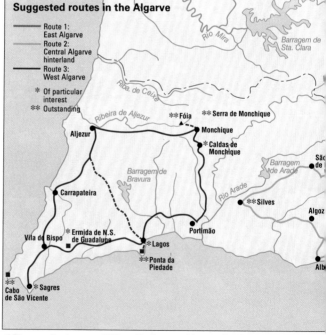

Suggested routes in the Algarve

- Route 1: East Algarve
- Route 2: Central Algarve hinterland
- Route 3: West Algarve
- * Of particular interest
- ** Outstanding

Rio Mira · Barragem de Sta. Clara · Riba. de Ceixe · Ribeira de Aljezur · **Fóia · **Serra de Monchique · Monchique · *Caldas de Monchique · Barragem de Arade · São de · Aljezur · Barragem de Bravura · Rio Arade · **Silves · Algoz · Carrapateira · *Ermida de N.S. de Guadalupe · Portimão · Vila do Bispo · *Lagos · **Ponta da Piedade · Alb · **Cabo de São Vicente · *Sagres

◄ The massive towers of Silves Castle are evidence of its former importance

Route 1: East Algarve (190 km)

Adding up to a fairly long day's drive, this route explores the scenic contrasts of the eastern Algarve. Beyond São Brás de Alportel lies some remote mountain country; and at the eastern extremity a delightful stretch of the Guadiana valley. The mountain roads tend to be very winding and progess therefore slow, leaving little time to visit the coastal towns on the final section of the route; they are perhaps best left for another day.

From ★★**Faro** take the N 2 via Estói to São Brás de Alportel. At first there is a fair amount of traffic, but soon the road becomes quieter. Setting out in good time allows a brief stop right at the start of the tour to visit the palace gardens in ★**Estói** and/or the Roman ruins at Milreu. Beyond Estói the route passes through a charming garden landscape continuing all the way to **São Brás de Alportel**, a pleasant small country town. At the large crossroads keep on the N 2 which now heads north towards Almodôvar and Lisbon. A little way along, at Pousada de São Brás, there is a fine view over the countryside. In due course the N 2 reaches the remote village of Barranco Velho, a few kilometres beyond which one forks right onto a road through the mountains to Cachopo. The scenery on this stretch is exceptionally beautiful, as indeed it is south of Barranco Velho. The road follows a convoluted course through lonely hill country, passing few villages. Cachopo is worth a short stop. There

Faro

São Brás de Alportel

Cachopo

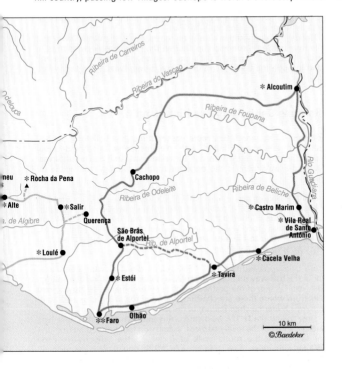

is not much to see but it does show just how very isolated and out of the way Algarve villages can be. Afterwards head east on the N 124, now making somewhat quicker progress. The poverty of this part of the Algarve is all too evident from villages such as Vaqueiros, Martim Longo and Giões along the way.

Alcoutim

Continue until eventually arriving at ★**Alcoutim**, a little town on the banks of the Guadiana. Here the fortress and the alleys beneath the fortress walls are well worth visiting, not to mention the riverside cafés with views across the water to Sanlúcar de Guadiana in Spain.

From Alcoutim a quite delightful, albeit narrow, road runs southwards parallel to the river, the banks of which are gently undulating on both the Portuguese and Spanish sides. For most of the way the road runs a little above the river, dropping down to the water from time to time. Guerreiros do Rio is a particularly charming village with a small historical and natural history museum. Joining the wider but no less quiet

Odeleite

N 122 south of Odeleite, head next for Castro Marim from where the IP 1 invites a quick return to Faro. Those with time and energy to spare could take this opportunity to look around ★**Castro Marim** and perhaps

Vila Real de
Santo António

visit ★**Vila Real de Santo António**. Returning to Faro by the coast road (N 125) there are several possibilities. Some time could be spent on the beach at Manta Rota, or at ★Cacela Velha, a little seaside spot with

Olhão

(almost) no tourists; alternatively ★**Tavira** and **Olhão** could be the final ports of call.

Other options

Instead of returning to Faro by the busy coast road, a detour can be made from Tavira on the N 270 through very pretty countryside. At São Brás de Alportel turn left again for Faro.

Holidaymakers based in resorts on the east coast between Tavira and Vila Real de Santo António can shorten the tour slightly by taking the N 397 direct from Tavira to Cachopo. Even so, allow plenty of time: the road through the lovely Serra de Alcaria is very twisting and therefore slow.

Route 2: Central Algarve Hinterland (125 km)

For most of its length this route passes through a delightful, largely cultivated landscape, dotted with picturesque villages and small towns, before ending with a visit to the ancient Arab capital of Silves. Along the way there is the opportunity for a walk on the Rocha da Pena.

Albufeira

Leaving **Albufeira** take either the N 125/N 270 or the IP 1 eastwards to ★**Loulé**. If on the N 270, pull in just short of the town to visit the pilgrim chapel of Nossa Senhora da Piedade, a little way up from the road, on the south side (good view). Loulé's daily lunchtime market brings a real splash of colour to the area around the market hall. The old town is in any case well worth visiting.

Salir

From Loulé proceed north to ★**Salir**, either direct or with a detour at about the half-way point to Querença, a village in a picturesque setting. Salir itself is one of the prettiest villages in the Algarve, occupying two hills from where there are charming views of the little farms and holdings which are the chief feature of the landscape.

Now follow the N 124 westwards. Anyone keen to stretch their legs and see some of the lovely *baroccal* scenery on foot rather than from the car will enjoy the round walk of 5 km on the ★Rocha da Pena

Alte

(479 m). Otherwise drive straight on to ★**Alte**, one of the showpiece villages of the Algarve hinterland, with pretty white houses and on the east side an interesting church and spring.

A traditional calling: fishermen in Albufeira

Next comes **São Bartolomeu de Messines**, a small country town where a brief stop is recommended to explore the old centre (some may prefer not to stop here, so leaving more time for Silves). The almost deserted road then cuts across some very remote country, passing scarcely a single village. A short distance to the north lies the Arade reservoir, its water level pitifully low after the failed rains of recent years. Soon ★★**Silves** comes into view away in the distance. Its red sandstone castle and walls are particularly impressive, dominating the townscape. Immediately outside Silves, on the right of the road, stands a Manueline wayside cross protected by a roof. To do real justice to the town requires a fairly lengthy stop. There is the cathedral, chiefly notable for the number of Gothic features that survived the 1755 earthquake more or less unscathed; there is the imposing castle, dating back to the Moors, where visitors can walk along the walls around the courtyard; and there is the archaeological museum offering a good insight into the cultural history of the region.

São Bartolomeu de Messines

Silves

For the last lap of the tour follow the N 269, a quiet country road, eastwards through tranquil countryside to Algoz, a typical Algarve village worlds removed from the bright lights and bustle just a few kilometres away on the coast. From there it is only 11 km back to Albufeira.

Algoz

Route 3: West Algarve (160 km)

This tour of the western Algarve encounters some exceptionally varied scenery. Foothills merge gradually into the Serra de Monchique in which rises the highest peak in the Algarve. The *serra* in turn gives way to the

View from Fóia, the highest peak in the Algarve

barren landscape of the far west, quite different from anywhere else in the Algarve and counting among its wonders Cabo de São Vicente, the most south-westerly point of the Continent. An early start is required to have enough time to enjoy the sights of Lagos. And if stops are made in some of the villages en route, Cabo de São Vicente should be dropped from the itinerary (shortening it to about 100 km).

Portimão

Leaving **Portimão**, take the N 266 northwards towards Monchique. Soon the road enters relatively sparsely populated countryside and as it gains height one splendid view succeeds another. A few kilometres before Monchique a very special little place is reached – ★Caldas de Monchique, a spa considerably smaller but rich in history and with much more atmosphere than Monchique itself. Anyone already wanting to rest need look no further than one of the several charming cafés here.

Monchique

The small town of **Monchique**, regional centre for the ★★**Serra de Monchique**, spreads up a hillside, its steep alleys inviting ascent and a backward glance down into the valley. Virtually every street in the north-west of the town offers a gateway to lovely mountain scenery and it is well worth allowing time for a walk.

Not to be missed either is the short detour (16 km in all) to ★★Fóia (902 m), the highest peak in the Algarve. The summit, reached by a road starting in Monchique, commands a magnificent panorama of almost the entire coastline and a fine view inland towards the Alentejo to the north.

Returning to Monchique by the same road, head south again, branching left after only 3 km onto the N 267 running west. At first it winds with numerous bends through most pleasing mountain scenery, but as it nears Aljezur the landscape becomes increasingly barren and monotonous, the influence of the Atlantic being more and more reflected in the vegetation.

Rather than spend time in **Aljezur** some may prefer to make a detour to the coast. Places like Praia de Monte Clérigo give a good idea of how the west coast of the Algarve differs from the more tourist-orientated south coast. About 6 km south of Aljezur the N 120 veers inland offering a fast run direct to Lagos some 24 km away. The alternative is to continue south-west on the N 268 with detours to the sea at either Carrapateira or **Vila do Bispo**. In due course the main road reaches ★**Sagres**. Just south of the town is the Fortaleza de Sagres, and 6 km west ★★Cabo de São Vicente. Standing on the cape gazing out to sea, it is easy to imagine what emotions the Portuguese seafarers of the 15th c. must have felt as they set sail on their voyages beyond the horizon.

Aljezur

Sagres

From Cabo de São Vicente return by the same route through Sagres to Vila do Bispo and branch off eastwards onto the N 125 which in these parts carries very little traffic. A few kilometres beyond the little town of Raposeira a historical gem stands hardly noticed by the roadside – the ★Ermida de Nossa Senhora de Guadalupe, the oldest surviving church in the Algarve.

Vila do Bispo

Finally ★**Lagos** is reached. The town centre is relatively small, so visitors can choose between a more or less comprehensive tour, which might even take in the Igreja de Santo António and the museum, or a less arduous stroll through the streets in the centre of town. There are a great many cafés and restaurants to choose from. ★★Ponta da Piedade, about 2 km south of Lagos, boasts perhaps the strangest rock formations in the Algarve. From Lagos it is then another 17 km back to the starting point at Portimão.

Lagos

The tour of the western Algarve can just as well be done in reverse which has the advantage firstly that Lagos can be explored while one is still relatively fresh, and secondly that the day can be brought to an agreeable conclusion in the little spa of Caldas de Monchique, so full of character. The only disadvantage is that a decision has to be made early on as to whether to include Cabo de São Vicente or not.

Alternative route

Sights from A to Z

Albufeira F 5

Capital of the administrative district of Albufeira
Population: 17,000

The town of Albufeira lies on the southern coast of the Algarve about
35 km west of Faro. Albufeira is the first town of any size in the east of
the Barlavento, and is located on one of the bays surrounded by rocky
cliffs that characterise this region. Once a village, Albufeira remained
relatively unaffected by the initial influx of tourists in the 1960s and
1970s, but this idyllic situation did not last long, and by the end of the
1970s it, like many other places in the Algarve, attracted the attention of
large holiday companies and quickly developed into one of the Algarve's
major tourist centres. Together with the surrounding beaches, it is now
dominated by tourism and the infrastructure that goes with it. All kinds
of water sports can be enjoyed here, as well as tennis, golf and horse
riding.

History   Albufeira looks back on a long and eventful past. The Romans settled
here in the first half of the 2nd c. BC – however, its ideal location suggests
that there had been settlements here long before that. The Romans
erected a fort on the cliffs, named their settlement Baltum and built salt-
extraction works by the sea, salt being needed to preserve fish. In the
5th c. AD the Visigoths came to the region, only to be driven out by the
Moors in 716. They named the town Al-Buhara or Al-Buhera, from which
the present name of Albufeira (meaning lagoon) was derived. Albufeira
became an important port as a result of trading with North Africa.
Occupation by Christian troops in 1189 lasted a mere two years, and it
was the middle of the 13th c. before Albufeira was conquered by knights
of the Order of Santiago and subsequently fell to the Portuguese. Trade
with North Africa declined and the town lost its importance.

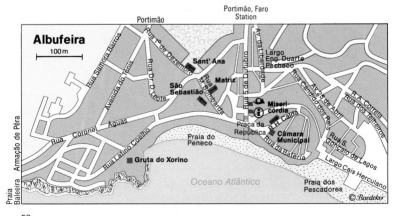

Rua 5 de Outubro – a popular street in Albufeira

In the 16th c. the people of Albufeira successfully withstood repeated attacks by Moorish, British and French pirates. The earthquake of 1755 caused much devastation, and floods destroyed many houses near the coast. Civil war in the 19th c. was Albufeira's next disaster; guerrilla troops led by the infamous Remexido, a supporter of the absolutist King Miguel I, besieged the town and finally set fire to it.

Albufeira still occupies an impressive amphitheatre-like location on the slopes of the rocky bay. The wide beach is crowded with tourists, but also fishermen moor their boats here and go about their daily business. However, modern buildings and tourism now dominate and little remains of the old fishing village.

Traffic, which for a long time plagued the narrow streets, has been banished to the outskirts, and the town centre is now a large pedestrian zone. The streets are laid with typical Portuguese mosaics, and the little whitewashed houses give the centre of the town an appealing atmosphere. Souvenir and jewellery shops and boutiques abound, while in the evening Albufeira is an eldorado for night-life. Sounds and rhythms of all kinds emanate from the houses, and those who enjoy a pub-crawl will find many to choose from. The same goes for restaurants and cafés; some streets seem to be full of them, especially the Rua Cândido dos Reis. Less noisy and to be recommended is a stroll from the indoor fish market up the narrow Rua da Bateria along the steep coast.

Townscape

Sights

Before going on a tour of Albufeira visitors should enjoy the view over the bay and the old town from the viewing site above the beach to the

★View

east. This superb panorama is perhaps the most-beautiful experience the small town has to offer.

Tour

From here steps lead down to the beach and to the Largo Cais Herculano. After following the Rua da Bateria as far as the busy Rua 5 de Outobro, either continue westwards or join the crowds in Rua 5 de Outobro and the centrally located Largo Engenheiro Duarte Pacheco.

Hospital

Near the old Town Hall with the unusual metal construction on its tower stands the hospital. A plaque indicates that the entrance gate to the fortress once stood here.

Igreja da Misericórdia

In nearby Rua Henrique Calado the little Igreja da Misericórdia is almost hidden in a row of houses. Only the Manueline door of red sandstone makes it stand out from the others.

Igreja Matriz

The Igreja Matriz was rebuilt after the earthquake by Francisco Gomes de Avelar, the then Bishop of the Algarve. In 1993 the whole building was renovated but has not really benefited from this.

Igreja Sant' Ana

The Igreja Sant' Ana on the corner of Rua 1° de Dezembro by the Largo Jacinto d'Ayete, on the other hand, is an extremely pretty church. This typical, whitewashed Algarve building dates from the 18th c. and provides an almost rural element in its urban surroundings. Of note are the crossing cupola and the baroque gables on all four sides.

Igreja de São Sebastião

This church still has a small Manueline side door from a previous church.

Largo Engenheiro Duarte Pacheco

The Largo Engenheiro Duarte Pacheco is Albufeira's main square. This is the busy hub of the town, the meeting place of locals and tourists alike. It is lined with cafés, restaurants and snack bars, interspersed with postcard stands and fashion jewellers. The town's churches are portrayed on the fountain in the square, and a tile picture provides a view of old Albufeira. Among the pretty herbaceous borders old Portuguese men sit under a rubber tree and survey the scene.

Gruta do Xorino

The Gruta do Xorino in the south-west of Albufeira is where the liberals fled when the town was besieged by the monarchist Miguelites in 1833. They reached the caves through an underground passage, and from there continued their flight by boat to Faro. Fishermen offer boat trips to the Gruta do Xorino from Albufeira's town centre; it is also possible to reach the caves by a path along the cliffs.

Beaches

Municipal beach

From Rua 5 de Outobro a tunnel leads to Albufeira's municipal beach. The tunnel was cut through the massive rock between 1932 and 1935. The engineer in charge of the project was Duarte Pacheco, who was minister of construction under Salazar. For a municipal beach it is perfectly acceptable, although in summer it is generally overcrowded. Above the beach is a short promenade lined with flags of all nations, where cafés provide a welcome change from the throng below.

Beaches to the west

To the west of Albufeira lie several small beaches in attractive bays as well as the long Praia da Galé that extends as far as Armação de Pera. Everywhere there are small and large catering establishments together with good facilities for water sports – diving, surfing, waterskiing. The Praia da Galé is preferred by surfers, while the best beaches for diving and snorkeling are those between Albufeira and the Praia do Castelo, namely, the popular Praia de São Rafael and the Praia da Baleeira.

The beaches of Albufeira are popular in the summer

Attractive smaller beaches in the east of Albufeira include Oura, Balaia and Maria Luisa, which form part of the tourist suburbs of Montechoro and Areias de São João. All beaches offer good water sports and catering facilities.

Beaches to the east

Olhos de Água lies 7 km east of Albufeira on the coast. The name stems from the freshwater springs that can be seen on the beach at low tide and which the local inhabitants describe as "water eyes". The beach, somewhat rocky in parts, is very attractive but tends to become crowded in high season.

Olhos de Água

The Praia de Falésia is another well-tended beach some 12 km east of Albufeira. It is noted for its high rock-wall that extends for several kilometres along the coast and shines colourfully when the light is favourable. There is plenty of room on the beach, despite the presence along the cliffs of one of the Algarve's largest holiday parks with its apartments, bungalows and a hotel, covering an area of 35 ha. Originally only a few small holiday homes were built here in 1973, followed by a huge hotel in 1978. The last bungalows were completed in 1992.

★Praia da Falésia

Surroundings

Tunes, some 10 km north of Albufeira, is a sleepy village known only for its railway station. Its name suggests that it might have been settled by immigrants from Tunis in North Africa.

Tunes

The village of Paderne is located 12 km north-east of Albufeira in the midst of some beautiful, slightly hilly countryside. This picturesque spot offers a peaceful escape from the hustle and bustle on the coast. Known

Paderne

61

to the Moors as Badirna, it was conquered by the Portuguese under Dom Paia Peres Correia in 1248. The parish church, built in the 16th c., still shows some Manueline features from this period.

Also of interest are the ruins of a Moorish castle about 2 km south of the village. You reach the castle on a gravelled path marked "Castello", which branches off the main road to the south at the western exit of the village near the cemetery. It leads underneath the highway and you can see the castle from a good distance. It was bought by the government in 1998 and is to be restored in the near future, together with the nearby "Roman bridge".

Boliqueime

Boliqueime, a village 10 km north-east of Albufeira, has been somewhat spoiled by modern development. It was the birthplace of Cavaco Silva, who was prime minister of Portugal for a number of years. Lídia Jorge (► Famous People), one of Portugal's best-known authors, also grew up here. In her novel *The Day of the Miracles* she describes everyday life in the sleepy village during the Salazar period and the hope that first sprang from the Carnation Revolution.

Guia

In Guia, 6 km north-west of Albufeira, stands the Igreja de Nossa Senhora da Guia, built in the 19th c., the interior of which is decorated with beautiful tiles.

Zoomarine Park

Near Guia lies the well-known Zoomarine Park, which attracts some 400,000 visitors a year and is laid out with small lakes, gardens and restaurants. Among the various birds and animals are parrots, which include some droll items in their repertoire, but mainly – as the name implies – different marine animals. There are several ponds and aquaria with many varieties of fish, including sharks, as well as performing sea lions, dolphins and seals. There is a large swimming pool suitable for children and adults, together with roundabouts, a Ferris wheel and cinema shows. Just to see the main attractions and the many animals will take at least four hours.

Open mid-Mar. to Oct. daily 10am–6pm, to 8pm in summer; Nov. to mid-Mar. Tue.–Sun. 10am–5pm.

Algoz

Algoz is a typical small Algarve country town about 10 km north-west of Albufeira and 15 km east of Silves. It lies in the middle of very beautiful countryside, some of which is almost completely unspoiled. It is well worth making a short detour to the Ermida de Nossa Senhora do Pilar on a hill on the edge of town. From up here there is a splendid view of Algoz and its surroundings.

Krazy World

North of Alvor on the road leading to São Bartolomeu de Messines you reach Krazy World, a theme park with an ingenious mini-golf course, a pet zoo, snake pond, crocodile enclosure and many other attractions as well as a restaurant and a swimming pool.

Open Jun.–Sep. daily 9.30am–7.30pm, Oct.–May daily 9.30am–6pm.

Alcoutim   L 3

Capital of the administrative district of Alcoutim
Population: 3,500

Alcoutim is beautifully located in the north-east of the Algarve on the right bank of the Guadiana, which here forms the frontier between the

View of the Guadiana and the Spanish town of Sanlúcar ➤
from the castle ruins of Alcoutim

Algarve and Spanish Andalusia. 40 km further south the Guadiana enters the Atlantic. In the town the Ribeira de Cadavais flows into the Guadiana.

The town's charm lies in its seclusion; only a few tourists stray this far. Some come by boat: when conditions are favourable excursion boats from Vila Real de Santo António (see entry) continue on to Alcoutim.

There is only a modest degree of tourist infrastructure. Alcoutim and its western and southern surroundings form part of the most remote regions in the Algarve. Population density is low and poverty levels high as there is little work available.

Opposite the town to the east, on the Spanish bank of the river, lies the town of Sanlúcar de Guadiana, presenting a tranquil picture, far removed from the military battles and enmity that existed between the two towns in centuries past.

History

Alcoutim was a river port back in Phoenician times, and it is thought that there was also a Celtic settlement here. In the 2nd c. BC the town was Roman and known as Alcoutinium. In AD 415 the Alans took Alcoutim, followed shortly afterwards by the Visigoths; the Moors ruled the town in the 8th c. In 1240 the Portuguese under Sancho II succeeded in taking Alcoutim, and in the early 14th c. Alcoutim was handed over to the Knights of the Order of Santiago. In 1371 Portugal and Castille concluded the Treaty of Alcoutim: after a festive meeting on the river Fernando I and Henrique II of Castille signed the treaty, temporarily ending the wars between the two countries. In the 17th c. Alcoutim again became the scene of battles between Spain and Portugal after Portuguese nobles had initiated the restoration of Portugal's independence from Spain by means of a revolt in 1640. It was 1668 before Spain finally recognised Portugal's independence, and until that date there were frequent attacks from both sides of the river. Alcoutim suffered its last political conflicts at the time of the Miguelite Wars in the 1830s, when liberals and absolutist Miguelites fought one another on the Guadiana.

Townscape

Alcoutim with its shining white houses stretches beneath the castle as far as the river bank. A stroll through the little streets of this still unspoiled town is well worthwhile. On the river bank and in the town itself there are some attractive squares, and several churches and the castle bear witness to the town's turbulent past.

Sights

Castelo

Because of its location Alcoutim played an important strategic role early in Portuguese history. The present castle dates back to an 11th c. Moorish fort, but there were probably larger defensive walls here before that. In 1304 Dom Dinis I provided the town with funds to renovate the town walls and the castle.

The castle has not been used for military purposes since 1878. Since then it has served various needs, including being an abattoir at one time. In 1973 archaeologists began to take an interest in its history and undertook extensive digs and restoration projects based on the original plans. Today there is an exhibition of archaeological finds open to visitors, and the old foundations which were revealed during the digs can also be inspected.

Ermida de Nossa Senhora da Conceição

The Ermida de Nossa Senhora da Conceição lies higher up to the west of the castle site. A semicircular flight of steps leads up to this simple edifice. The chapel dates from the 16th c.; all that remains of the original is a Manueline doorway. The building was extensively restored in the first half of the 18th c., and the baroque altarpiece from that period is particularly striking.

The parish church is charmingly located on the bank of the Guadiana. Between 1538 and 1554 the former small, single-aisled chapel was replaced, with help from the Knights of the Order of Santiago, with a triple-aisled church in early Renaissance style; the Renaissance portal has been preserved. Inside the church, note the capitals and the baptistry with a 16th c. bas-relief.

Igreja Matriz

The inconspicuous Ermida de Santo António also stands by the river. This little chapel with an archaic-looking circular window above the doorway dates from the 16th c.

Ermida de Santo António

The small Igreja da Misericórdia on the Praça da República was built at the beginning of the 16th c. but underwent numerous restorations and renovations in later years.

The site has been flooded on several occasions over the centuries. A mark on the outside wall shows the level reached by the waters during one of the worst floods in 1876.

Igreja da Misericórdia

Surroundings

From Alcoutim a road leads southwards along the bank of the Guadiana through beautiful countryside. In the sleepy village of Guerreiros do Rio, which is idyllically located on the banks of the river some 12 km south of Alcoutim, the Museu do Rio has been opened in the former primary school. A small exhibition provides information on the history, fauna and flora and life of the people living by the river. The fishermen in Guerreiros offer scenic boat trips on the Guadiana.

Guerreiros do Rio

8 km west of Alcoutim is the N 124, and 25 km along this road is the village of Giões. On the edge of the village stands the 16th c. parish church, which houses some attractive portraits of saints, including one of Nossa Senhora das Relíquias (16th c).

4 km east of Giões, near Clarines, can be found the remains of a pre-Roman settlement known as Cerro das Relíquias.

Giões

30 km west of Alcoutim lies the isolated village of Martim Longo, which was settled in Roman times. Remains of 16th c. wall-paintings can still be seen in the parish church. The hills in the vicinity are ideal for gentle walks.

Martim Longo

In the middle of the Algarve mountains, about 10 km south-east of Martim Longo, lie the houses of Vaqueiros. The most striking building in the village is the 16th c. church, which renovated in the 18th c. Its attractively painted side-altars are of particular interest.

Vaqueiros

Cachopo is a pretty, secluded Algarve village that very few tourists visit. From Martim Longo, follow the N 124 to the south. On the edge of the village you can see the barns that are typical of this region and are reminiscent of Celtic roundhouses.

Cachopo

Aljezur   C 4

Capital of the administrative district of Aljezur
Population: 5,500

The small town of Aljezur is located in the west of the Algarve about 40 km north of Sagres. The N 120 from Lagos passes through Aljezur, continues north through the Alentejo region and on towards Lisbon. Far away from the busy holiday centres, Aljezur is an ideal destination for those looking for a different kind of holiday with less emphasis on comfort and a good tourist infrastructure and more on enjoying nature at its best. The climate is somewhat harsher than in the east of the Algarve, and the vegetation in particular differs from that in the south-east. It is markedly more barren, with no pretty gardens but more in the way of low undergrowth and *macchia* bushes. The peace and quiet the region has enjoyed to date is due mainly to the fact that the whole of the coastal strip south and north of Aljezur is a nature reserve. However, even in the Costa Vicentina nature park tourist projects are planned, albeit on a small scale.

History

It is assumed that Aljezur was founded by the Moors. In 1246 it was conquered by the Portuguese Order of Santiago led by Dom Paio Peres Correia. Because of its secluded location Aljezur never became of great importance.

Townscape

The most attractive side of Aljezur is seen when entering it from the north after first crossing a small river, the Ribeira de Aljezur, and then reaching the town centre. The major public buildings, some banks and cafés and restaurants line the main street. Up on a hill lie the remains of a castle that dates back to Moorish times. Over the centuries it fell more and more into decay and was finally completely demolished in an earthquake and never rebuilt. From here there is a superb view of the surrounding countryside.

Beaches

There are some excellent beaches near Aljezur, but some are difficult to get to and the wind and sea are rougher here than on the south coast of the Algarve. Strong currents mean that conditions vary from year to year. The isolated and extensive Praia de Carriagem, the semicircular Praia de Monte Clérigo and the Praia da Arrifana, with the remains of an old fortress, are of scenic beauty. Also very popular are the beaches near Carrapateira and the beach at Odeceixe in the north-west of the Algarve. Odeceixe itself is a pretty village. The beach lies 2 km further west at the mouth of a small river.

Almansil   G 5

Administrative district: Loulé
Population: 6,000

Alamansil (or Almancil), 13 km north-west of Faro, has been somewhat spoiled by development. The busy N 125 bisects the town and leaves it looking disorganised and divided. Nevertheless, with its numerous shops and banks Almansil is the shopping centre for the nearby luxurious holiday resorts of Vale do Lobo and Quinta do Lago. Above all, however, Almansil is well known for two reasons – the Igreja de São Lourenço is one of the most artistically and historically interesting churches in the Algarve, and the Culture Centre near the church has also made a name for itself with art and music-lovers.

Sights

★Igreja de São
Lourenço

The Igreja de São Lourenço stands outside the town on the road to Faro, and is visible from afar. It is thought to date back to the 15th c., when a small chapel was first built here. From the outside the present baroque church appears rather plain; only the dome above the choir really stands out.

The church is renowned for the extraordinary glazed tile decoration in the relatively small interior (➤ p. 42). Architecture and decoration

The church of São Lourenço contains splendid azulejos *decoration*

blend together into a harmonious whole. The walls, vaulted ceiling and even the dome are all clad in blue and white *azulejos*. A warm contrast is provided by the high altar in *talha dourada* with a figure of St Lawrence. The six tile-paintings on the side-walls depict scenes from the saint's life. In the front on the left is shown a conversation between St Lawrence and Pope Sixtus in which St Lawrence is complaining that he is not to die a martyr's death. He then learns that he will become a martyr within the next three days. The following tablets show the martyrdom of the saint whom the authorities caused to be burned to death because he had given to the poor money intended for building a church.

The tile-paintings have been dated to 1730. At that time the production of large paintings in tiles was very popular in Portugal. Political events, town views, allegories and even biblical scenes were portrayed on tiles. The *azulejos* in São Lourenço were the work of the baroque artist António Oliveira Bernardes, but it is not known in which factory the tiles themselves were made; possibly they were imported from Italy or Holland.

Open Mon. 2.30–6pm, Tue.–Sat. 10am–1pm, 2.30–6pm.

The Centro Cultural São Lourenço, a short distance down from the church, was fitted out in the early 1980s by a German firm. In the beautiful interior – when restoring the building traditional Algarve architecture was preserved – is a gallery with seven rooms in which temporary exhibitions are held. Concerts, ranging from classical to jazz, are held in the culture centre with, now and again, avant-garde music included in the programme. There is also a sculpture garden and a patio where open-air performances are held.

Centro Cultural
São Lourenço

Surroundings

★Quinta do Lago   Quinta do Lago, the "country estate by the sea", is an extremely exclusive holiday resort 6 km south of Almansil. Elegant villas and bungalows have been built on this spacious area of land, some of them privately owned and some available for hire as holiday accommodation. Between the houses broad lawns have been laid out with small artificial waterways and decorative umbrella pines. There are several golf courses and tennis courts, and the beach, which is wide, relatively empty and clean, offers facilities for various water sports. The restaurants are first class. In 1989 Quinta do Lago was chosen as the venue for the NATO Assembly.

★Vale do Lobo   Wolf's Valley, a few kilometres west of Quinta do Lago, is an equally luxurious holiday resort, with attractive villas with small gardens and swimming pools, broad lawns and pine trees. Here too there are golf courses and tennis courts and a wide range of similar leisure pursuits, but not much in the way of organised entertainment is provided. The little centre of Vale do Lobo is attractively laid out, and one can pass a pleasant hour or so in one of the cafés or restaurants – some with a view of the sea.

The beach between Vale do Lobo and Quinta do Lago is suitable for long walks, and there are some beach restaurants.

★Alte   F 4

Administrative district: Loulé
Population: 500

Alte is an extremely attractive village in the Algarve hinterland at the foot of the Serra de Caldeirão, north of Albufeira and at least 20 km from the coast. The easiest access is via the quiet country road that leads from São Bartolomeu de Messines eastwards into the foothill region. The countryside around Alte is relatively unspoiled and hilly. The delightful "Algarve gardens" stretch this far; north of Alte the landscape becomes a little more barren. Olives, figs, oranges, lemons and, above all, almonds thrive in the fertile soil; in spring luxuriant gardens come into bloom everywhere.

Alte is known for its festival held on May 1st each year, when the streets and lanes are decorated with flowers. There are flower processions through the streets and a grand dance festival which attracts folk-dancing groups and spectators from far and wide. Picnics are traditionally held in and around Alte on this day. Somewhat quaintly perhaps, in February the Festa dos Chouriços, or Sausage Festival, is celebrated in honour of the village saint and patron saint of animals, São Luís.

Townscape   In recent years this picturesque little village has attracted increasing numbers of tourists. Coachloads of holidaymakers visit it, and one can only hope that its delightful and quiet image will not change too drastically. Not only is Alte's location captivating, the village itself with its whitewashed little Algarve houses, small lanes, flower gardens and planted containers at the gates is quite entrancing. Hibiscus, geraniums and oleander bushes bloom everywhere, and visitors can follow twisty and cobbled lanes through the village. Away from the hustle and bustle of the coast, a stroll through Alte will give a good insight into rural life in the Algarve.

Sights

Igreja Matriz   In the village centre towers the Igreja Matriz, built in the early 16th c.

The Ermida de São Luís in Alte

Some features from that time remain, such as the simple Manueline doorway. The pretty village church is usually open, the entrance being on the right-hand side via the sacristy. In the three-aisled interior note the beautiful wooden ceiling and Manueline arch that separates the choir and high altar from the nave. A glance up at the choir ceiling shows three bosses: the front one symbolises the Portuguese voyages of discovery, the central one in the shape of a moon symbolises discoveries in the Orient, and the rear blue one the sea routes to India discovered by the Portuguese. There is an attractive pulpit with steps made of *azulejos*. In the baroque side chapels in the left and right aisles are portrayals of numerous popular saints – at the front in the left aisle are São Jorge, São Francisco and São Vicente, at the back John the Baptist, Mary and Christ, in the right aisle São Miguel with a pair of scales and São Sebastião. In the Capela de Nossa Senhora de Lurdes a black saint can be seen in the left aisle. This side-chapel is clad in rare tiles from Sevilla.

The road to the Fonte das Bicas leads past the Ermida de São Luís. This baroque chapel with a simple façade is usually closed. It is dedicated to the patron saint of Alte. | Ermida de São Luís

The Fonte das Bicas is an idyllic little place on the eastern edge of the village. As well as verses by the poet Cândido Guerreiro (1871–1953), who hailed from Alte, there is a tile picture of St Anthony. | Fonte das Bicas

At the taps (*bicas*) the villagers fill their plastic bottles with fresh spring water; people even come from far and wide, as it is believed by many that the water has healing powers and is said to be the reason why the inhabitants of Alte live so long.

A short distance along the river lies the Fonte Grande, (Great Spring). | Fonte Grande

Tables and benches invite visitors to picnic, while a kiosk supplies drinks. There is also a restaurant nearby.

Queda do Vigário Those wishing to extend their walk can continue out of the village and along the river. After 2 km you reach Queda do Vigário, the largest waterfall in the Algarve.

Surroundings

★Salir The peaceful village of Salir 15 km to the east is as pretty as Alte. It is located on two hills, on the western one of which a few traces of a Moorish castle can still be seen. The importance of these fragments lies in the fact that this is one of the few places in the Algarve with authentic Moorish remains. The little Castelo quarter with its tiny white houses and many flowers is quite idyllic. The larger part of the village lies on the second hill, dominated by the water tower and the plain village church. From the church square there is a fine view of the mountainous countryside where smallholdings abound on the rich red soil.

★Rocha da Pena Between Alte and Salir a signposted minor road leads north off the N 124 to the Rocha da Pena, a small mountain 479 m high. This region with its varied flora and fauna has been designated a nature reserve. A circular route 4.7 km long starts at a round flowerbed with an old carob tree in the centre. The route, not in the best of conditions and badly signposted, climbs up past good viewing points and a small cave to which the Moors are said to have fled during attacks by Christian soldiers in the 13th c. After the walk visitors can seek refreshment in the das Grutas bar at the starting point.

Malhão For those who prefer to discover the region by car, a detour (of about 20 minutes from Salir) is recommended to Malhão and its centre of Tibetan buddhists (**Centro Budista Tibetano**). From the road from Salir to Alte a small pathway branches off to Malhão and the north, about 1 km outside Salir. At first it winds along a small riverbed and then, as a wide and well-made road, leads up to the village of Malhão, in the shadow of the mountain of the same name, 537 m high. A road sign points to the right and the Centro Budista Tibetano, the meditation centre Hum Kara Dzong. From here is a fantastic view of the Serra do Caldeirão.

Alvor D 5

Administrative district: Portimão
Population: 5,000

Alvor is a tourist fishing village on the south coast of the Algarve. It lies about 1 km inland, between Lagos and Portimão, on the wide Baia de Lagos (Bay of Lagos). To the west of Alvor is a lagoon formed at the mouths of four rivers where many of the villagers work as fishermen.

History It is thought that Alvor dates back to the 5th c. In the Moorish period – when the village was known as Albur – there was probably a castle here, which was captured by the Portuguese in 1250 during the reign of Afonso III. Alvor gained a place in Portuguese history when King João II died here in 1495. His body was buried in Silves Cathedral and later transported to Batalha. Alvor was almost completely destroyed by the 1755 earthquake and the resultant flood.

Townscape Alvor is a prosperous place lying as it does between the two holdiay centres around Portimão and Lagos, and although itself tourist orientated it has retained its attractive appearance. The centre of the village with its small lanes features some low whitewashed fishermen's houses. There are a few restaurants, cafés and souvenir shops, but all in all it remains relatively rustic. Some streets lead down to the water. Particularly attractive is the harbour with its fish market and simple taverns and cafés along the bank. To the east of Alvor, however, near Torralta and by the Praia dos Três Irmãos, there are some larger hotel blocks.

Sights

The Igreja Matriz is one of the village's highlights. Dating from the 16th c., it is a typical Algarve village church which retains some of its original architectural features. The Manueline main and side doors are worthy of note. Other Manueline features can be found inside – the arch above the chancel is adorned with a turned stone ribbon, the delicate capitals on the six pillars consist of stone fishing ropes and plant ornamentation. The altarpieces are framed sparingly in *talha dourada*.

Igreja Matriz

Alvor's "own" beach is the kilometre-long Praia de Alvor stretching to the west and east of the village. There are hotels on the Praia dos Três Irmãos further west.

Praia de Alvor

Surroundings

Mexilhoeira, 4 km north-west of Alvor, has retained its rustic character. At its highest point stands the Igreja Matriz with a Renaissance doorway and a Manueline side doorway. The bell tower, too, has a small doorway decorated in Manueline style. The courtyard in front of the church, from where there is a superb view towards Alvor and the sea, is attractively planted with trees.

Mexilhoeira

For those with archaeological interests there are two excavation sites near Alvor worth visiting. For the **necropolis** of Alcalar leave the N 125 near the exit to Alvor and follow a small narrow road northwards to Alcalar and Casais. After 5 km a road sign (Necropole) points to the right. Follow this road for about 50 m then take a footpath to the left towards the excavation site (always accessible) about 150 m away. It is believed that the burial site of Alcalar was developed between 2000 and 1600 BC.

Alcalar

Roman remains can be found near Abicada. Near the village of Figueira a track signposted Ruinas romanas branches off to the south. Follow the uneven but well-defined path a further 1.5 km to the coast (if in doubt at any turnings, keep to the right). The path at first runs parallel to the railways line, passes a deserted country estate and ends near a group of houses. Directly below is the excavation site of Abicada. The area is fenced in, but you can have a good look from all sides. The site of the villa, probably inhabited from the 1st to the 4th c. AD, was in those days most likely directly on the edge of the sea. Its mosaic floors are well preserved.

Abicada

Armação de Pêra   E 5

Administrative district: Silves
Population: 3,000

Armação de Pêra, with its high-rise hotels and apartments, lies on the south coast of the Algarve between Portimão and Albufeira, about 45 km west of Faro.
    Surprisingly, just a few kilometres to the north lies countryside that, if

The white Ermida de Nossa Senhora da Rocha stands out against the blue sea and sky

not completely uninhabited, is still extremely attractive. Those approaching Armação de Pêra from the north along the N 125 will initially not anticipate anything undesirable at all – until suddenly behind a hill the bizarre skyline of the town comes into view.

Townscape

Apartment blocks, huge hotels and other high-rise buildings in course of construction together with giant cranes combine to give Armação de Pêra a sorry appearance. The long, broad beach stretching for several kilometres to the east of the town may compensate for all this. The small, colourful fishing boats drawn up on the sands are most picturesque, and the promenade is quite attractive.

There is still a little of the old village to be seen – the remains of the 17th c. fort with the little Capela de Santo António. The most pleasant side of Armação de Pêra lies to the east of the coast road.

Surroundings

To the west there are rows of hotels and holiday accommodation. In part these are attractively laid-out apartment villages on the cliffs above beautiful sandy bays. Between large rocky headlands there are deep bays, which the waters of the Atlantic have shaped into cliffs over thousands of years. Popular small sandy bays include the Praia dos Beijinhos, the Praia de Salomão, the Praia da Cova Redonda and the Praia Maré Grande.

★Ermida de
Nossa Senhora da
Rocha

On a high rocky outcrop 1 km west of Armação de Pêra stands a little jewel of a building – a marked contrast to its surroundings. The little Ermida de Nossa Senhora da Rocha has been built on a cliff 35 m above the sea. Gleaming white, it stands out against the blue sea, and a *miradouro* (viewpoint) juts out into the sea. From there you can clearly see the neighbouring headlands.

The chapel shows traces of early Gothic. The entrance between two columns leads into a small vestibule. The capital of one pillar is still well preserved, while the second has weathered over the centuries. A few candles always burn in the small anteroom – many Portuguese come here to pray to the Senhora da Rocha. The unusual hexagonal spire above the chancel can be seen from afar. There is a well nearby.

Below the chapel of Our Lady of the Rocks lie two narrow sandy bays, linked by a tunnel. Both beaches are relatively quiet.

Praia de Nossa Senhora da Rocha

Pêra, 2 km inland from Armação de Pêra, is still a pretty village with practically none of the turbulent atmosphere of the coastal strip nearby. The villagers keep themselves to themselves. Beautiful too is the surrounding countryside with its small country estates and orange and lemon groves. In front of one of the two churches is a square with a view of the sea.

Pêra

The village of Alcantarilha, 3 km north of Armação de Pêra, was founded by the Moors, and the name is Arabic for small bridge. The busy N 125 cuts through the village, but nevertheless there are some attractive corners to discover. The interior of the pretty parish church still displays some Manueline features. Adjoining the church is a charnel house.

Alcantarilha

Together with Tavira, Moncarapacho and Loulé, Porches is a centre of Portuguese ceramic manufacture. The village is located on the N 125 4 km north-west of Armação de Pêra. Along the road there are numerous sales centres offering ceramic articles of all kinds.

Porches

Between Porches and Alcantarilha you will find the bathers' paradise known as "The Big One" (➤ Practical Information, Aquaparks).

Carvoeiro   C 7

Administrative district: Lagoa
Population: 4,000

Until recently the coastal town of Carvoeiro was a pretty fishing village, but of late this idyllic spot has also developed into a sprawling tourist centre. Initially many Portuguese chose Carvoeiro as their summer resort, and then in the early 1980s a building boom began. In spite of everything, however, the town has managed to retain something of its former atmosphere.

The town centre above the little bay still consists of narrow streets and lanes. The houses are traditionally whitewashed, and new villas and small apartments have been built among the old fishermen's cottages. The buildings around the former village display an appealing degree of sympathy with their surroundings, and many of the holiday centres reveal hints of Moorish architecture in their construction. Carvoeiro has gained its good reputation from its overall planning. However, building has now spread to the extent that almost all the coastal strip around Carvoeiro has been developed. The infrastructure is more than adequate: cafés and restaurants abound and on the beach fishermen offer trips along the coast in their small boats. From the sea there are fantastic views of the rocks and cliffs: the Atlantic has pounded them for thousands of years, carving bizarre shapes in the soft limestone.

Townscape

Surroundings

Near Algar Seco, 2 km east of Carvoeiro, visitors can admire some particularly grandiose rock formations. In the course of time wind and weather have shaped a unique landscape. It is best to explore on foot – walking through a labyrinth of plateaux, rock pillars, narrow openings and natural archways and past a pool that rises and falls with the tides. Below, the sea bubbles through hidden caves and fissures. As the light changes, the limestone takes on a wide range of colours. Protected by walls of rock but with a view of the sea is a small café in the midst of this world of limestone.

★★Algar Seco

To the east and west of Carvoeiro are a few beautiful sandy bays; some of them, however, are difficult to reach. Access to the beach in the Vale de Centianes is by way of some steps near the Hotel Cristal. The small Praia do Carvalho is reached from Alfanzina, also by means of steps.

Beaches

Castro Marim

L 4

Capital of the administrative district of Castro Marim
Population: 5,000

Castro Marim lies in the south-east of the Algarve, some 4 km north-west of the border town of Vial Real de Santo António. The town is located on small hills rising up out of the fenland plain of the Guadiana, which flows past Castro Marim about 3 km further to the east. Around Castro Marim there are salt works, and to the south lies a protected marsh region, the Reserva Natural do Sapal de Castro Marim, with a rich variety of flora and fauna.

The name Castro Marim (Castle by the Sea) suggests that at one time

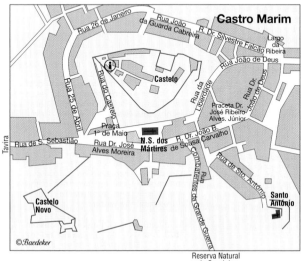

Reserva Natural
do Sapal de
Castro Marim

◄ *The attractive modern development at Carvoeiro*

The Order of the Knights of Christ

At first glance Castro Marim appears to be the very cradle of the Knights of Christ. The order – which played a decisive role in the story of Portuguese expansion during the 15th and early 16th centuries – was founded in 1319 and set up its headquarters on a hill near the town. The members of the order stayed on the right bank of the Guadiana until 1356, when they moved to the former Templar castle in Tomar.

This "flying visit" concealed an ingenious chess move. The Knights of Christ were no less than the former Templars, who had been suppressed in 1312. The Knights Templar had been founded in 1119 to protect pilgrims in the Holy Land and had played a definitive role in the medieval crusades. Not only did the Pope support the order, he also bestowed sundry privileges on it. The standing and power of the Templars grew apace, and soon they were able to call large tracts of land their own. In Portugal they settled by the Rio Nabão and built the well-known fortress of Tomar with its Templar church.

In France, too, the Templars acquired considerable influence and owned large areas of land – much to the annoyance and envy of Philip IV. In the early 14th c. he sought a means to suppress them. He accused the members of the order of heresy and of having links with Islam. The Pope, who was dependent on France, declared the accusations justified, and the Templar order was henceforth banned from all Christian countries.

In Portugal, however, the dissolution of the order was purely superficial.

Soon after the suppression of the Order of Knights Templar the Order of Christ was founded. The members of the order were the same: they merely changed their name and the design of the cross on their white robes. What had previously been a purely red cross with eight points now had a smaller white cross set into the red. The possessions and property of the Templars passed to the Knights of Christ – in principle, everything remained as it was. Only their headquarters was moved for form's sake to the Algarve. After a few years, when everything had quietened down, there was nothing to prevent them moving back to Tomar.

When the order was founded its members had sworn to defend the Christian faith, fight Islam and help to expand the Portuguese sphere of influence. Now they had the opportunity to carry out these promises. In the centuries that followed, the Knights of Christ exercised considerable influence on Portuguese history and eventually on the history of the world. Some of the major seafarers of the 15th and 16th c. were members of the order – Bartolomeu Dias, Vasco da Gama, Pedro Álvares Cabral. Henry the Navigator was a Grand Master of the order from 1418. Several kings also belonged to the Order of the Knights of Christ, in particular Manuel I. The symbol of the time, the cross of the Knights of Christ, was displayed on the sails of the caravels and on the dress of the mariners – and so became known throughout the world.

Its conversion to an order of monks in 1523 marked the beginning of the end. In 1789 the order was secularised and dissolved in 1910 when the Portuguese republic was proclaimed.

there was a settlement directly by the sea and that the present-day hills could even once have been islands.

Archaeological finds have proved that there was a pre-Roman settlement at Castro Marim. The Phoenicians probably established a trading port here. The name of the town also suggests the presence of Iberian Celts; fortified Celtic settlements on the peninsular were known as *castros*. Both in Roman times – when it was known as Castrum Marinum – and under Moorish rule, Castro Marim was of importance because of its location on a major link road. In 1319 Dom Diniz I declared the town the main seat of the Knights of Christ, the order which played such a decisive role in the Portuguese voyages of discovery and conquest. In 1356 the order moved its seat to Tomar, but for centuries afterwards Castro Marim remained a fortified town of strategic importance in guarding the frontier with Spain. In the 14th and 17th c. the fortifications were extensively enlarged. During the period of the Inquisition Castro Marim was a much-feared prison camp. As a result of the destruction caused by the 1755 earthquake and the rebuilding of the nearby Vila Real de Santo António in 1744, Castro Marim lost much of its importance within a short space of time.

History

The centre of Castro Marim lies between several small hills with castles on top. The town centre around the long and prettily laid out Praça 1° de Maio with its benches and plants and the Igreja de Nossa Senhora dos Mártires is very attractive.

Townscape

Sights

From the Praça 1° de Maio steps lead up to the Igreja de Nossa Senhora dos Mártires. This church was built in the 18th c. by the Knights of Christ, and an example of their work is the side balustrade

Igreja de Nossa Senhora dos Mártires

The main square of Castro Marim

displaying typical Knights of Christ crosses. The beautiful dome is very striking.

★Castelo

Above the little town centre stands the extensive castle complex, which can be reached in a few minutes from the Praça 1° de Maio. Originally 13th c., it was extended by the Knights of Christ after 1319. Within the fortified walls lie the ruins of an older Moorish castle, square in plan with circular towers at the corners. Also part of the complex is the Igreja de Misericórdia with a pleasing Renaissance doorway. From the castle walls there is a superb view of the town and of the newer castle opposite and also over the Guadiana towards Spain.

Within the castle walls there is the information office for the Sapal nature park (see below); here too are sundry exhibits relating to the history of Castro Marim.

Castelo Novo

The Castelo Novo or Castelo de São Sebastião stands above the town centre to the south. It was built in the 17th c. during the wars of restoration between Spain and Portugal.

Igreja de Santo António

On a third hill to the east stands the Igreja de Santo António containing some interesting portrayals of the saint.

Surroundings

Reserva Natural do Sapal de Castro Marim

To the south between Castro Marim and Vila Real de Santo António lies the marshy nature reserve of Sapal de Castro Marim. This is the breeding ground of oystercatchers, herons, storks and ospreys; many species of fish also live in the waterways. The flora in this largely unspoiled region is also very diverse. Guided tours are available (details can be obtained from the information office in the castle).

Estói   H 5

Administrative district: Faro
Population: 600

Estói is a village typical of the eastern Algarve hinterland. The main buildings and some pretty houses are grouped around the church. It is known chiefly for its palace and for the Roman excavations nearby.

Sights

Igreja Matriz

The 17th c. parish church appears almost too large for this little village. Dedicated to São Martinho, it was badly damaged in the 1755 earthquake. In the early 19th c. the then bishop of the Algarve, Francisco Gomes do Avelar, had the church rebuilt to plans by Francisco Xavier Fabri, the Italian architect he had invited to south Portugal after the earthquake to give expert advice on rebuilding the damaged cultural possessions of the Algarve. The internal structuring of the church was carried out mainly in the 1840s by local craftsmen. The church's most valuable possession is the 55 cm high monstrance of gilded silver. The 17th c. figure of St Vincent with the Raven on the right-hand altar was saved from the damaged church.

★Palácio de Estói

Immediately north of the church lie the parklands belonging to the Palácio de Estói. The palace is located in wonderful surroundings with extensive orange plantations, and it is worthwhile taking a walk along

Azulejos *decoration on the steps of the Palácio de Estói*

the palace wall to the north-west. Two *noras*, typical old Algarve fountains, can be seen; however, these no longer function.

The Palácio de Estói was built as a small rococo palace at the end of the 18th c. by the Visconde de Carvalha. Later it passed into the possession of another nobleman, and since 1989 it has been owned by the municipality of Faro. There are plans to restore it and to use the rooms for concerts. For the time being, however, it is not open to visitors, but the surrounding park (albeit not very large) is open. Laid out in the 18th and 19th c., the gardens are on several levels. Through the present main entrance – originally a side entrance – an attractive avenue of palms leads initially to the terrace on the middle level with a small pavilion and a pool, in the centre of which stands a group of Italian statues. The square is decorated with several tile pictures of allegorical and mythological scenes. Leda with the Swan is particularly fine. Busts of some Portuguese politicians and writers, including the Marquês de Pombal, Luís de Camões and Almeida Garrett line the walls.

Steps lead down to a slightly overgrown part of the garden. Here too there is a wall with attractive blue-and-white *azulejo* paintings. The Casa da Cascata, standing out amid the lush greenery, is clad in mosaics from nearby Milreu. A statue of the three Graces, modelled on the famous group by the Italian Antonio Canova, also catches the eye. An avenue of old trees links this part of the garden with the former main entrance.

From the middle level, steps lead up to a locked gate. From here there is a view of the somewhat sober façade of the palace with an open staircase on both sides. In the background the tower of the palace church can be seen.

Open Mon.–Sat. 9am–noon, 2–5pm.

Surroundings

On the western outskirts of Estói, alongside the road to Santa Bárbara de Nexe, lies the Milreu archaeological site. Digs have been going on here since excavations were started by the historian and archaeologist Estácio da Veiga in 1877. In Roman times Milreu was a summer residence for wealthy families from Faro, then known as Ossonoba. Sometimes Milreu is also called by the Roman name Ossonoba. The foundations of a Roman villa and baths have been discovered. They possibly date from the 1st c. AD. Relatively well preserved are the walls of an early Christian basilica that was built on the foundations of a Roman temple. A later small chapel was also built here.

Remains of a Roman road divide the area into a northern and a southern half. To the south of the Via Romana stands a semicircular walled ruin. Here the Romans erected a shrine, a **water sanctuary** (*nymphæum*), which was unique in that it was constructed like a Roman ambulatory temple – an exceptional feature on the Iberian Peninsula. Extraordinary too is the fish frieze of coloured tesserae. This find was sensational for two reasons: first, the decoration of an exterior wall is very rare; secondly, this discovery refuted the earlier theory that there was a shrine to Venus near Milreu. It has now been agreed that here a sea-nymph was revered as the tutelary goddess.

High inside the temple lies the platform (*podium*) with the shrine (*cella*), in the centre of which there was once a pool. In the entrance area another semicircular pool was found.

In the 5th c. AD the Visigoths erected a Christian church within the walls of the Roman shrine. A font and the remains of a mausoleum dating from that period have been preserved.

On the north side of the Via Romana lies the excavation site of the patrician house which a rich Roman probably had built. It has the typical ground-plan of a Roman **villa**, with a peristyle, or pillared courtyard, around which living, dining, and recreation quarters were grouped. Still to be seen are some mosaic floors where the archaeologists again stumbled upon fish and sea-creature motifs. The most important items found in the villa, a bust of Hadrian and one of the Empress Agrippina Minor, are now in the Archaeological Museum in Faro. A bust of the Emperor Gallienus is kept in the museum in Lagos.

To the west of the villa were the hot **baths** with a changing room (*apodyterium*), a warm bath (*caldarium*) and a cold bath (*frigidarium*). Remains

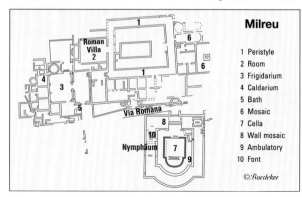

Milreu

1 Peristyle
2 Room
3 Frigidarium
4 Caldarium
5 Bath
6 Mosaic
7 Cella
8 Wall mosaic
9 Ambulatory
10 Font

©*Baedeker*

The most-important Roman remains in the Algarve – the ruins of Milreu

of underfloor heating in the warm bath and its boiler room were also discovered. A small pool decorated with fish mosaics is well preserved.

Open Tue.–Sun. 9.30am–12.30pm, 2–6pm, 5pm in winter.

The little village of Santa Bárbara de Nexe is located 6 km west of Estói in some beautiful fruit-growing country. From here there is a view of the nearby hills. **Santa Bárbara de Nexe**

The 15th c. parish church has three aisles and is one of the few smaller churches in the Algarve which are open every day. It is charmingly sited above the village street and has a pretty and inviting forecourt. The chancel is divided from the nave by a Manueline pointed arch decorated with rope and coral motifs. Spanning the choir is a Manueline ceiling with rope and Gothic net decoration. Some side-chapels – the middle one in the left-hand aisle contains an impressive statue of Santo Amaro – are embellished with *talha dourada*.

★Faro   H 5

Capital of the administrative district of Faro
Population: 30,000

Faro is the capital of the historic province of the Algarve and also of the district of Faro, thus making it the administrative and economic centre of the Algarve region. It is a port and to a moderate degree an industrial town, as well as having its own university.

Faro lies in the south-east of the Algarve in the north of an extensive system of lagoons – several islands that here form the coastline lie offshore. 10 km west of the town centre is the Algarve's international

airport, where the whole year round chartered and scheduled flights
from a number of European countries land each day, bringing holidaymakers to the south of Portugal. In spite of this, Faro is not really a
tourist centre. Most visitors merely arrive and depart from here but
spend their holiday elsewhere in the Algarve and may just make a day
trip into the town.

History

Faro has had a very varied history. The town is presumed to have been
founded by the Phoenicians, who set up a small trading post on the
south coast of Portugal. Under Roman occupation – when it was called
Ossonoba – Faro developed into an important administrative town and
the port also grew in significance. To the north of Faro there was at that
time apparently a kind of summer residence, and in Milreu remains of a
Roman shrine and of a villa with baths can still be seen. In AD 418 the
Visigoths conquered the south Portuguese port, and Faro became an
episcopal see for the first time. The Visigoths began to build a church
dedicated to the Virgin Mary. Because of the cult of the Virgin Mary,
which played such a major role in those days, the Visigoths named the
town Santa Maria de Ossonoba. From 714 to 1249 Faro was Moorish,
and the capital of the province of Al-Gharb (Algarve) at that time was
Xelb, now Silves.

King Afonso III of Portugal conquered Faro in 1249. That year saw the
end of Moorish rule in south Portugal, and in 1250 the Algarve towns
were affiliated to the kingdom of Portugal. In 1577 the Portuguese transferred the episcopal see from Silves to Faro. Subsequently the town was
twice largely destroyed – in 1596 following an attack by the count of
Essex, and in 1755 by the great earthquake that also completely laid
Lisbon to waste. In 1756 Faro was named the capital of the province of
the Algarve. In the early 19th c. the town again had to suffer foreign
occupation when Napoleonic troops invaded in 1808. Since the mid-
20th c. Faro has developed into the major centre in south Portugal.

Name

It is thought that the town's present name may date from the Moorish
era; in the 11th c. Ben Said Ben Hárum founded a principality here, and
the word Faro may well be a corruption of his name. On the other hand,
there is clearly a possible link with the Portuguese word *farol* (lighthouse).

Townscape

Generally speaking, in Faro the Portuguese go about a normal everyday
life. They are used to tourists, but the town is not, like so many other
places in the Algrave, exclusively dominated by tourism. At first sight
Faro is not particularly appealing. Upon entering the town the first
things the visitor sees are dismal commercial areas and then high-rise
apartments. The town centre, on the other hand, is extremely inviting.
Most houses date from the 18th and 19th c. and a large part of the inner
town is a pedestrian and shopping zone. Here you will find some good
stores as well as numerous street cafés and restaurants in which to
unwind. The pavements are inlaid with typical Portuguese black-and-
white mosaics. Everywhere there are smaller or larger squares with
attractive trees or parks. Particularly idyllic is the historic quarter around
the old cathedral, only a short distance from the pedestrian streets and
surrounded by a town wall.

Sights

Tour

A tour through Faro will give a general impression, following which the
visitor can devote time to a particular sight or place of interest. The
starting point can be the central Praça de Dom Francisco Gomes by the
harbour basin. From here proceed via the Jardim Manuel Bivar park to

The symbol of Faro: the Arco da Vila ➤

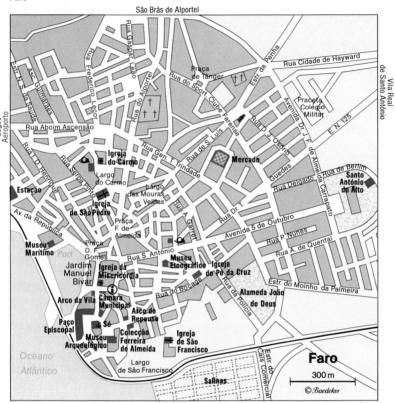

São Brás de Alportel

Faro

300 m

© Baedeker

the historic centre with the cathedral and the Museu Arqueológico. Leave the old town walls through the Arco do Repouso, continue to the Praça da Liberdade with the Museu Etnográfico and finally to the Praça Ferreira de Almeida. This is the business centre of Faro. After resting in one of the many cafés or restaurants, simply enjoy a stroll through the small streets and mews or go on a shopping expedition. The tour could then be followed by a visit to the Igreja do Carmo and/or a walk to the Museu Marítimo in the harbour.

Praça de Dom Francisco Gomes

On the busy Praça de Dom Francisco Gomes stands an obelisk erected in 1910 in memory of the diplomat Ferreira d'Almeida, who was born in Faro in 1847 and during his period in office as minister of naval affairs established a naval college and actively promoted the fishing industry.

Jardim Manuel Bivar

The Jardim Manuel Bivar to the south of the square is much more peaceful. In the gardens, with their pretty flower beds, tall palms and jacaranda trees, sit mainly elderly Farense citizens reading, writing, having a rest or just watching the world go by.

On the eastern side of the park stands the Igreja da Misericórdia, a 14th c. church that was rebuilt after the 1755 earthquake. The tourist information office will be found on the opposite side of the adjoining Rua da Misericórdia.

At the south end of the park there is the Arco da Vila. Built in the 18th c. by the Italian architect Francisco Xavier Fabri, it has a bell tower and a statue of the patron saint of Faro, St Thomas Aquinas. The gateway leads into the beautiful historical centre of Faro which is partly enclosed by a 13th c. town wall. It is well worth having a good look around here. Galleries, antique shops, cafés and restaurants can be found in the little streets, and those who visit in the spring will be able to see storks' nests built on many towers and ledges. The parent storks fly over Faro's old town while the beaks of the young can be seen poking out of the nests.

★★ Centro Histórico

In the spring too the Largo da Sé shows its most beautiful side. This magnificent square, which unfortunately serves as a car park during the day, is lined with orange trees that flower in March and April and give off a pleasant aromatic scent. On the north and west sides of the Largo da Sé lies the Paço Episcopal, the Bishop's Palace. When it was decided in the late 18th c. to incorporate a priests' seminary here, the original building was extended by Fabri in the form of the long west wing. After 1974 the building served provisionally as a reception centre for the *retornados*, those returning from the former Portuguese colonies. Since 1986 priests have again received training here. In 1940 a memorial was erected on the square in front of the building to Bishop Francisco Gomes do Avelar, who in the late 18th c. promoted the idea of a priests' seminary and campaigned vigorously for the rebuilding of the numerous churches destroyed in the earthquake. In the north-east corner of the Largo da Sé stands Faro's town hall (*câmara municipal*).

Largo da Sé Paço Episcopal

The bell tower of Faro Cathedral

Faro

★Sé

The most striking building on the Largo da Sé is the cathedral. A part of its history can be seen from the outside – large sections of the original Gothic church were destroyed in the 1755 earthquake and then rebuilt. Only the tower and one window on the south side remain from the earlier church. The Visigoths built the first Christian church in honour of Santa Maria – probably on this site. Later a mosque was supposed to have stood here, on the foundations of which – as so often happened after the Moors had been driven out – the Portuguese again built a church.

Gothic, Renaissance and baroque features can all be found on the cathedral. Its Gothic origins are seen mainly on the entrance doorways. The north side is unusual in that there is no uniform area of wall: instead it is made up of three side-chapels, the centre one of which has a dome.

The interior of the church, which was rebuilt in the 18th c., is striking as a result of its light and almost hall-like character. It has three aisles each separated almost imperceptibly from its neighbour by three slender columns. The choir has a coffered barrel- vaulted ceiling. António Pereira da Silva, bishop of the Algarve from 1704 to 1715, had his tomb built in the Capela de Santo Lenho on the right near the chancel. The side walls of the cathedral are asymmetrical with three or four side chapels of different dimensions. The tile cladding in the chapels is predominantly 18th c. The baroque organ above the entrance to the high choir is striking; it was painted by Francisco Cordeiro between 1716 and 1751. Open Mon.–Fri. 10am–1pm.

Arco da Porta Nova

Continue by way of the south-west corner of the Largo da Sé to the Arco da Porta Nova, another preserved gateway in the old town wall. It was built in 1630 and restored in 1992. The Arco da Porta Nova leads directly to the sea. Ferries to the offshore islands leave from this point, and the railway line from Vila Real de Santo António to Lagos runs past here.

Cloisters of the former Convent of Poor Clares – now an archaeological museum

Portuguese Coffee-House Culture

A true coffee-house culture is probably the last thing you would expect to find in Portugal. And there isn't one either – at least not in the classical Austrian sense of the term. What you will find, however, is a genuine coffee-house culture Portuguese-style. Cafés have always played an important role in Portuguese public life, something that is perhaps little known abroad. A certain set would meet in the café, people who felt themselves linked by age, profession, sport, political leanings or other factors. The men met in one café, the women in another. They drank a *bica* (a small cup of black coffee), a *galão* (white coffee in a glass) or a clear *medronho* (fruit brandy) and simply chatted or held more serious discussions. For the most part it was adherents of a certain political persuasion who came together in one café, while in another café on the next corner sat the "opposition". It was sufficient just to order a *bica* in order to be allowed to sit at a table for a whole morning.

A piece of this culture still lives on in the Aliança in Faro. It is one of the oldest cafés in Portugal, having been established by the merchant José Pedro da Silva in 1908. At that time it was considerably smaller than it is today. Over the years additional rooms have been built on, and as a particular feature a sort of kiosk (part of which still stands) was built in which newspapers and magazines were sold and from which telephone calls could be made. From all the good coffee houses in Faro that existed after the turn of the century, the Aliança is the only one to have survived. Its interior fixtures and fittings are no longer the originals, these having been destroyed by fire in the 1920s. However, the rooms have been beautifully restored; stucco decorates the ceilings, and the walls have again been clad in heavy wood panelling. From that date, too, are the wrought-iron tables with marble tops.

Being the first café in Faro, the Aliança also served drinks on the pavement. At that time the Praça de Dom Francisco Gomes had a completely different atmosphere from that of today. It was the scene of much that went on in public life – demonstrations, parades and rallies were held in the square, and patrons of the Aliança had a ringside seat.

In its history the Aliança has seen some illustrious guests. Cavaco Silva, for many years prime minister of Portugal, was a frequent visitor during his student days, and Simone de Beauvoir came here in 1942, as did Lídia Jorge. The poets Fernando Pessoa and Mário Sá-Carneiro and the multi-talented artist Almada Negreiros were also among its patrons, although they met mainly in Lisbon, but often travelled south. And of course Cándido Guerreiro, one of the few Algarve poets, came here, too, from the village of Alte.

When the Aliança came into contact with the artistic sets, it – like the Brasileira café in Lisbon – provided the painters, graphic artists and caricaturists with space in which to exhibit. It is no doubt from this tradition that the "photo gallery" has developed, which today is very popular with visitors. On display are photographs of the Algarve which today no longer is. Many black-and-white photos, some of which are already slightly yellowing, give visitors an idea of the seaside towns and the inland villages as they were before the region changed in appearance.

From the Largo da Sé it is also worth making a detour through the arched gateway at the end of the Rua do Arco. A courtyard leads to the architecturally tasteful Arco gallery.

Museu Arqueológico e Lapidar Infante Dom Henrique

East of the cathedral there is the small Praça Afonso III. A memorial to the king, during whose reign the Moors were driven out of Faro and other Algarve towns, has been erected on a lawned area in the centre.

On the south side lies the relatively plain façade of the former Convent of Nossa Senhora da Assunção, a house of Poor Clares endowed in 1518 by Dona Leonor, the third wife of Manuel I, and completed in 1561 to plans by the architect Diogo Pires. The small two-storey cloister is very lovely. Since 1973 the archaeological museum has been housed in a part of the building around the cloister. On display are some Roman finds – busts, gravestones, glass and coins – as well as architectural fragments mainly from the Manueline period. The most beautiful Roman exhibits are a bust of the Emperor Hadrian from the 2nd c. AD and one of the Empress Agrippina Minor from the 1st c. AD, both finds from Milreu. A Roman mosaic that was uncovered in Rua Infante dates from the 3rd c. Open Mon.–Fri. 9am–noon, 2–5pm.

Further rooms surrounding the cloister house the very comprehensive private collection of the diplomat and art lover Ferreira d'Almeida. Particular items on display are 19th c. paintings, including some portraits of members of his circle of friends, 18th c. prints, old views of Lisbon and Coimbra, porcelain, silver and glass. There is also a small museum section in which paintings by mainly Portuguese artists are displayed, including views of the Algarve from the first decades of the 20th c.

Arco do Repouso

To the east of the convent stands the Arco do Repouso. Tradition has it that, after seizing Faro, Afonso III first rested here (*repouso* means rest or repose). In the 18th c. a small chapel was built into this very beautifully restored gateway. Afonso III is portrayed on several tile pictures on the town wall outside the gate, including one showing the taking of the town.

Igreja da São Francisco

Continue along Rua D. Teresa and Rua de Caçadores to the Igreja de São Francisco on the often empty Largo de Francisco. This square changes dramatically, however, when Faro's annual markets are held here. The Igreja de São Francisco was originally 17th c., but was rebuilt following the earthquake. Military personnel at present occupy the adjoining former Franciscan monastery. The church is open only for fairs. Inside, the *azulejo* paintings with scenes from the life of St Francis are very attractive. Another tile-painting shows the Coronation of the Virgin Mary.

Igreja do Pé da Cruz

On the Largo do Pé stands a little 17th c. church of the same name. It is thought to have been built on the site of a former synagogue.

Alameda João de Deus

Those seeking a little rest are recommended to walk to the Alameda João de Deus. This park is beautifully laid out with flower beds, tall trees, ornamental ponds and a basketball pitch, and there are small kiosks at which to sit and enjoy a drink. The park is named after perhaps the best-known Portuguese educationalist, on whose model – related to the Montessori method of teaching – a large number of kindergartens were established in Portugal.

Museu Etnográfico Regional

Well worth a visit is the Museu Etnográfico Regional on the busy Praça da Liberdade. Anyone interested in knowing more about everyday life and culture in the Algarve before tourism took over and how the region looked in the early decades of the 20th c. will particularly enjoy seeing the photographs and everyday objects on display in this lovingly assembled collection. Especially interesting are the photographs showing old

Igreja do Carmo with ...   *... the Bone Chapel*

town views and landscapes that have since disappeared. Preserved on film are Algarvios at work in the salt works, in the fields, fishing, weaving baskets, washing clothes and transporting water. There is also a picture of a genuine donkey cart used as an *aguadeiro*, or water carrier, as well as several items of fishing and agricultural equipment. Lastly some rooms from Algarve houses have been faithfully reproduced.

Open Mon.–Fri. 10am–12.30pm, 2–5.30pm.

In the northern part of the inner town, in the little square of the same name, stands the Igreja de São Pedro. It was built in the 16th c. to replace a church to St Peter, when the development of this part of Faro led to the formation of a new community. A figure of São Pedro is carved into the Renaissance doorway. The interior is triple-aisled, the choir is spanned by a barrel-vaulted roof, and in the first chapel in the right-hand aisle can be seen a tile painting reassembled after the earthquake.

Igreja de
São Pedro

Near the Igreja de São Pedro to the north is the Largo do Carmo on which stands the Igreja do Carmo, a baroque church built in 1719 and flanked by two low campaniles. In this church a meeting was held in 1808 to plan the revolt against the Napoleonic occupation of the town.

★Igreja do Carmo

The interior is dominated by the over-extravagant use of *talha dourada* on the high altar and side altars. Simpler, on the other hand, is the sacristy where various statues of Christ are displayed in small wooden niches. Notice also the wooden ceiling of the sacristy with its 24 differently painted tablets.

The sacristy leads out to a cemetery and the **Capela dos Ossos** (Bone Chapel), consecrated in 1816, which is known far beyond the boundaries of Faro. The vault and walls are "decorated" with human bones and skulls. The chapel was built by monks, and the skeletons come from earlier graves in the cemetery. Open Mon.–Fri. 10am–1pm, 3–5pm.

Mercado

Outside the commercial district and to the east of the Igreja do Carmo lies Faro's indoor market, which is open in the mornings. On sale are fish, meat, vegetables and fruit.

Capela de Santo António do Alto

On a small hillock on the eastern edge of town stands the Capela de Santo António do Alto. The adjoining museum houses a collection including portraits of St Anthony and books about him. Climb the church tower and enjoy the beautiful view of Faro.
Open Mon.–Fri. 10am–12.30pm, 2–5.30pm; visitors need to ring the bell!

Museu Marítimo Almirante Ramalho Ortigão

The Museu Marítimo Almirante Ramalho Ortigão in the north-west corner of the harbour houses a collection of exhibits on the theme of the Sea. Various ship models – from the caravel to the steamship – are displayed, together with information about various methods of catching sardines, cod and squid or octopus, and visitors can also admire a small shell collection. Open Mon.–Sat. 2–4pm.

Café Aliança

Those who feel in need of a rest and refreshment after a tour of the town have plenty of opportunity to enjoy these in the centre of Faro. Among the many cafés and restaurants the Café Aliança on the Praça D. Francisco Gomes, on the corner of Rua 1° de Maio, is the richest in tradition. It is one of the oldest cafés anywhere in Portugal, having been opened in 1908 (➤ Baedeker Special, p. 87).

Surroundings

★Praia de Faro

The municipal beach is the Praia de Faro, about 10 km by road from the town centre. It is reached along the same road that leads to the airport. Shortly before the airport turn right and proceed over a small bridge direct to the beach, which stretches for several kilometres to the east and west.

Ilha da Barreta

There is a ferry link from Faro to the Ilha da Barreta, a spit of land off the lagoon islands. The boats leave from the landing stage near the Porta Nova (Centro Histórico).

Lagoa   E 5

Capital of the administrative district of Lagoa
Population: 6,500

Lagoa is located 8 km east of Portimão. Also 8 km away, but to the north, is Silves, the old capital of the Algarve, and it is 5 km from Lagoa to the coast at Carvoeiro. The busy N 125 passes to the south of the town, so Lagoa has remained a typical small Portuguese town.

Wine-producing region

The Lagoa region is well known as a wine-producing area. It is one of the last wine districts to survive in the Algarve. A large proportion of the Algarve farmers used to earn their living from viniculture, but land prices went up when, with the onset of tourism, many of them took the opportunity to sell up. In the countryside surrounding Lagoa relatively full-bodied red wines are produced. Famous are the dry Algar Seco, the sweet Algar Dolce and the Aguardente Afonso III, which is stored in oak casks and drunk as an aperitif. Lighter wines of certified origin and quality are sold under the Lagoa label, young country wines under the name

Porche's. Wines can be tasted and purchased at a wine-merchant store on the edge of town (Adega Cooperativa de Lagoa, on the N 125).

Not much is known about the history of Lagoa. Only the name gives a clue as to the earlier location of the town; Lagoa means "lagoon" or "inland sea" and so it is assumed that there was once a stretch of water here on the banks of which a settlement developed.

History

Lagoa is not a particularly attractive town. Nevertheless it is worth a brief visit, as here visitors can obtain an idea of what Portuguese everyday life is really like, something they will not find in the nearby tourist centres. On the small Praça da República, a few steps away from the noise of the main street, is a busy indoor market, which is worth exploring.

Townscape

Sights

In the Igreja Matriz, the main façade of which dates from the 19th c., there is a statue of Nossa Senhora da Luz by the major Portuguese baroque sculptor Machado de Castro. The church forecourt is planted with jacaranda and araucaria trees, and in the centre is a memorial to the soldiers who died in the colonial wars in Guinea, Mozambique and Angola.

Igreja Matriz

In the building of the former Convento de São José near the parish church there is a gallery in which temporary exhibitions are held. The Torre-Mirante, the bell tower of the old convent with its characteristic narrow row of windows, spans the small street.

Torre-Mirante

The church of Estômbar near Lagoa: the Manueline doorway

Surroundings

Estômbar

Estômbar is a small country town prettily situated on a hill 3 km west of Lagoa. José Joaquim de Sousa Reis, who went down in Algarve history under the name Remexido (► Famous People), was born here in 1797. He was the leader of a group of monarchists who terrorised many places in the Algarve and in southern Alentejo in the struggles against the liberal forces during the civil wars of the early 19th c.

The church of Estômbar, situated on a slight hill, is very beautiful. It has a baroque façade with a well-preserved 16th c. Manueline portal.

Between Estômbar and Lagoa lies the Slide and Splash aquapark (► Practical Information, Aquaparks), which is particularly attractive to younger visitors.

★Lagos   C/D 5

Capital of the administrative district of Lagos
Population: 11,000

The town of Lagos is located on the south coast of the Algarve in the western area known as the rocky Algarve. It is barely 40 km from here to Cabo de São Vicente (Cape St Vincent), the south-westernmost point of the European continent. The N 125, part of which is an expressway, provides a rapid road link with Faro, 90 km away, and the international airport, while the railway line that serves the whole coast as far as the Spanish frontier at Vila Real starts in Lagos.

The Ribeira de Bensafrim enters the Atlantic near Lagos; the river narrows just before its mouth and has been made into a channel. Lagos lies at the western end of a wide bay, the Baia de Lagos, which to the southwest is protected by the Ponta de Piedade and in the east extends as far as Portimão. In the north-east of the town the flat Meia Praia stretches over several kilometres, while the coastline south and west of Lagos, on the other hand, consists of bizarre rock formations and small, sandy rock-encircled bays, which make this region attractive to tourists.

All the countryside around Lagos is tourist orientated. To the east holiday centres continue to expand, although a few kilometres to the west of Lagos it is much more peaceful. Lagos is the last large town on the west of the Algarve coast. The hinterland becomes increasingly barren: near Lagos there are still fig and almond trees, but further west the delightful garden-like Algarve landscape of the central and eastern parts gives way to scrubland.

The tourist infrastructure in and around Lagos is excellent. There are numerous apartment blocks, hotels, guest houses, as well as campsites. Restaurants and cafés abound in Lagos and near the beaches. With all that, however, some of the population still make their living from trade and fishing. The main fish caught are tuna and sardines. Near the fish harbour in Lagos there is a modern yacht station, only completed in 1995.

History

The town of Lagos is historically one of the richest in the Algarve. The Phoenicians established an important trading centre here as long ago as the 1st c. BC. Lagos was well suited for a base of that kind; for traders from the Mediterranean who sailed the whole of the Iberian Atlantic coast the Bay of Lagos offered the first sheltered harbour when coming from the west and the last when coming from the Mediterranean. The Greeks and Carthaginians, too, used this favourable anchorage. In Roman times, from the 2nd c. BC, the town was known as Lacóbriga. Under the Moors it was named Zawaya, meaning "fountain" or "lake". Under Abderraman the Moors began to protect the town with strong walls. In 1189 it was taken by Portuguese troops led by Sancho I and

One Horse for Ten Men

The year 1444, when slaves were first sold in Lagos, was not a very laudable time for Portugal. The Portuguese had just discovered the mouth of the Senegal and had come upon black Africans for the first time. As evidence of the landing and almost as a sort of souvenir from this African region, some of the natives were forced to make the degrading voyage back to Portugal. In 1444 the black slaves were exhibited in Lagos just as if they were ordinary items of merchandise.

The slave trade then quickly became a very lucrative business. Together with the spice trade, the selling of slaves was for a time Portugal's main source of income. In the 16th c. one third of the cost of its sea voyages and expansion in Africa, Asia and America was financed by this trade in human lives. After the discovery and conquest of Brazil the Portuguese also took African slaves to South America. For a long time the Cape Verde Islands served as an assembly camp for Africans and were the centre of the slave trade between Africa, Europe and America.

The black Africans' misfortune lay in the fact that they were strong and robust. Work of all kinds – in the house and in the fields – fell to them. The sparsely populated Algarve in particular needed an additional workforce. At the time of Portuguese expansion many Portuguese left their homeland to trade or seek employment in the newly discovered countries, which they knew because as seafarers they had seen them on voyages or had been shipwrecked there. Those in need of workers made their way to the Praça da República in Lagos. Here slaves could be obtained by barter; in exchange for a horse, for example, one could obtain ten men, although bartering values varied according to requirements and "quality". As a

The former Slave Market in Lagos

rule slaves baptised into the Christian faith were worth more than "heathens".

Before the black Africans came to Lagos to be sold they would have endured terrible voyages. After being captured and torn at night from their families, they were transported across the sea in overladen ships under the most inhuman conditions. Because of the lack of hygiene and medical care one in every four died on the voyage.

English Quakers were the first to publicly denounce the brutality of this enterprise. Many Jesuits in Portugal followed their example, but it was not until the 18th c. that trade in human beings was finally prohibited. In the Cape Verde Islands, which then still belonged to Portugal, such trade was still going on as recently as 1878.

supported by German and English soldiers, and two years later it was recaptured by the Moors.

The town was finally taken by the Portuguese during the reign of Afonso III in the middle of the 13th c. From then onwards it was called Lagos, from the Portuguese *lago* (lake). Lagos was ceded to Bishop Dom Roberto as a territorial possession and developed into an important centre in south Portugal. In the 13th c., and again in the 14th c. under Afonso IV, the town walls were rebuilt to withstand Moorish attacks. In the second half of the 14th c., under Pedro I, the town was given a new form of legal administration making it independent of Silves, which at that time was the more important town.

The town's real heyday was in the 15th and early 16th c. Lagos was the departure harbour and thus the centre for the great voyages of conquest and discovery, which at that time made Portugal one of the foremost countries in Europe. Large numbers of shipyards were built where the famous Portuguese caravels were constructed, their designs being drawn up in nearby Sagres under Henry the Navigator. In 1434 the navigator Gil Eanes (➤ Famous People), who was born in Lagos, set out from his home port on what was to be the first voyage by a European round Cape Bojador in West Africa. Great riches came to Lagos as a result of the numerous discoveries made, the booty plundered and the new trading links established. There was also trade in human beings – the first slave auctions were held in Lagos in 1444.

Although the town was made the capital of the Algarve in 1577 it had by then already begun to lose much of its former importance. A large proportion of the Portuguese caravels were no longer launched in Lagos but in Belém near Lisbon. The real decline of Lagos, however, went hand in hand with that of Portugal as a whole. For over 100 years Portugal and Spain had been the leaders in sailing the seas of the world but they failed to use the resultant riches to their best advantage. Money was spent building large numbers of prestigious buildings while the nation's

The attractive waterfront outside Lagos tourist office

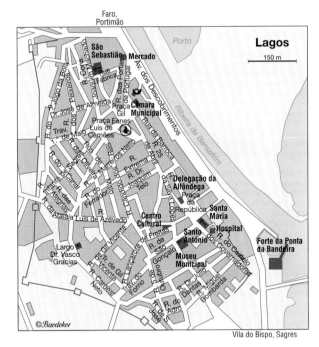

Faro, Portimão

Vila do Bispo, Sagres

general prosperity suffered. In 1578 Dom Sebastião sailed from Lagos in an attempt to undertake a crusade in North Africa. He was killed in the first battle of Alcácer-Quibir and in the resulting dispute over succession to the throne Spain occupied the whole of Portugal.

During the 60 years when Spain ruled Portugal in the 16th and 17th c. Lagos became a second-rate town. In 1755 the strong earthquake caused much destruction and the resulting flood inundated the lower quarters of the town. One year later Faro superseded Lagos as the capital of the Algarve, and Lagos became little more than a provincial township. When tourism made an impact in the second half of the 20th c., Lagos regained some of its importance.

The outer districts of Lagos are unattractive, with skyscrapers and large blocks of flats. The immediate suburbs are also heavily populated and not very inviting. The centre of Lagos is far more appealing, however. Although geared to tourism it has retained its own particular charm. In many places the Old Town is still surrounded by the medieval walls. It is also worthwhile strolling through the side streets of the inner town off the main thoroughfares. Here Lagos is not particularly colourful or picturesque but a plain residential town. A small area in the centre around the Praça Gil Eanes and the Praça da República has been turned into a pedestrian zone. There are lots of small shops as well as restaurants and cafés where visitors can sit outside and watch the world go by. Despite this, however, Lagos has not over-emphasised its tourist side. Locals sit here together with holidaymakers and live their lives as they have always done. The palm-lined coast road between the harbour channel and the inner town was opened in 1961 and is known as the Avenida dos Descobrimentos (Avenue of Discoveries).

Townscape

Sights

Tour

Sights in Lagos are limited to a few buildings in the town centre. The starting point can be the central Praça Gil Eanes. The Igreja de São Sebastião just north of the square is worth visiting. Then proceed south and down the pedestrian street to the Praça da República, followed by a detour to the sea and along the shore to the Ponta da Bandeira fortress. Finally, visit the well-known Igreja de Santo António and the Museu Municipal, and then continue westwards to the town wall. Pass through the town gate to experience the totally different atmosphere outside the walls. Then return through the small, quiet streets of the western inner town to the starting point. Alternatively, a tour of Lagos can equally well begin outside the town gate.

Praça Gil Eanes

The Praça Gil Eanes is one of the two main squares in the centre of Lagos. In the middle stands a well-known statue of the "longed for" King Sebastião (► Famous People: Dom Sebastião set out from Lagos in 1578 to conquer North Africa but never returned). The statue was carved in 1973 by the famous Portuguese sculptor João Cutileiro. On the east side of the square stands the town hall, and a little further on the main post office. Those who arrive in the morning should not fail to visit the indoor market, built in 1924 on the marine promenade. All kinds of freshly caught fish are sold here every day.

Igreja de
São Sebastião

From the Praça Gil Eanes the street sweeps round via the small Praça Luís de Camões to the Igreja de São Sebastião a bit further north. Steps lead up to the attractive church forecourt. A start was made on building the church in the 15th c., but changes were made later. In 1755 it was badly damaged in the earthquake. Still standing is the 16th c. Renaissance doorway on which can be seen the Portuguese crown, and

Santa Maria Church in the Praça da República

this motif is repeated further up on the façade. The three-aisled interior is divided by tall pillars with beautiful capitals. It is said that the crucifix on the left of the altar was taken to Alcácer-Quibir and is one of the few items saved from that fateful battle (1578) and brought back to Portugal. The portrait of Nossa Senhora da Glória in one of the side-chapels comes from a wrecked ship. A small garden next to the church leads to a charnel house built into the side wall.

A second central square is the Praça da República at the southern end of the pedestrian zone. The square opens onto the Avenida dos Descobrimentos and the harbour channel. On a stone base stands a statue of Henry the Navigator – gazing out to sea. This memorial was erected in 1960 on the 500th anniversary of his death (► Baedeker Special, p. 118).

Praça da República

On the southern side of the square stands the Igreja de Santa Maria, the successor to an older 14th c. church that was rebuilt after the earthquake. In 1460 Henry the Navigator was interred in the older church, but later his coffin was moved to the Capela do Fundador in Batalha.

Igreja de Santa Maria

Behind the church stands the former Governor's Palace, which is partially integrated into the town wall. Until 1756 the province of the Algarve was administered from here.

Palácio dos Governadores

The northern side of the Praça da República is taken up by the narrow building of the Delegação da Alfândega (customs authority). It was here that the first auction of black African slaves was held in 1444. They were placed in manacles under the arcades where potential buyers could inspect them.

Delegação da Alfândega

Continuing south along the Avenida dos Descobrimentos parallel to the harbour channel parts of the old town wall can be seen. There is a memorial to Gil Eanes who was born in Lagos and in 1434 set out from here to sail round Cape Bojador. At one place along the wall a Manueline window has been preserved; it was part of the Governor's Palace and it is said that it was from here that Dom Sebastião heard his last mass before sailing to North Africa.

Avenida dos Descobrimentos

The fortified Ponta da Bandeira with its four round corner towers was built in the 17th c. to defend the harbour. The narrow drawbridge provides access to the inner courtyard and to the Museu Marítimo on the left. In another part of the fortress there is a restaurant. Open Tue.–Sat. 10am–1pm, 2–6pm, Sun. 10am–1 pm.

Forte da Ponta da Bandeira

The Igreja de Santo António is one of the most-impressive churches in the Algarve. It was built as the regimental church of the troops stationed in Lagos whose patron saint was St Anthony. Exactly when it was founded is not known, but it is thought that it was constructed during the reign of João V between 1706 and 1750. After the earthquake it was rebuilt in accordance with the old plans.

Igreja de Santo António

The small interior is in typical baroque style. It is almost completely clad with *talha dourada*, the gilded carved wood with which church walls and altars throughout Portugal were decorated in the 18th c. after the Portuguese discovery of gold mines in Brazil. The altar wall is particularly opulent. On the high altar stands a statue of Santa António with an officer's sash, staff of command and the child Jesus on his arm. Between the Solomon pillars St Elói can be seen in the niches on the left and St Joseph on the right.

The side walls above the base are clad in *azulejos*, richly embellished with *talha dourada*. The painted panels depict scenes from the life of St Anthony, including the healing of a blind man and the replacing of a severed foot. The many wooden cherubs and figures under small corbels, who appear to be bearing the weight of the pilasters, warrant close

*Bizarre rock
formations on
the Algarve
coast – Ponta
da Piedade
near Lagos*

inspection. Surmounting all this gilded magnificence is a barrel-vaulted roof painted with the Portuguese coat of arms. Before leaving take another look at the underside of the gallery: the three virtues – faith, hope and charity – look down from all the gilding upon those entering and leaving the church.

Museu Municipal de Lagos

Since 1934 the building adjoining the church has housed the very original collection of the Museu Municipal de Lagos. As well as a collection of *azulejos* and some religious exhibits there is a small archaeological section where finds from the Neolithic, Bronze and Iron Ages are displayed. There are a few Roman finds, including a bust of the Emperor Gallienus from Milreu, together with ceramics, receptacles and oil lamps from the Moorish period. The history of Lagos is also portrayed, including a collection of German inflationary banknotes. Finally, the whole of the Algarve is represented by everyday items and craft objects made from agave and coconut fibre, wood and ceramics, small dolls and the chimneys typical of the region. Open Tue.–Sun. 9.30am–12.30pm, 2–5pm.

Centro Cultural

Those interested in modern art should visit the Culture Centre opened in 1992. Theatrical and dance performances are arranged as well as exhibitions. A cafeteria adjoins the centre. Open daily 10am–midnight, winter to 8pm.

Surroundings

Meia Praia

The beaches near Lagos provide extremely charming scenery but are usually crowded in the summer. North-east of Lagos the Meia Praia curves gently for several kilometres around the Baia de Lagos. It offers plenty in the way of water sports. Access to the beach is by bus or a small boat from Lagos, or alternatively on foot past Lagos railway station.

Praia do Camilo ★Praia de Dona Ana

In the south of the town are the small Praia do Camilo and the well-known Praia de Dona Ana with small rocky islands lying offshore. The latter is the most beautiful of the bays around Lagos, although it too gets very crowded in high season. Steps lead down to the Praia de Dona Ana which is divided into two small bays by a rocky promontory. At high tide it is impossible to get from one bay to the other without getting wet feet. Above the Praia de Dona Ana are various large hotels as well as some foodstalls and restaurants.

★★Ponta da Piedade

From the Praia de Dona Ana visitors can drive or walk – a path runs intermittently along the top of the cliffs – the 2 km to the Ponta da Piedade in the south. Here you will probably find the most beautiful rock formations anywhere in the Algarve. They can be seen from the shore but better still from the sea. Boats to Ponta da Piedade sail from Lagos (from where there are also boat trips to various caves nearby) and in the high season from Praia de Dona Ana. The Ponta da Piedade is an impressive section of foothills falling steeply away into the sea at the southern end of the Baia de Lagos. The rocks rise to 20 m at their highest point. Rocky overhangs, crags and towers form a beautiful yet bizarre landscape. Marking the entry and exit to the Bay of Lagos is a lighthouse with steps down to the sea.

Praia do Porto de Mós

To the west of the Ponta da Piedade stretches the Praia do Porto de Mós with bars and beach cafés, a wide sheltered bay with few breakers but good conditions for water sports. There are small bays everywhere which can be reached only by boat and are therefore usually quiet.

Luz

Luz is a former small fishing village about 5 km west of Lagos, which has now developed into a tourist centre. It boasts the beautiful Praia de Luz where there are good conditions for water sports – surfing, waterskiing, diving or pedalos. Above the beach is a pretty restaurant housed in a former fortress and from which there are fine views of the sea.

The village of Odiáxere is located 6 km from Lagos. It has suffered badly from the N 125, which passes straight through it. Leaving the main road, however, there is a sense of how rural and peaceful it must once have been here. Odiáxere has a charming village church, which was rebuilt after the 1755 earthquake. The Manueline doorway of the old church has been preserved. Immediately behind the church there stretches fertile countryside with gardens and smallholdings.

Odiáxere

In Odiáxere a road branches off the N 125 northwards to Barragem da Bravura or Barragem de Odiáxere. For about 10 km the road winds through some superb countryside, first through meadows and orange groves and then over a plateau and a sea of white and yellow roses. Towards the end of the journey the landscape becomes more hilly and suddenly the road comes to an artificial lake surrounded by forests of eucalyptus trees. The Barragem da Bravura forms part of a number of reservoirs that Salazar had built in the late 1950s and which are popular with the Portuguese for a day out but not so attractive to tourists. There is a beautiful lookout with a view over the lake and a small restaurant. Barragem da Bravura is not suitable for bathing or water sports.

Barragem da Bravura

★Loulé   G 5

Capital of the administrative district of Loulé
Population: 9,000

Loulé, 15 km north-west of Faro in the *barrocal*, the foothills of the Algarve mountains, is surrounded by hilly countryside with many fig, almond, olive and fruit trees; in spring the fields are full of poppies. The region's beauty has persuaded many Portuguese and foreigners to build weekend retreats or holiday homes here. As a result this region, which for a long time remained unspoiled, has become increasingly populated in recent years.

Loulé is a busy centre, with its colourful and bustling Saturday market attracting people from far and wide. A characteristic feature is the large number of individual craftsmen still working here. Blacksmiths, silversmiths, potters and saddlers producing artistic or everyday objects have their workshops in Loulé, particularly in Rua 9 de Abril and Rua da Barbaça.

From archaeological finds it is assumed that the Loulé region was inhabited in Celtic times. There are also traces of occupation by Romans, Visigoths and Moors. How Loulé was actually founded is not clear. Some researchers believe it was founded by the Carthaginians in 404 BC, while others hold the view that it dates from Roman times. Under the Moors it was named Al-Ulyá, which probably became Laulé and then later Loulé. One legend has it that the town's name is derived from a laurel tree, *laurus* in Latin, which is said to have stood near the castle. In 1294 Loulé was taken by Portuguese troops under Dom Paio Peres Correia. The latest important event in its history was being granted its town charter in 1988.

History

Loulé is a very attractive small town with some magnificent, almost citylike avenues and squares and a pretty Old Town full of interesting corners. The little whitewashed houses in the Old Town make parts of this quarter seem almost like theatrical backdrops. More vibrant, on the

Townscape

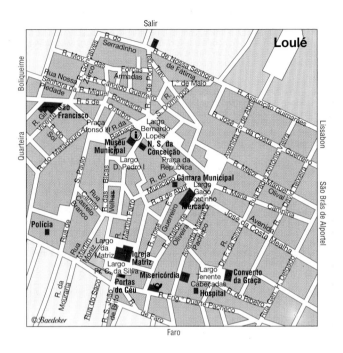

other hand, are the neighbouring streets round the Praça da República, Largo Gago Coutinho and Avenida José da Costa Mealha. There are numerous shops in Rua 5 de Outubro, a pedestrian zone.

Carnival

The small town is famous throughout Portugal for its lavish and colourful carnival celebrations, which include the Almond Blossom Festival (➤ Practical Information, Events). The carnival floats are literally covered in almond blossoms made of paper.

Sights

Tour

A short tour of Loulé could begin at the Largo Bernardo Lopes near the tourist office, continuing past the castle walls and further south through the narrow streets of the Old Town to the Igreja Matriz de São Clemente. From there go via Rua Engenheiro Duarte Pacheco and Avenida Marçal Pacheco to the Igreja da Misericórdia and – after making a detour to see the remains of the Convento da Graça – to the indoor market. Visitors should then visit the pilgrimage chapel of Nossa Senhora da Piedade outside Loulé to the west.

Castelo

A few remnants of the walls that once marked the boundary of the Old Town are all that remain of the ancient castle. Near the tourist office some stone steps lead up to the castle walls, from which you have a beautiful view of Loulé and the surrounding countryside as far as the sea.

Convento do Espírito Santo

Nearby is the Museu Municipal, housed in a section of the tastefully restored Convento do Espírito Santo. The convent was founded in the late 17th c., partly destroyed in the 1755 earthquake and dissolved in 1836.

The Museu Municipal consists mainly of one room with displays of traditional Algarve kitchen fittings and utensils. Other rooms, which originally would have been the convent kitchen and refectory, now house the municipal art gallery. Open Mon.–Fri. 9am–12.30pm, 2–5pm.

Opposite the convent you can see the simple façade of the Ermida de Nossa Senhora da Conceição. The chapel was built in the middle of the 17th c. in gratitude for the regaining of independence from Spain. The striking altar, decorated with *talha dourada*, was carved by a sculptor from Faro in the middle of the 18th c. The cladding of the interior walls with tile paintings depicting scenes from the life of Mary dates from the same period.

Ermida de Nossa Senhora da Conceição

Loulé's main church lies in the Old Town between Largo da Silva and Largo da Matriz. Its origins can be traced back to the second half of the 13th c. and it was probably commissioned by the archbishop of Braga in north Portugal. Parts of the church were destroyed in the 1755 earthquake and it suffered further earthquake damage in 1856 and 1969. First to catch the eye in the three-aisled church are the capitals on the columns. Some of the side chapels were built in the 16th c., including one with a Manueline pointed arch dedicated to São Brás and one with Manueline ribbed vaulting dedicated to Nossa Senhora da Consolação.

Igreja Matriz de São Clemente

The gardens in front of the church invite you to take a rest. Tall palm trees provide welcome shade and there are beautiful flowers to admire as well as a good view of the newer part of the town.

South of the church leave the Old Town through one of the old gateways, the Portas do Céu (Gate of Heaven). A small chapel is built above the archway.

Portas do Céu

Portas do Céu and ...   *... archway of the Convento da Graça*

Igreja da Misericórdia	From here, access to the Igreja da Misericórdia is by way of Rua Engenheiro Duarte Pacheco and Avenida Marçal Pacheco. The Manueline doorway, reached by a broad flight of steps surmounted by a granite crucifix, stands out clearly against the façade. Thick ropes carved in stone surround the finely worked frame of the doorway.
Convento da Graça	Although little remains of the former Convento da Graça, what is left is impressive. Between new houses a relatively well-preserved Gothic doorway still stands.
★Mercado	Loulé's interesting indoor market, built in the neo-Moorish style, is on the busy Largo Gago Coutinho. A daily market is held here, with fruit, vegetables, fish and poultry for sale, and the neighbouring streets are a hive of activity.
Igreja de São Francisco	The Igreja de São Francisco outside the Old Town is known for its pelican-shaped tabernacle.

Surroundings

★Capela de Nossa Senhora da Piedade	2 km west of Loulé on the Boliqueime road stands the Capela de Nossa Senhora da Piedade. A pilgrims' way leads up the hill, on top of which stands the old Renaissance chapel housing the statue of the Senhora da Piedade, which is carried in procession every year two weeks after Easter. The chapel has a wooden vault, and above the altar hangs a small lantern. It is always open, and during the week people from Loulé often visit their patron saint. On the walls are scenes depicting the stations of the Cross. A large, gleaming white domed church has been built near the old chapel where mass is celebrated for the pilgrims. From the church forecourt there is a superb view of the hilly Algarve landscape to the north and of the sea far away to the south.
Querença	10 km to the north-east of Loulé, in a sparsely populated region, lies the village of Querença. The countryside here is less attractive, the fertile Algarve gardens being further to the south. Surrounding Querença is woodland, and the road is lined with expanses of cistus shrubs, while on some hilltops only macchia grows. The road leads up to the Old Town on a hill and then appears to end at the church forecourt. Actually the small parish church stands at the highest point and all the village roads lead down from it. With luck the 16th c. church may be open. It has an attractive font and several statues of saints carved by Algarve sculptors. On the broad courtyard in front of the church there are two small restaurants, which offer country cuisine and are popular at weekends. On weekdays they are the only place where the people of Querença can meet in their leisure time. Near Querença, it is worth making a trip to the cave at Salustreira and the spring at Benémola.

Monchique   D 4

Capital of the administrative district of Monchique
Population: 8,000

Monchique is the capital of the Serra da Monchique, the mountain range that marks the boundary between the western Algarve and the Alentejo. The town is 458 m above sea level and nestles in pretty wooded countryside. The vegetation includes spruce, eucalyptus, mimosa and strawberry trees.

The volcanic Serra de Monchique contains several hot springs, which are used for healing purposes in the Caldas de Monchique thermal baths. Monchique is a traditional centre for arts and crafts such as textiles, basketwork, woodcarvings and ceramics. This region is also known for the production of *medronho* brandy made from the fruit of the strawberry tree. However, a large proportion of the population is now employed in service industries along the coast.

Monchique is picturesquely located on a hillside. Steep streets and narrow lanes wind through the Old Town and from everywhere there are superb views of the surrounding mountains. The town itself caters for day visitors and there are plenty of cafés and restaurants, most of which are well frequented. Pleasant accommodation can be found in small establishments in the surrounding countryside.

Townscape

Sights

The Largo 5 de Outubro is Monchique's central square, though it is somewhat lacking in atmosphere. There are cafés and an attractive gallery, and a modern fountain splashing in the middle of the square represents a *nora*, which formed a part of the irrigation system introduced to the Algarve by the Moors.

Largo 5 de Outubro

The Igreja Matriz, Monchique's small parish church, is worth a visit. Its most striking feature is the 16th c. Manueline entrance door with a five-section fanlight. The three-aisled interior is relatively broad and plain. The tiled frieze is of new *azulejos* but depicts a traditional *ponta da diamante* pattern which was popular in Portugal in the 17th c. The pillars carry unusual capitals of turned stone bands. On the high altar stands a statue of Nossa Senhora da Conceicão attributed to the famous Portuguese baroque sculptor Machado de Castro.

Igreja Matriz

A little way up from the parish church stands the Igreja de São Sebastião, in which the Senhora do Desterro, the Madonna of Banishment, is revered.

Igreja de São Sebastião

You will find the short walk to the ruins of the Convento de Nossa Senhora do Desterro more rewarding than the neglected ruins themselves. In the town, follow the trail symbols showing a camera and telescope, then once outside the town take the stony woodland path through tall trees. The ruins of the convent, which are reached after a 15-minute climb from the town centre, are surrounded by old cork oaks. There is a wonderful view of Monchique from up here.

Convento de Nossa Senhora do Desterro

Surroundings

Monchique is famous for its warm springs, the Caldas de Monchique, which are of volcanic origin and lie 6 km to the south (➤ Practical Information, Spas). The Romans knew of the healing properties of the waters and built a thermal bath here named Mons Cicus. The hot springs are good for rheumatism, inflammation of the liver, disorders of the urinary and respiratory tracts and gastro-intestinal problems. The most famous patient seeking a cure here was King João II, but he died shortly afterwards (which of course means nothing!). Dom Sebastião is also said to have visited the Caldas de Monchique.

★Caldas de Monchique

Bottles of the healing waters of Monchique are on sale all over Portugal. Small though it may be, the Caldas de Monchique is one of the most idyllic and inspiring places in the Algarve. It has retained a late 19th c. charm that one would not believe possible a few kilometres away on the coast. The tiny village centre lies in a narrow valley under tall, shady trees, while a quiet square with a café and restaurant invites visitors to rest awhile. The few small houses dotted around,

Caldas de Monchique – a fashionable spa in the early 1920s

guest houses, have a cosy and friendly feel about them. Behind the village the hillsides are covered in lush grass and flora which can be enjoyed on a walk from the central square and out alongside the bubbling brook; first one will pass a picnic area, then it becomes more isolated.

Olhão   H/J 5

Capital of the administrative district of Olhão
Population: 25,000

The town of Olhão is located in the south-east of the Algarve, on the edge of the Ria Formosa lagoon region. Between the town and the sea the dune islands of Farol and Culatra extend west almost as far as Faro, while in the east the island of Armona stretches to the village of Fuzeta.

To date tourism has not reached Olhão and the town lives mainly from fishing. The fishing port on the eastern edge of town is the largest in the region; only Portimão in the Faro district boasts comparable catches. Ships also embark from here on deep-sea fishing expeditions along the coasts of Africa and Newfoundland.

History

Compared with other Algarve towns, Olhão is relatively young, and it was not until the 14th c. that a fishing village first developed here. At that time there were numerous freshwater springs in the Olhão region, which were known as *olhos* (eyes) and from which the place gets its name. Many seafarers and fishermen used to stop off in the village to replenish their water supplies from the springs. The job of *aguadeiro*, or water carrier, was a typical occupation in Olhão for many years.

A noteworthy action on the part of some fishermen has gone down in Portuguese history. In the early 19th c. the people of Olhão took up the fight against the Napoleonic forces in an attempt to regain their independence. After the French had finally been driven out, a group of Olhão fishermen set sail in a small fishing boat, the *O Bom Sucesso* (*Good Success*), and crossed the Atlantic to Brazil to bring the good tidings to the exiled royal family. João VI thereupon bestowed on the village the title of Olhão da Restauração (Olhão of the Restoration).

The mid-19th c. saw an upturn in the town's fortunes as a result of the expanding fishing industry, and the port increasingly grew in importance. As Olhão is so dependent on fishing, it has suffered badly from the decline in this section of the economy in recent years.

Olhão differs from other Algarve towns both in its townscape and its general atmosphere. It has been described many times as the most North African of the Algarve towns and one certainly detects a strong Arab influence. This impression results above all from the characteristic cube-shaped houses; the fishing quarter in particular consists of straight rows of such two- or three-storey square dwellings. They are all very similar, but none is exactly the same as any other. Common to all are the *açoteias*, the flat roofs used as terraces. Almost all the roofs also have a small tower up to which the women were said to climb to watch for their menfolk returning from the sea. The North African influence on the architecture can be attributed to the close trading links between Olhão and places on the coast of North Africa. Such styles of building were also regarded as suitable because of the similar climatic conditions. Large parts of the town were built in the 19th c., while newer buildings can be seen further inland towards the N 125.

In its general atmosphere the town is perhaps the most unusual that the Algarve coast has to offer. Olhão has a daily life all its own, which

Townscape

Traditional houses in Olhão

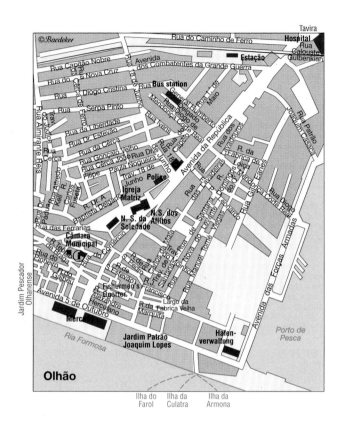

has nothing whatsoever in common with the tourist-dominated existence experienced elsewhere in the Algarve. In the early morning the fishermen roar along to the harbour on their mopeds and after doing their work seek refreshment with a coffee or something stronger in one of the small breakfast bars. Beneath it all, however, poverty and social deprivation still exist. Perhaps the visitor will not take to Olhão at first sight – but very soon they will be fascinated by the genuine and very typical liveliness of the town.

Sights

Tour

There are not many sights and places of interest in Olhão. Rather it is the atmosphere that holds the attention. Those who wish to see some buildings of interest would do well to follow the main street, the Avenida da República, in the direction of the sea – past the parish church, the Capela de Nossa Senhora dos Aflitos and the Capela de Nossa Senhora da Soledade, and then continue through the pedestrian zone to the two indoor markets and the marine promenade.

Igreja Matriz de Nossa Senhora do Rosário

Financed by fishermen, the foundation stone of the Igreja Matriz was laid in 1689. The link with fishing and seafaring in general is clear from

108

the red navigation light in the seaward side, which is lit in the evenings. The single-aisled interior with its barrel-vaulted roof is relatively plain, the most striking feature being the baroque high altar decorated with *talha dourada*.

A climb up the church tower is a must. From the top there is a magnificent view over the rooftops of Olhão and far into the lagoon countryside and the open sea beyond. As a rule the tower is kept locked, but you can ask the verger for the key.

At the rear of the Igreja Matriz there is the Capela de Nossa Senhora dos Aflitos. This chapel consists of a room open on one side but protected by a grille and with an interior clad with tiles and where candles are always burning. Flowers are placed here and stacked up are votive gifts such as wax arms, legs, feet and heads. Fishermen's wives visit this popular chapel to pray for their menfolk's safe return during stormy seas and bad weather in winter.

Capela de Nossa Senhora dos Aflitos

The Capela de Nossa Senhora da Soledade has an attractive dome. Our Lady of Solitude hears the prayers of the lonely.

Capela de Nossa Senhora da Soledade

The Rua do Comércio is the main street in a small pedestrian and shopping zone. The shops are simple and some are quite cheap.

Rua do Comércio

Parallel to the shore lies the Avenida 5 de Outubro. From the town centre go direct to the two indoor markets, where fresh fish, meat, vegetables and fruit are sold each morning. Each of the large halls has four corner towers containing small shops and cafés. Around the two indoor markets a large open-air market is held on Saturdays.

Mercado

On the east side of the indoor market halls is the Jardim Patrão Joaquim Lopes, where you can sit on one of the benches and enjoy a view of the mud flats. Ducks and geese swim in an enclosed pond, and there is a memorial to the man who gave the gardens their name. A little further away from the town lies the landing stage for boats going to the islands of Farol, Culatra and Armone.

Jardim Patrão Joaquim Lopes

East of the berth there is the beginning of the port of Olhão. Many small fishing boats moor near the landing stage and nearby is the large harbour with fish-processing works.

Porto

Surroundings

Since 1987 a part of the coast, 60 km long and covering 18,400 ha, between Faro and Manta Rota has been a nature reserve known as the Parque Natural da Ria Formosa. The flora and fauna of the lagoon region with its vast dunes and salt marshes is unique. Birds in particular abound here, with many rare species and joined in the winter months by numerous birds from northern Europe that winter here. Other migratory birds stop over on their way to and from Africa. All in all, more than 200 species of bird have been sighted in the nature reserve.

★Parque Natural da Ria Formosa

You will get a first impression of the area by visiting Quinta de Marim, about 1 km east of Olhão harbour and near the campsite. The way to Quinta de Marim is signposted from the N 125 ("Parque Natural"). Open daily 9am–noon, 2–5pm.

Quinta de Marim

Plan at least two hours to explore the area of Quinta de Marim on foot and to have a look at the visitor centre. It provides details of the lagoon region of the Ria Formosa, its flora and fauna as well as general information on environmental and conservation issues. Temporary exhibitions are held, there is an auditorium and library and a pleasant cafeteria. The walk leads then further down to the coast, to the tide-driven mill (*moinho de maré*). The first mill of this kind was

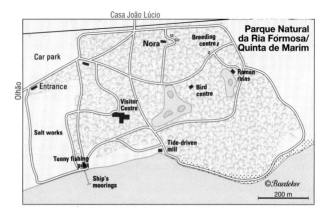

Casa João Lúcio

Parque Natural da Ria Formosa/
Quinta de Marim

Nora

Breeding centre

Car park

Roman ruins

Olhão

Entrance

Bird centre

Visitor Centre

Salt works

Tide-driven mill

Tunny fishing

Ship's moorings

© Baedeker

200 m

built in France in the 12th c., and they were introduced into Portugal at the end of the 13th c. The Quinta de Marim mill, one of the last tide-driven mills in existence, was built in 1885 and in use until 1970. The mills usually included living quarters for the miller and his family and a stable.

Excavations in the east of the area have unearthed remains of Roman salt works. There is also a building here where sick and injured birds are cared for. Finally you will reach the area used for agriculture – the Quinta de Marim practises a limited amount of farming in accordance with soil association standards – where a *nora*, a well dating back to Moorish times, can be seen. At one time it was operated by animal power and later mainly by electric motors. Nearby is a breeding centre for the *cao de agua*, which comes from this region and is in danger of dying out. This poodle-like dog was at one time a true companion and helper of the fishermen. It is the only species of dog to have webbed paws. It is also said to be an expert diver, reaching a depth of about 4 m.

**★Farol
Culatra
Armona**

These three lagoon islands can be reached by boat from Olhão several times daily from June to September and three times daily in winter. Farol and Culatra, the smallest island, in the west are visited on one trip, while another boat goes to Armona in the east. The landing stage is near the harbour in Avenida 5 de Outubro.

All three islands are flat dunes with excellent sandy beaches. Few people live on the islands, but there are some simple restaurants and cafés. Farol, recognisable from afar by its lighthouse, is the least populated of the three islands, with only a few small houses and two cafés.

Fuzeta

Fuzeta is a small fishing village about 8 km west of Olhão. It lies fairly high and there is a wide view over the mud flats and the island of Armona. The village is not strikingly pretty but does give an impression of vibrancy and originality. It has a harbour and an indoor market, and its cubical houses resemble those in Olhão. At the northern end of the village is a typical Portuguese cemetery with graves like small houses laid out in proper little streets.

Moncarapacho

North of Olhão there is a beautiful stretch of countryside with fruit plantations, orange groves and small villages. A slightly larger village typical of this region is Moncarapacho, 8 km north-east of Olhão. It boasts two churches – the parish church with a beautiful Renaissance doorway and nearby the Santo Cristo chapel, adjoining which is a small open-air museum with an archaeological collection. Open Mon., Wed., Fri. 11am–3pm.

North of Moncarapacho stretches the Serra de Monte Figo, which rises to 410 m at São Miguel. A very narrow road leads up to the mountain; on a clear day there is a beautiful view from the top over the coastal strip of the eastern Algarve.

Serra de Monte Figo

Portimão   D 5

Capital of the administrative district of Portimão
Population: 30,000

Portimão is located 60 km west of Faro at the mouth of the Rio Arade. To the south, towards the coast, it has expanded so that it almost joins the tourist centre of Praia da Rocha (see entry) with its high-rise hotels. While the whole region south-west and south-east of Portimão is tourist dominated, the northern suburbs are relatively unaffected. This is clearly seen when coming from the Faro direction and crossing the long bridge over the Rio Arade. Looking towards the coast it is built up as far as the eye can see, while to the north there are unpopulated hillsides.

Apart from the Guadiana, the Rio Arade is the major river in the Algarve. However, over the years the river has become increasingly silted up so that only flat-bottomed boats can navigate it as far as Silves and then only shortly before and after high tide.

In the north of Portimão a railway bridge and an old road bridge cross the Arade and lead to the town centre. For many years the road bridge was the only way across the river and consequently a permanent bottleneck. Eventually a new bridge was built further north and now this takes the N 125 expressway.

Together with Faro and Olhão, Portimão is one of the three largest towns in the Algarve. Foremost it is an industrial and harbour town and a shopping centre only second. For a number of years Portimão was the centre of Portuguese sardine fishing and its highly subsidised processing industry. Until the mid-1970s more than 70 fishing trawlers regularly set sail and fish was processed in a total of 61 factories. After the end of the Salazar regime subsidies were drastically cut. Now there is only one fish-canning factory in Portimão while six trawlers still fish; the river banks are lined with sardine factories that have been forced to close down. In the north of the town are some shipyards.

Tourism also contributes to the economy of Portimão, and there are several hotels and guest houses, numerous restaurants and popular cafés catering mainly for day-trippers coming to Portimão from the nearby tourist centres. The town is a good place for shopping and in the centre north-west of Praça Manuel Teixeira Gomes there are row upon row of shops.

Portimão traces its history back to a Phoenician trading post. Greeks and Carthaginians also settled at the mouth of the Arade, and two place names have come down from Roman times, Portus Magnus and Portus Hannibali; the former survives in the present name. Under the Moors Portimão was already an important fishing port; the Moors were skilled sailors and set out from Portimão on long fishing trips.

In 1242 Portimão, like the neighbouring towns of Silves and Alvor, was captured by Christian Knights of the Order of Santiago. In 1476 Afonso V made a gift of the town to Count Gonçalo Castelo Branco as a reward for his honourable military service, and at the end of the 15th c. the count had strong walls built around it. The port of Portimão grew in importance as a result of the voyages of discovery and conquest undertaken in the 15th and 16th c, when shipbuilding broke all records. Wood for the caravels was cut from forests on the nearby Monchique mountains. In 1487 Bartolomeu Dias set out from here on the voyage which was to see the first European sail round the Cape of Good Hope. There

History

was an official embarkation ceremony for him in a sheltered bay on the Rio Arade north of Portimão. After the route to India had been discovered in the early 16th c. ships returned laden with spices and landed in Portimão harbour. In the 16th and 17th c. Portimão was attacked by British, Dutch and North African pirates, and for this reason the entrance to the harbour was safeguarded by means of the defensive installations of Fortaleza de São João, on the opposite side of the mouth of the Arade, and Fortaleza de Santa Catarina, the remains of which can be seen near the Praia da Rocha.

The 1755 earthquake devastated Portimão as so many other places in the Algarve, and the town took a long time to recover from the disaster. A rapid economic upswing began with the growth of the fishing industry in the middle of the 19th c.

Townscape

Portimão is a vibrant town with an authentic everyday life which is not devoted solely to tourism although foreign visitors do play a part, and one can detect something of the atmosphere of a harbour town around the approach to the old road bridge. Here there are many simple cafés and restaurants, small family businesses offering superb fresh fish, especially sardines of course. Further to the south lies an attractive area on the river bank with lovely squares where tourists can while away the time in cafés, and gardens where the children can enjoy rides on the mini-railway. In the busy town centre the buildings are taller than in other Algarve towns, and in the afternoons the streets are choked with traffic.

Sights

Tour

Portimão only has a limited number of interesting places to see. Nevertheless a stroll through the town is well worthwhile. It is best to

Azulejos *decoration on houses in Portimão*

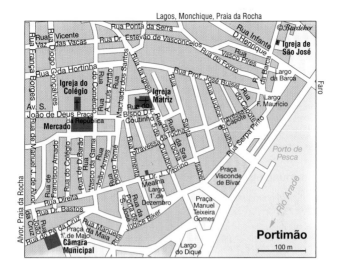

Portimão

100 m

begin at the riverside promenade where there are several very different squares, including the Praça Manuel Teixeira Gomes and the Praça Visconde de Bivar. From here head for Largo 1° de Dezembro, take a look around the shopping area, view the Igreja Matriz and perhaps make a detour to the Praça da República. Those interested in the harbour area can then return to the river bank and continue north.

The Praça Visconde de Bivar on the banks of the river is attractively laid out as a small park. From here you have a beautiful view across the Arade to the opposite bank and the town of Ferragudo. The best thing to do is to spend awhile sitting on a bench or in a café. There is a children's railway that goes through the park and round the statue of the Visconde de Bivar.

Praça Visconde de Bivar

Next to the Praça Visconde de Bivar lies the comparatively plain Praça Manuel Teixeira Gomes, the centre of tourist Portimão. Here you can book boat trips to the grottoes and river excursions along the Arade to Silves. Organised walks can be booked, too, and there are several cafés, including the popular Casa Inglesa, which has become the regular stop of many locals and tourists. There is a fountain in the centre of the square with a statue of Teixeira Gomes, a diplomat who was born in Portimão and who was also an author. In 1924 he was elected president of the republic.

Praça Manuel Teixeira Gomes

The Largo 1° de Dezembro has a completely different atmosphere. Almost rectangular in shape, it is laid out as a small park and has a comfortable feel. There is a fountain surrounded with beautiful flower beds. Quite striking are the ten benches with *azulejo* pictures portraying important events in Portuguese history, including the capture of Ceuta on August 21st 1415, the discovery of Brazil by Pedro Alvares Cabral on April 24th 1500, the regaining of independence from Spain in 1640 and the proclamation of the Portuguese republic in 1910.

Largo 1° de Dezembro

North of the Largo 1° de Dezenbro towers the Igreja Matriz. Before the 1755 earthquake a 14th c. church stood on this site, and its Gothic doorway has been preserved and stands out clearly within the new façade.

Igreja Matriz

113

Note the weathered capitals portraying various heads. The interior is three-aisled, and there are statues of saints, some of which were saved from the ruins of the old church. Above the main altar is a beautifully painted vault.

The church is used as an occasional concert centre, and events forming part of the international Algarve music festival are held here.

Praça da República

Portimão's old indoor market, nowadays partly used as a gallery, stands on the busy Praça da República. Opposite is the single-aisled Igreja do Colégio, which once belonged to a Jesuit college. It dates originally from the 17th c. and was rebuilt following the earthquake. Nearby stands an senior citizens' day centre together with the Museu Diogo Gonçalves, an art gallery.

Surroundings

Praia da Rocha

The neighbouring town to the south of Portimão is the tourist centre of Praia da Rocha (see entry).

★★Ferragudo

On the opposite side of the Rio Arade to Portimão there is the fishing village of Ferragudo, a popular subject for picture postcards. As well as its impressive church standing on a hill, it boasts the Fortaleza de São João, built in 1622 to protect the river entrance; the fort is now in private ownership. A villa nearby belongs to the Portuguese Rei sem Reino (king without a kingdom), a descendant of the Bragança family, which belonged to the last king.

Ferragudo is like an oasis of the past – little narrow streets with fishermen's houses, a few simple guest houses and inns, and a pleasant atmosphere. But even here many houses have been sold in recent times

Ferragudo: a charming fishing village

and it is feared that in the near future Ferragudo too will fall chiefly into the hands of non-Portuguese. The tall skyline of Praia da Rocha, lying opposite Ferragudo, is a constant reminder of what can happen to popular Portuguese tourist resorts.

South of Ferragudo lies the Praia Grande, which, as the name suggests, is an extensive beach. A breakwater makes bathing safe here, and it is very popular with surfers. It also has restaurants and cafés.

Praia da Rocha   D 5

Administrative district: Portimão
Population: 2,000

The tourist centre of Praia da Rocha is a suburb that comes under the administration of Portimão (see entry). Its skyline and oppressive atmosphere are similar to those of Quarteira and Armação de Pêra. No longer does it possess the aura of the stylish seaside resort that it was in the first half of the 20th c. Today it has a good tourist infrastructure with plenty of facilities for sports and amusement as well as numerous restaurants, cafés and bars. The reason for this escalation in development is the magnificent beach that extends to the mouth of the Rio Arade.

It has to be said that with its faceless apartments and hotels Praia da Rocha is one of the real eyesores of the Algarve. Above the main beach, nearly 2 km long and almost 100 m wide, runs the Avenida Tomás Cabreira, lined with hotels, restaurants, cafés, boutiques and shops. At the eastern end of the Avenida, the Fortaleza de Santa Catarina, a 17th c. defensive installation, stands guard over the mouth of the Rio Arade. Today it houses a restaurant and café with a terrace. From here you have a fine view towards Ferragudo on the other side of the river and the Fortaleza de São João opposite.

Alternatively, from the western end of the Avenida Tomás Cabreira, you can enjoy a splendid view of the steep coastline of Praia de Rocha.

Townscape

Praia da Rocha's main beach is quite picturesque and accordingly gets crowded. To the west lie a row of idyllic sandy bays, most of which are divided from one another by rocky reefs and arches. Here too it is difficult to find a quiet spot.

★Beaches

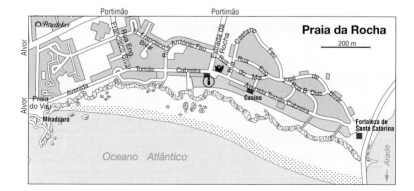

115

The wide sandy beach at Praia da Rocha

Boat trip

A boat trip from Praia da Rocha, along the steep coast with its bizarre rock formations as far as the Praia dos Três Irmãos (Beach of the Three Brothers; ➤ Alvor), is of particular interest.

Surroundings

Praia do Vau

The beach neighbouring Praia da Rocha to the west is the Praia do Vau. Although the hinterland here is also heavily populated, it is nevertheless almost tranquil compared to Praia da Rocha.

Quarteira   G 5

Administrative district: Loulé
Population: 9,000

The tourist centre of Quarteira lies on the coast about 15 km west of Faro. The long sandy beaches, the short distance from the airport and the wide range of amusement and leisure facilities seem to make Quarteira an attractive holiday destination. At any rate, the town is completely dominated by tourism, the hinterland back as far as the N 125 is heavily developed and there is also a great deal of holiday accommodation further north.

Townscape

Quarteira is one of those places that have given the Algarve its bad reputation. It is a town of high-rise buildings, with an unattractive appearance similar to that of Armação de Pêra or Praia da Rocha. The only compensation is the beach; accommodation on the coast road, the

Avenida Infante de Sagres, with a view of the open sea possibly offers some charm of its own. But for those whose accommodation lies within the main centre there is little to commend it. All the streets to the left and right of Avenida Dr. Sá Carneiro, the main street – named after a candidate for the presidency in 1980 who died in an air crash shortly before the elections – are lined with multi-storey concrete apartment blocks. The area around the Largo do Mercado in the west still has a few little old houses, but these are completely unable to hold their own against the competition. There are still a few nice beach cafés along the coast road on the edge of the beach.

Near Quarteira there are two aquatic sports and leisure parks, the Atlântico Park on the N 125 and the Aqua Show on the N 396, which leads north-east from Quarteira.

Atlântico Park
Aqua Show

Sagres   B 5

Administrative district: Vila do Bispo
Population: 2,000

From Sagres it is only 5 km to the Cabo de São Vicente, the most south-westerly point of the European continent. Both Sagres and the Cabo de São Vicente lie on a rocky plateau that terminates abruptly at the coast to form steep cliffs up to 150 m high. The plateau is divided into two constituent parts, one ending at the Ponta de Sagres south of the town of the same name and the other further north-west where the Cabo de São Vicente falls away into the sea. Between the two headlands there is the Bay of Beliche, a relatively sheltered anchorage. Further east, on the other side of the Ponta de Sagres, the Sagres bay offers excellent shelter, especially when the wind is in the north. Like the climate, the countryside around Sagres is harsh and barren with only a few low-growing macchia bushes.

Sagres is known largely through its history. The town played an important role when the Portuguese adventurers sailed the seas in the 15th and 16th c., and to a large extent the region is still trying to live off that reputation. Tourism has gained only a small foothold to date. There are admittedly some hotels and some private accommodation in and around Sagres, but the tourist infrastructure is not comparable with that in the holiday centres further east. However, those who just want a quiet holiday in natural surroundings with some isolated beaches may well find here what they are looking for.

Archaeological investigations have shown that this region of Europe must have attracted settlers as far back as the Stone Age. Traces have been found of grave sites dating

117

Henry in the Light of Research

Dom Henrique O Navegador is back in the limelight. This time, however, under different circumstances. Although his memory was honoured in 1960, 500 years after his death, Portuguese historians have for some time been engaged in studying him more closely as a person. Who was Henry in real life? Is the picture painted of him in the 19th c. – when people loved to glorify historical figures so much – the right one, or in retrospect was he falsely idealised?

It is possible that the much-vaunted and still quoted school for seafarers near Sagres, where the latest techniques of navigation were said to have been taught to young sea captains from the 15th c. onwards, was in truth simply a figment of the Portuguese imagination. That was the first unpalatable suggestion put forward by researchers. Then came the realisation that in fact personal interests had been allowed to play a prime role in what for a long time had been thought of as purely altruistic motives behind Henry's financing of voyages of discovery. He was apparently involved with a trading company in Lagos, which at that time had a monopoly on all the new wares coming to Portugal from Africa. He himself had held a monopoly on tuna fishing for some time already. Finally it also became obvious that Henry was financing exploration not only with money from the Order of Christ but also to a considerable degree from taxes imposed on the ordinary people of the Algarve. Last but not least, research now shows that Henry pursued his aims with such rigour that he did not even bother to save his own brother when the latter was taken prisoner by the Arabs and could have been freed in exchange for Ceuta. Henry refused to get involved and his brother Fernando died in an Arab gaol.

So, what remains of the romantic picture we have of the man? What nobody can or will dispute is that Henry the Navigator was one of the most-important figures of the early period of Portuguese discovery and had a great thirst for knowledge. Born in Oporto on March 4th 1394, Henry was just 21 years old when, following the capture of Ceuta, he listened eagerly to tales and reports by Arab traders who had sailed along the coasts of Africa or had undertaken trade journeys on the African mainland. He wanted to know exactly what this distant country looked like. Gradually it dawned on him that south of the Cabo Bojador in the *mar tenebroso*, the Sea of Darkness, there were in fact no lurking monsters that could harm seafarers. The sea there was apparently not always saltier, thicker, stickier or hotter, as people in Portugal had said it was. And the idea that ships on the far side of the cape of southern Morocco would be sucked into a whirlpool and would fall off the end of the earth now appeared comical to him. In the end it was the reports by the Arabs that appeared far more believable than the myths of his own countrymen.

The Portuguese rulers supported Henry's seafaring ambitions. In October 1443 he was granted sole rights to arrange all voyages south of the Cape of Bojador. A few days later the region of Sagres was assigned to him. Between 1443 and 1447 Henry frequently stayed in the Algarve, and from 1452 onwards preferred it to any other place of res-

south-western tip of Portugal, Henry assembled seafarers, geographers, navigators, astronomers and cartographers around him in order to pool all their knowledge and make use of it for practical seafaring purposes. However, at that time the Algarve was without doubt the centre of Portuguese seafaring. The voyages of discovery that he financed must have been well organised and very effective. The caravel, a new type of ship incorporating both Arab and north European ideas, was developed. It proved in practice to be extremely stable and manoeuvrable.

With his ideas that were so unconventional at the time, Henry the Navigator, who is known to have

The wind rose in the Fortaleza of Sagres dates from the 15th c., the time of Henry the Navigator

idence, such that from 1457 he lived mainly in Sagres.

At that time, apart from the fortified walls, there were just a few houses there. Various contemporary reports indicate that Henry intended to realise an ambitious port project here. However, there are no documents to support this: it is merely assumed that in Sagres, on the

made only one sea voyage himself to Ceuta, distanced himself from the medieval beliefs of his age – and this is a contribution to history that nobody would question. Henry did not live to experience the results of his efforts. Probably he did not even foresee that after him the world would change irretrievably. He died in 1460 – before the Portuguese had even crossed the equator.

Earthenware vessels used by the fishermen of Sagres for catching squid

History (cont.)

from the 3rd c. BC that are of Celtic or Iberian origin. An early written reference to the Cabo de São Vicente was by the Greek geographer and historian Strabo, who wrote of the "holy mountain range". From Pliny the Elder too we read that this region was known to the Romans as Promontorium Sacrum (Holy Foothills). The Romans believed that this isolated place must have been the home of the gods. The prevailing notion that this was "the most westerly point not only of Europe but of the whole of mankind", as Strabo describes it, explains the reverence and all that it inspired. This exposed region was also occupied by the Moors who built a shrine here. Through the Portuguese it finally gained an important place in European history (➤ Baedeker Special, p. 118).

Townscape

The modest houses of this port and fishing town are spread over a barren and windy plateau. A town centre in the normal sense of the word does not exist, and the main street ends at the busy harbour.

Beaches

The beaches around Sagres are suitable for bathing and sunbathing but only to a limited degree. The best protection from the wind is offered on the Praia do Martinhal 4 km to the north-east, not least favoured by windsurfers. Scenically more attractive is the Praia de Beliche to the west. Here, however, there is little protection from the mainly strong west winds.

Surroundings

★Fortaleza de Sagres

2 km along a road running south from Sagres is Ponta de Sagres with the Fortaleza de Sagres. Considered the very hub of the history of

Portuguese exploration and conquest in the 15th and 16th c., it is thought that there was an academic centre here in the time of Henry the Navigator (► Famous People) which taught the theoretical principles employed in sailing the oceans of the world. Only scanty remains of the early fortifications still exist from this period within the Fortaleza de Sagres. The walls in their present form date from 1793 and are among the most impressive fortifications in the whole of Portugal. In recent years extensive restoration has taken place here. Open daily 10am–6.30pm, in summer to 8.30pm.

After having entered the Fortaleza through the massive gateway, you will see a large circle of stones to the left, measuring 43 m in diameter and known locally as the *rosa dos ventos* (wind rose). For centuries it lay concealed and overgrown and it was only uncovered by chance in 1921. It is thought to date from the 15th c., but its original function is uncertain. For a long time the stone circle was thought to be a wind rose or compass face, but it is unusual in being divided up into more than 40 irregular segments whereas other wind roses have a maximum of 32.

On the other side there is the small 16th c. Igreja de Nossa Senhora de Graça. It is believed that previously a church also dedicated to the Virgin Mary stood on this site.

The row of houses that you encounter when leaving through the gateway includes (from left to right) a water tower from the 15th and 16th centuries, a building for holding exhibitions, a souvenir shop and a cafeteria. Towards the back there is a small building where gun powder was formerly kept.

Above Sagres harbour there are the remains of the walls of a former fort which guarded Baleeira harbour. They must date from before 1587 but were badly damaged by Sir Francis Drake and rebuilt in the early 17th c., only to be destroyed again in the 1755 earthquake.

Fortaleza de Baleeira

The lighthouse on Cabo de São Vicente

Fortaleza de Beliche

The Cabo de São Vicente lies about 6 km west of Sagres. The road crosses the inhospitable rocky plateau with scarcely a tree or bush on either side – which gives the feeling of being at the end of the world. About half-way to the cape there is the Fortaleza de Beliche. The original fort, whose date of construction is not known, was almost completely destroyed during an attack by Sir Francis Drake, and an inscription indicates that the present building dates from 1632.

On the site a small chapel dedicated to St Catherine stands high above the sea. The fort now houses a restaurant and a few hotel rooms belonging to the Pousada de Infante.

★★Cabo de São Vicente

The Cabo de São Vicente is the south-westernmost point of the Iberian peninsula and thus of the European continent. The Portuguese dedicated the cape to St Vincent, because according to legend the body of this Christian martyr was washed ashore here in an empty boat in the year 304.

The road to the cape ends at a lighthouse rising 60 m above the sea that crashes against the rocks below. The present lighthouse was built in 1846 on the instructions of Maria II. The fortifications dotted around date from the 16th c. when the bishop of Silves had the first lighthouse, defensive walls and a convent built here. The convent was run by Hieronymites until 1516 and was then taken over by the Order of Santa Maria de Piedade. Accommodation was provided for pilgrims who came to this remote spot. In 1587 a large part of the buildings was destroyed during an attack by Drake's fleet.

São Bartolomeu de Messines   F 4

Administrative district: Silves
Population: 8,500

São Bartolomeu de Messines is a friendly small town in the Algarve hinterland, about 20 km north of Albufeira. Although lying very close to the motorway that leads north from the Algarve, São Bartolomeu de Messines nevertheless appears quite secluded and gives the impression of an authentic Portuguese town with no trace of the rampant tourism found on the coast. It is attractively located in a broad valley at the foot of the Penedo Grande, part of the Serra do Caldeirão, and is surrounded by hilly countryside with fig, olive and carob trees. A few kilometres further north flows the Rio Arade which rises in the Serra do Caldeirão and enters the Atlantic near Portimão.

João de Deus, a well-known 19th c. writer (➤ Famous People), was born in São Bartolomeu de Messines and there is a memorial to him in the town.

Another famous son of the town was José Joaquim de Sousa Reis, known as Remexido (➤ Famous People). He rose to prominence during the civil wars in the 19th c. as leader of an Algarve guerrilla group that fought on the side of the absolutist Miguelites and caused havoc in southern Portugal. He faced a firing squad in Faro in 1838.

History

In the Moorish era São Bartolomeu de Messines was known as Masîna or Mussiene. During the 19th c. the theory was put forward that emigrants from the Sicilian port of Messina landed here and named the town Messines. After capturing it from the Moors the Portuguese dedicated the town to St Bartholomew, who has been its patron saint ever since.

Townscape

São Bartolomeu de Messines is a typical small country town with a not especially attractive centre. Those who like to experience something of Portuguese everyday life, however, should visit this place. It is particularly vibrant on market days (with an animal market, on the last Monday of each month).

Sights

The Igreja Matriz, which traces its origins back to an earlier 14th c. church, is worth a visit. The present church is 16th c., with marked changes made in the 18th c. The baroque main front in red sandstone and dating from 1716 is striking. The entrance is framed by two turned columns – a rarity in the Algarve. The three-aisled interior is worth seeing for its pillars which are reminiscent of early Manueline stone-rope pillars. Manueline ceilings have been preserved in some of the side chapels. There is a beautiful small pulpit made from local marble.

Igreja Matriz

A short way outside the town to the north-west stands the little Ermida de São Pedro which is normally closed. Architecturally nothing out of the ordinary, it is pleasantly located on a small hill.

Ermida de São Pedro

Surroundings

15 km north-west of São Bartolomeu de Messines lies the village of São Marcos da Serra, with a small church at its highest point. Near the village the motorway and the railway line run north from the Algarve and are the main arteries linking the south with Lisbon. The Miguelist guerrilla Remexido is said to have been captured on a hill to the east of São Marcos da Serra.

São Marcos da Serra

São Brás de Alportel   H 5

Capital of the administrative district of São Brás de Alportel
Population: 8,000

São Brás de Alportel nestles in gently undulating countryside in the mountain foothills about 17 km north of Faro at the junction of the N 2 and the N 270. A short distance to the north the hills of the Serra do Caldeirão rise to 500 m above sea-level. Surrounding São Brás de Alportel is some lovely garden country, and the region is particularly worth a visit when the almond trees are in blossom in February and March. Apart from almonds, fig, carob and olive trees grow here together with small lemon and orange groves.

São Brás de Alportel depends mainly on agriculture, while tourism plays a minor role in a quiet and rural manner. 2 km north there is a pousada from which there are fine views of the foothills. In the first half of the 20th c. São Brás de Alportel was a popular holiday resort because of its dry and mild mountain climate.

Archaeologists have found traces of Roman remains in the region. It is also believed that there was a Moorish settlement called Xanabus or Xanabras on the site of the present town. The first recorded mention of the place was in 1517; this related to the small chapel dedicated to St Blasius around which a few houses were built. The earthquake in the mid-18th c. caused great damage in the town, so that most of the buildings are post-1755.

History

São Brás de Alportel is a typical little Algarve town with small buildings. Its centre is the Largo de São Sebastião, which forms the junction between the N 270 and the N 2 and is accordingly very busy. The Avenida da Liberdade is also quite lively, with shops, cafés, a provincial cinema and a gallery. South-east of the Largo de São Sebastião in the direction of the church there is a quiet and pleasant residential quarter.

Townscape

Sights

Igreja Matriz

From the Largo de São Sebastião the Rua Gago Coutinho leads directly to the Igreja Matriz on the edge of São Brás de Alportel. From the attractive church forecourt you have a fine view of the garden countryside around. In the 15th c. there was a small chapel here dedicated to São Brás. It was extended and altered several times, and in 1725 a start was made on extensive restoration work that took over 26 years to complete. During that time the choir and roof were replaced and other detailed interior work carried out. Sadly, a few years after work was completed large parts of the church were destroyed in the 1755 earthquake. In 1792 the then bishop of the Algarve, Francisco Gomes do Avelar, initiated further rebuilding. The church is three-aisled and has three barrel vaults, while slender columns divide the interior. On the left in the choir is a mid-20th c. copy of an early 18th c. painting of the Trinity. The copy was done in Rome and presented as a gift to the church community of São Brás de Alportel in 1991. At the front of the left aisle is a striking neoclassical side altar in marble, a rarity in both form and material in this region. It was probably designed by the Italian architect Francisco Xavier Fabri, who undertook much work in the Algarve after the earthquake.

Palácio Episcopal

After the episcopal see had been transferred from Silves to Faro in the 16th c. São Brás de Alportel was considered as the site for a summer residence for the bishops. However, nothing was done until the iniative was taken first by Simão de Gama and then by António Pereira da Silva, two bishops who held office in the late 17th and early 18th c. Today all that can be seen is a reconstruction of those parts of the former episcopal palace, which were rebuilt in the first decades of this century. One section of the building houses a school. The palace once had a small garden, and visitors can still see the pretty, domed pavilion, the former Fonte Episcopal (Episcopal Fountain).

Museu Etnográfico do Trajo Algarvio

Somewhat set back on the left-hand side of Rua Dr. José Dias Sancho going in the Tavira direction is the Museu Etnográfico do Trajo Algarvio. In this small museum, so typical of Portugal, temporary exhibitions of clothing, items of furniture, household objects and examples of Algarve customs and traditions are lovingly laid out. For those who wish to learn something about rural Algarve in days gone by, this museum should not be missed. A permanent exhibition covers old agricultural implements such as cork presses and cork-boiling pans, blacksmiths' tools, carriages and donkey carts. Open Mon.–Fri. 10am–1pm, 2–5pm, Sat., Sun. 2–5pm.

Surroundings

Barranco Velho
Ameixial

Further north the little-used (but very winding) N 2 passes through some lonely and largely unspoiled countryside. Only occasionally do you come across a village – Barranco Velho, a typical small place, after 10 km and the secluded hamlet of Ameixial after 30 km.

★★Serra de Monchique   D/E 3/4

The Serra de Monchique ridge of mountains stretches from east to west, forming a protective wall in the north of the coastal plateau of the western Algarve. It creates an effective barrier against cold weather from the Atlantic and thus helps to maintain the coastal region's North African climate.

Beautiful scenery in the Serra de Monchique ➤

Geologically, the massif presents itself as a boldly structured eruptive mass deposited on the uneven subsoil and bisected by the Ribeira de Odelouca, forming a western and an eastern block. Thanks to the largely impermeable nature of the ground, rainfall collects in streams and rivulets and finds its way to the coastal plain. As the mountains are volcanic there are several warm springs.

Landscape

The Serra de Monchique is a beautiful hilly region, its two highest mountains being the Fóia (902 m) and the Picota (774 m). Its varied and rich flora is locally unique. The slopes are covered with eucalyptus trees, cork oaks, spruces and mimosa; further up are low shrubs and rhododendrons. In the foothills of the Serra to the south there are beautiful orchards with orange, lemon, almond and olive trees.

Sights

Monchique

The chief town in the Serra de Monchique is Monchique (see entry); just below it in a wooded valley lies the spa of Caldas de Monchique.

★★Fóia

A ride up to the Fóia peak, at 902 m the highest mountain in the Serra de Monchique, is well worthwhile. From Monchique a very scenic and winding road first leads up the south side of the mountain. Here the road is lined with houses, some very neat in appearance, and several tourist restaurants. A brief stop at a *miradouro* (viewpoint) with a small well will be rewarded with a panoramic view of the entire Algarve coast. Directly below lies Portimão and to the west the Cabo de São Vicente and the west coast, while to the east you can see Faro on a clear day. Higher up the mountain the vegetation becomes increasingly sparse, with some cistus shrubs and rhododendrons, while herds of sheep and goats roam the valleys. After a further bend in the road there is a view northwards to the Alentejo.

Having arrived at the peak you will find it rather desolate. Portuguese Telecom, the RDP broadcasting station and the air force are all stationed here under a forest of antennae. There is also a café and a souvenir shop.

★Silves   E 4

Capital of the administrative district of Silves
Population: 12,000

Silves, the old Moorish capital of the Algarve, is located in the hinterland about 8 km north-east of Portimão. The little town extends along the right bank of the Rio Arade and is visible from afar. It is surrounded by gently undulating countryside, the southern foothills of the Serra de Monchique (see entry). Here, the hinterland is no longer as delightful and garden-like as that in the east of the Algarve, although there are orange and lemon groves, fig and almond trees, eucalyptus, cork oaks and cistus shrubs.

Little remains of the town's former greatness. Silves has the appearance of a rather sleepy little place although it can still boast a few historically significant buildings and it therefore attracts considerable numbers of day visitors. However, there are not many restaurants and cafés.

History

It seems likely that Celtiberian tribes settled in this region. Silves was of interest to the Phoenicians as a river port. They established an important trading post here that provided good links between the interior and the Mediterranean. The Carthaginians and the Romans also valued the site and named it Silbis.

In the 8th c. Moors, assumed to have originated from the Yemen and Egypt, ruled Silves which they called Xelb. During the Moorish era Xelb was known far beyond the Iberian peninsula; its importance resulted primarily from its location – a sheltered harbour near the sea and within easy reach of North Africa. Lively trade between the climatically favourable south-west of the Iberian peninsula and Mediterranean countries promoted a strong economy. The Moors introduced their established methods of irrigation and were thus able to farm the land very efficiently. Xelb is believed to have had a population of some 40,000 at that time and became the capital of the province of Al-Gharb, then under the control of the emirate and later caliphate of Córdoba. Historians, jurists, philosophers, writers and musicians all helped the town to gain a good reputation far beyond its borders; it became famous in song and verse and is said to have been a finer town than Granada. Its prosperity attracted the attention of enemies as well as that of friendly admirers, and in 922 Vikings sailed up the Rio Arade and tried to take Xelb but were cut off.

Troops of the Portuguese King Sancho I conquered Xelb in 1189. Taking part in the campaign were renowned knights, including Frederick I (known as Barbarossa, or Redbeard) and Richard the Lion-Heart, who had entered into an alliance with Portugal. Immediately after the town had been captured, a Flemish priest was appointed bishop. Two years later the Moors won Xelb back again, but the Portuguese, who had already conquered the greater part of present-day Portugal with the help of the crusaders, were determined to advance all the way to the south coast. A few years later they moved down from the north and encircled the Silves region for two decades. In 1242, under the leadership of the Master of the Order of Santiago, Dom Paio Peres Correia, the Portuguese finally captured Xelb and renamed it Silva. The last Moorish ruler of Xelb was Aben Afan.

The withdrawal of the Moors saw the beginning of the region's economic decline. The small town enjoyed a short-lived flowering in the early

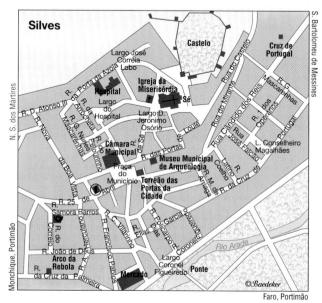

Faro, Portimão

16th c. at the time of the Portuguese voyages of discovery and conquest, when ships laden with pepper and other wares sailed up the Rio Arade to Silves. However, the Arade became increasingly silted up and this spelled the end for the port.

In 1577 the episcopal see was transferred from Silves to Faro. Lagos became the capital of the Algarve. In 1755 Silves was badly ravaged by the earthquake, and many of the buildings and other treasures that could have borne witness to the town's earlier cultural and economic standing were destroyed. Silves drifted into comparative insignificance.

Townscape

The central Praça do Município is still magnificent, and the cathedral and the castle with its battlements still bear witness to the town's former greatness. Between the town hall and the castle small streets with old whitewashed houses line the side of the hill.

Sights

Tour

A tour of Silves can commence at the Praça do Município. From there continue up the hill to the cathedral and the Igreja da Misericórdia opposite, and then on to the castle. After visiting the interesting archaeological museum refreshments can be taken at a café at the point where the tour began. A short visit to the famous Cruz de Portugal on the north-eastern edge of town is worthwhile. A little out of the way in the north-west of the town centre lies the small Ermida de Nossa Senhora dos Mártires, also worth a look. End the tour with a walk down to the Rio Arade.

Praça do Município

The town hall (*câmara municipal*) of Silves is more the type of building one would expect to find in a city, and it stands out against the rest of the townscape. An impressive arcaded walk is surmounted by two storeys. Impressive too is the Torreão das Portas da Cidade in the eastern corner of the square, a former watchtower that once formed part of the town wall and was also the town gate. More of the route taken by the old town wall can be detected on the other, western, side of the town hall. Near the former town gate stands a *pelourinho*, (pillory), which, like the tower, is built of the red sandstone that is typical of the region.

★Sé

The cathedral was built in the 13th c. in the Gothic style after the town had been captured by the Portuguese, and stands on the site of an earlier mosque. Many changes were made in the centuries that followed. From 1242 to 1577 Silves was an episcopal see and so the cathedral was then the major church in the Algarve.

Most of the nave was destroyed in the 1755 earthquake, but the crossing and choir were saved, and this can clearly be seen particularly from the inside, although from the outside too it is not difficult to recognise the medieval features that the earthquake left undamaged or that could be restored. The massive pointed doorway, of yellow sandstone from the coast, stands out clearly within the entrance façade. Note the heads of animals and people above the arch. The Gothic pinnacles in the upper section of the baroque façade are also of interest. Walking round the church, note the long Gothic windows in the south transept and the choir. The choir is built of red sandstone from the Monchique mountains.

The differing styles can clearly be seen in the interior. Much of the nave was repaired with red sandstone after the earthquake in such a way that it blends in very well with the undamaged parts. The sandstone pillars are very plain, as are the capitals, but their basic forms and simple plant motifs used in the decoration relate well to those Gothic capitals that remained undamaged. The pure Gothic decoration and the choir with its ribbed vault are unique in the Algarve, since all the other Gothic buildings were more seriously damaged than this one. Moreover,

The imposing castle at Silves

apart from Silves Cathedral, only the Sé in Faro was of comparable size. One of the keystones in the choir bears the Portuguese coat of arms. On the plain altar stands a statue of the Senhora de Conceição. Set in the floor of the choir you can see the tombstone of João II, who died in Alvor to the south-west of Silves in 1495 after having taken the waters in Monchique. In 1499 his body was moved to the Capela do Fundador in the convent church of Batalha. Tombs of crusaders and bishops can be seen in the north transept and the main choir.

The Igreja da Misericórdia dates from the 16th c., and on the rather plain side facing the Sé can be seen some Manueline decoration from that period. The main doorway is in a classical style. Inside there are some 17th c. paintings; that by the high altar was the work of a well-known 19th c. amateur artist from the Algarve.

Igreja da Misericórdia

The dominant feature of the townscape and visible from afar is the castle with its walls of red sandstone. There are believed to have been fortifications on this site during the Phoenician, Celtiberian and Roman eras.

★★Castelo

The present castle dates back to the Moors, but its appearance is the result of work done in 1940. Archaeological excavations in the inner courtyard have revealed parts of the Moorish castle. Other remains include the wells and underground storage chambers. Because they had these good facilities for food storage and access to fresh water, the Moors could withstand long sieges. The Cisterna Grande (Great Well) was built in the 13th c. and served as the main water reservoir of Silves even in the 20th c. It was restored and is now accessible for visitors, occasionally being used for exhibitions. The Cisterna dos Cães (Well of Dogs) was probably built by the Romans. On the castle site there is also the shaft of a former mine from which the Romans and the Moors

The inner courtyard of the Castelo

obtained copper. The broad inner courtyard is attractively planted with trees and bushes that the Portuguese introduced from abroad: jacaranda trees with their trumpet-shape blue flowers and pepper trees from Brazil, cedars from Bolivia, Japanese medlars with their yellow fruits, and date palms from the Canaries. In the courtyard stands a memorial to Sancho I, who in 1189 set out from Xelb on the first successful voyage of conquest.

Visitors can walk round the walls of the whole complex and climb the little turrets, from where there are fine views of the countryside around Silves. In the north you can see fruit plantations and to the north-east modern Silves. To the east a former British cork factory, which operated until 1901, can be easily picked out. Corks for port bottles were made here, but today the premises are used only for the storage of cork. In 1999 an attractive new gastronomic and amusement centre was opened in the former cork factory. Every summer the traditional Festival da Cerveja (Beer Festival) is held here.

The castle precincts are used for cultural events such as jazz concerts, exhibitions, operas, medieval banquets and much more. Open daily 9am–5pm, 7pm in summer.

Museu Municipal de Arqueologia

The Museu Municipal de Arqueologia in Rua das Portas de Loulé was opened in 1990. Before the earthquake a large private house stood on this site, and in the course of excavations below the remains of the old walls, a large number of utensils and everyday items were uncovered. The museum's exhibits are mainly finds from around the house and from the castle precincts as well as from Loulé and São Bartolomeu de Messines.

On a tour of the museum – the labels and captions are in Portuguese – visitors are taken in chronological order through an archaeological collection of exhibits from the Palaeolithic, Neolithic, Bronze and Iron Ages. As well as Roman finds, many items from the Moorish period are on display, together with objects from 1189 onwards, namely, those relating to Portuguese culture.

A particulary beautiful exhibit is to be seen at the start of the tour – a red sandstone *menhir*, or upright monumental stone, from the 4th or 3rd c. BC. Examples of Iron Age culture include several fragments of burial pillars from the period between the 8th and 6th c. BC. Roman remains include coins and vessels and the base of a statue of Jupiter. There is an interesting small collection of surgical instruments dating from between the 5th and 7th c. Mementoes of the Moorish era include ceramics and two 10th c. capitals as well as a 12th c. well with a shaft 10 m deep. On the lower floor are exhibits from 1189 onwards – coins, vessels, belt buckles, small thimbles and other sewing utensils. From the upper floor with its changing exhibitions there is access to the town wall. Open Tue.–Sun. 10am–6pm.

The well-known Cruz de Portugal, worked in white limestone in the 16th c., stands at the town exit leading to São Bartolomeu de Messines. This work of religious sculpture is an example of a Manueline Way of the Cross which is unique in the Algarve. On the front is a portrayal of Jesus on the Cross and on the back His Descent from the Cross. The year 1025 on the base of the cross has presented historians with something of a puzzle; it is assumed that this means that the lower section dates from the Moorish period.

★Cruz de Portugal

The Ermida de Nossa Senhora dos Mártires, to the north-west of the Praça do Município, dates back to a 12th c. building, from the time when Silves was first taken by the crusaders led by Sancho I. At that time those who died in the battles near the town were buried here. A second building dating from the Manueline epoch fell victim to the 1755 earthquake, after which it was rebuilt. The tomb inside is probably that of a 13th or 14th c. bishop.

Ermida de Nossa Senhora dos Mártires

Near a building in Rua da Cruz da Palmeira are remains of an original Moorish gateway. Apparently it was also the entrance to the town in the Portuguese period.

Arco da Rebola

The beautiful bridge over the Rio Arade can be traced back to a river crossing of Roman times. The present bridge dates from the Middle Ages and was strengthened in later centuries. Here the Rio Arade flows through idyllic scenery, and visitors may occasionally see a turtle basking on the river bank.

The indoor market near the bridge sees much coming and going throughout the week.

Ponte Mercado

Surroundings

A few kilometres north-east of Silves there is a dam across the Rio Arude – the Barragem de Arade. The intention was to create a reservoir for the Silves region and a recreation area with facilities for water sports, restaurants and cafés. Although a start has been made, the water shortage in the Algarve has now unfortunately become so serious that very little of the original project is likely to materialise. The catastrophic drought situation can clearly be witnessed here at the Barragem de Arade where the water level has dropped so much that already a large, arid and ravaged stretch of the river bank is visible.

Barragem de Arade

★Tavira   K 5

Capital of the administrative district of Tavira
Population: 10,000

Tavira

The small town of Tavira is located in the south-east of the Algarve a good 20 km from the Spanish frontier and along both banks of the Rio Gilão (or Rio Séqua) which here flows into the Atlantic. Tavira lies not by the open sea but in the lagoon region of the Ria Formosa; offshore to the south-west is the Ilha de Tavira, a lagoon island of dunes. The wide-ranging fruit plantations – mainly orange and lemon groves – in the hinterland of Tavira exude a delightful aromatic scent when in bloom in the spring.

Fishing is of some importance in Tavira – for a period it was the centre of the tuna industry on the Algarve coast – and so is salt production, as evidenced by the salt works at the mouth of the Rio Gilão. In spite of the beautiful sandy beaches nearby, tourism has not really gained a foothold in Tavira and there are no hotels of any size; this makes it all the more attractive for a day trip.

History

It is not wholly clear when Tavira was founded. It probably dates back to an Iberian settlement in the 2nd c. BC and the Phoenicians are also thought to have established a trading post here. The Romans found a settlement named Balsa at the mouth of the Rio Gilão and kept the name. The present name is derived from Tabira, as it was known under the Moors, under whom and until well into the Middle Ages Tavira was a major port. In 1242 the town was captured by the Portuguese led by Dom Paio Peres Correia – according to legend the treacherous murder of seven Portuguese knights by the Moors in spite of a ceasefire resulted in the town being taken by force by the Portuguese. In the colonial period the Portuguese army of occupation in North Africa received support and assistance from Tavira because it was so near to the Moroccan coast. The port lost its importance when the North African colonies were given up; the gradual silting of the harbour basin added to its problems, and Spanish subjugation of Portugal between 1580 and 1640 followed by plague in 1645–6 were the final blows to its prosperity. In 1755 the

Traditional houses in Tavira

Tavira – Birthplace of the Man who Never Was

Although he never really existed, Álvaro de Campos was born on October 15th 1890 in Tavira. He came from a Jewish family. After attending grammar school he became apprenticed to a shipbuilding engineer in Glasgow. A long voyage took him to the Orient. In 1914 he returned to Portugal and lived in Lisbon, where he devoted a large proportion of his time to doing nothing, and the remainder to writing. Álvaro de Campos was a follower of a "non-Aristotelic aesthetic" and produced poems based on this doctrine. He published numerous odes. He wore a monocle, was tall in stature, thin and with a slight stoop. He was described as irascible and even devoid of feeling. But – as we have already said – he never actually existed.

Álvaro de Campos was no pseudonym, no character in a novel, not even a fabricated person – Álvaro de Campos was a heteronym, one of several in whose existence the poet and writer Fernando Pessoa wrapped himself or divided or multiplied himself. The origins of the heteronyms of the best-known Portuguese writer of the 20th c. have aroused much speculation. Pessoa spent his childhood in South Africa, grew up bilingual there and even wrote English poems under another name. Perhaps his heteronyms stem from this time. It has also been suggested that the rather lonely Pessoa used this means to create a circle of friends and people to whom he could closely relate.

His main heteronyms other than Álvaro de Campos were Alberto Caeiro, described as a bucolic poet, and Ricardo Reis, a doctor from Oporto who wrote neoclassical poetry. Bernando Soares was a semi-heteronym, who always appeared when Fernando Pessoa was tired and sleepy. Each of them had a well-defined character, an unmistakable appearance, a date of birth, a birthplace and much more; Pessoa even produced horoscopes for them. The heteronyms could be readily interchanged, and they also held lively discussions with Pessoa.

Portrait of Pessoa *by Almada Negreiros*

Of Álvaro de Campos it is known that he moved in Lisbon's avant-garde circles, which caused considerable disquiet among the citizens of the city. He is said to have got on well with Alberto Caeiro, even to have dedicated a book to him and to have regarded him as the one man in the country who lived in the timeless present of children and animals and who had opened his eyes to the truth. He felt himself linked even more strongly with the poet Fernando Pessoa. This "spiritual relationship" must have been so close that in 1935, the year when Pessoa died, Álvaro de Campos also departed this life.

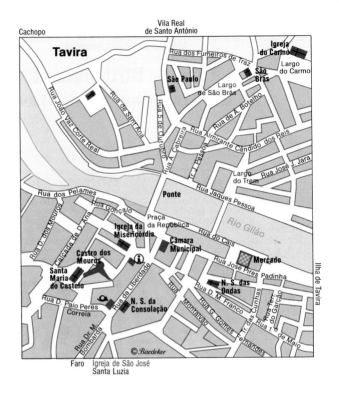

Tavira

Cachopo · Vila Real de Santo António

Igreja do Carmo · Largo do Carmo

São Paulo · São Brás · Largo de São Brás

Rua dos Fumeiros de Traz

Rua João Vaz Corte Real · Rua de Sant'Ana · Rua 5 de Outubro

Rua A. Cabreira · Rua Almirante Cândido dos Reis · Rua de A. Botellho

Largo do Trem · Rua José J. Jara

Rua T. J. Pessoa

Rua dos Pelames · Rua Gonçalo · Ponte · Rua Jaques Pessoa · Rio Gilão

Praça da República · Rua do Cais

Igreja da Misericórdia · Câmara Municipal

Rua dos Mouros · Calçada de D. Ana · Castro dos Mouros · Rua José Pires Padinha · Mercado

Santa Maria do Castelo · Rua da Liberdade · Rua · Rua José Pires Padinha · N. S. das Ondas · Ilha de Tavira

Rua D. Paio Peres Correia · N. S. da Consolação · Montavão · Rua D. M. Franco · Rua G. Gomes · Tr. das Cunhas · Rua de Garção · Rua 1 de Maio

Rua Dr. M. Bombarda · Fernandes

© Baedeker

Faro · Igreja de São José
Santa Luzia

earthquake destroyed large areas of the town and since then Tavira has remained of relatively minor importance.

Townscape

Tavira is one of the prettiest little towns in the Algarve. Because it was rebuilt following the earthquake, few of the buildings are more than 250 years old. Nevertheless, the uniform style of building employed lends Tavira a strong air of harmony. It is particularly picturesque along the banks of the Rio Gilão and the area here is sometimes compared with Venice (perhaps an exaggeration). Typical of Tavira are the characteristic hipped roofs of many old houses; similar roofs are now sometimes used on modern buildings. It is interesting to contrast the architecture with that of neighbouring Olhão, where building styles are basically quite different.

Sights

Tour

Tavira is a town where visitors can enjoy a quiet, relaxed stroll and just soak up the atmosphere. Those wishing to view a few of the sights could start at the Praça da República and see the south-west part of the town centre first. The Igreja da Misericórdia, the castle, the Igreja de Santa Maria do Castelo and finally the Capela de Nossa Senhora da Consolação are all worth a visit. Then cross the river and stroll through the pretty residential streets of the more-peaceful quarter on the other side. Here you will find the Igreja de São Paulo, the Capela de São Brás and the Igreja do Carmo, although these are often closed. The view across the river from Rua Jaques Pessoa, the riverside road, is not to be missed. There are several restaurants along the river bank.

On the south-west side of the river, a little way out from the town centre, the Igreja de São José and the Igreja de Nossa Senhora das Ondas are worth a visit.

The Praça da República, on the right bank of the river, forms the centre of Tavira. On the eastern side of the square lies a municipal park attractively laid out with flower beds and trees. At the south-east end of the square can be found Tavira's indoor market with some enticing cafés nearby. Rua da Liberdade, one of the main streets in the town centre, enters the Praça da República at its western corner. From the square there is a fine view of the Rio Gilão and the part of the town that lies opposite.

Praça da República

In recent years several bridges have been built over the Rio Gilhão and this has changed the character of the town centre. For centuries there had only been the one seven-arched bridge north of the Praça da República. This bridge is of Roman origin and all the traffic using the Roman road linking Faro and Mértola passed over it. The present bridge is a 17th c. reconstruction. In the winter of 1989–90 it was badly damaged by floods and had to be closed; since then it has been reopened to pedestrians only.

Ponte

The narrow Rua da Galeria branches off Rua da Liberdade and leads to the Igreja da Misericórdia. The Arco da Misericórdia next to the church is part of the old town gate dating to the time of the Moors.

In spite of the rebuilding work undertaken after the 1755 earthquake the church, originally dating from 1541, is still one of the finest examples

★Igreja da Misericórdia

Typical of many houses in Tavira is the exterior decoration

of Renaissance religious architecture in the Algarve. Details of the façade are of interest: under a projecting canopy, or baldachin, in the centre of the door you can see the Senhora da Misericórdia, the Madonna of Mercy, supported by angels. To the left are crowns and the Portuguese coat of arms, to the right the coat of arms of Tavira with the seven-arched bridge, a Portuguese king with his crown and a Moorish king wearing a turban. Various figures can be discerned in the door frame, including some little musicians. The two saints are St Peter on the left and St Paul on the right.

Spanning the triple-aisled interior are barrel-vaulted wooden ceilings. The blue-and-white *azulejo* pictures and the gilded high altar are very striking. Again the Portuguese crown and the coat of arms can be seen below the canopy. A closer examination of the capitals will reveal some masks. The small organ in the gallery is attractive – organs are something of a rarity in Algarve churches.

★Castro dos Mouros

A little way up from the town centre the Travessa da Fonte leads to the site of the former castle. Only fragments of the defensive walls remain of the original Roman fort and later Moorish castle, which was rebuilt after the Portuguese, under Dom Dinis I, had captured the town. Today a pretty garden has been laid out in part of the walls; it is privately owned but is open to visitors. From the gardens and from the top of the walls and the tower there are beautiful views over Tavira and the Rio Gilão. Open daily 9.30am–5.30pm.

★Igreja de Santa Maria do Castello

Near the castle garden stands the Igreja de Santa Maria do Castelo. It was constructed by the Portuguese on the site of a former Moorish mosque. Originally a 13th c. edifice, it was rebuilt after the earthquake in accordance with the old plans. Remains of the Gothic church include the entrance door and, inside, the interiors of some of the side chapels and the arch above the side altars.

In the choir can be seen the tombs of Dom Paio Peres Correia and the seven Portuguese knights who are said to have been murdered by the Moors during a period of truce, whereupon the town was attacked and taken by Christian troops. Note also the three side chapels on the left decorated with attractive blue-and-white tiles. The second side chapel still has some Manueline ceiling adornment and is clad in 18th c. *azulejos*.

Capela de Nossa Senhora da Consolação

The interior of the otherwise plain Capela de Nossa Senhora da Consolação in Rua da Liberdade boasts some 17th c. *azulejo* decoration and an altarpiece from the Flemish school (16th c.).

Igreja de Nossa Senhora das Ondas

This trapezium-plan church dedicated to the Madonna of the Waves stands on an acutely angled street corner near the Praça da República. Its 16th c. predecessor was destroyed in the earthquake, and the present church dates from the late 18th c.

Igreja de São José

An equally unusual plan is that of the Igreja de São José on the Praça Zacarias Guerreiro, south-east of the town centre, which is octagonal with unequal sides. The high altar is adorned with *trompe l'œil* paintings. Two side chapels are of Gothic-Manueline origin.

Praça 5 de Outubro/Igreja de São Paulo

After crossing the Rio Gilão by the old bridge, Rua 5 de Outubro leads to the Praça 5 de Outubro, a square that is attractively laid out with flower beds and trees. At its northern end stands the Igreja de São Paulo, originally a 17th c. Renaissance church with some beautiful 15th and 16th c. paintings.

Largo de São Brás/Capela de São Brás

The long Largo de São Brás with its small judas trees is another square with a lot of atmosphere. The sparingly decorated façade of the small Capelo de São Brás at the north-east end of the square is quite pleasing.

The dunes at Ilha de Tavira

A little way to the north-east of the Largo de São Brás you will find the unpretentious Largo do Carmo with the former Carmelite monastery and the Igreja do Carmo. Built in the 18th c., the church is notable for some important interior carvings and the magnificently decorated 18th c. choir-stalls.

Igreja do Carmo

Surroundings

The Ilha de Tavira, off the coast to the south-west, can be reached by boat during the holiday season. The ferry sails from the end of the riverside road that runs along the right bank of the Rio Gilão behind the indoor market. There is also a footbridge to the island, further west near Santa Luzia. The Ilha de Tavira has a sandy beach which is about 1 km long with flat dunes. The sea is not too rough and is suitable even for children to bathe.

★Ilha de Tavira

Santa Luzia, 2 km west of Tavira, is a fishing village that has been spoiled by modern development. The local inhabitants specialise in fishing for squid. They let earthenware jugs attached to a length of string down into the water; the squid, attracted by the absolute darkness they offer, swim into the jugs and are trapped. Colourful fishing boats lie along the mud flats, and on the far side there is the Ilha de Tavira. Near the holiday resort of Pedras d'el Rei on the western edge of Santa Luzia is a bridge leading to the island. Visitors can go on foot or direct to Barril beach by a little island railway.

Santa Luzia

Luz de Tavira is located 5 km west of Tavira near the busy N 125. The Igreja Matriz on the through road dates from the 16th c.; it is one of the few churches that survived the 1755 earthquake and an impressive

Luz de Tavira

example of Algarve Renaissance architecture. A number of Manueline features have been preserved, such as the attractive side doorway and the font. Mention should also be made of the *azulejo* decoration made in Sevilla in the 15th c. and found in the main chapel.

Torre de Ares

Near the coast, 2 km south-west of Luz de Tavira, some scanty remains of a medieval watchtower have survived. However, it is the journey here that is more rewarding than the place itself: a small group of typical little Algarve houses sit en route.

Conceição

The unspectacular village of Conceição lies 7 km east of Tavira. Close to the railway line between Lagos and Vila Real de Santo António stands an interesting parish church, which was originally Gothic.

Cabanas

Cabanas, lying about 2 km south of Conceição, is enjoying a tourist boom. The broad and mainly empty beach on a sandbank offshore is highly regarded by the holidaymakers staying in the large bungalow village at the edge of Cabanas. The beach can be reached by fishing boat or on foot in some places at low tide. On the coast road there are several small restaurants and cafés designed for tourists.

Vila do Bispo

B 5

Capital of the administrative district of Vila do Bispo
Population: 1,400

Although the village of Vila do Bispo in the extreme south-west of the Algarve is actually an uninspiring little place, it nevertheless acts as the region's administrative headquarters, a function once undertaken by,

Vila do Bispo Church

Praia do Castelejo: one of the beautiful beaches of the west coast

among other places, Sagres when it was more important than it is now. Far from the tourist world on the Algarve coast, Vila do Bispo could perhaps be described as being "at the end of the world", although the N 125 provides a good link with Lagos 26 km away.

In the Middle Ages the village was known as Santa Maria do Cabo and was often confused with Cabo de São Vicente 10 km away. Later it was gifted to the bishop of Faro and thus was named Vila do Bispo (Town of the Bishop).

Vila do Bispo is a quiet rural village without any particular features. Its church, built at the end of the 18th c. after the earthquake, is quite pretty. The interior is rich in 18th c. *azulejos* and *talhas douradas*.

Townscape

Surroundings

A number of places in the immediate vicinity and outlying areas include in particular Sagres (see entry) and the Cabo de São Vicente.

Sagres

The beaches west of Vila do Bispo, some rather remote, are very beautiful. They can be reached only by car along a small road from Vila do Bispo leading to the Praia do Castelejo which is often almost deserted during the week, while at weekends it is visited mainly by local people when the weather is good. A beach bar provides food and drink. From the little road to the Praia do Castelejo tracks (no signposts) lead to the Praia da Cordama and Praia da Barriga further north. There are also some beautiful bays with flat sandy beaches surrounded by high cliffs. The breakers of the Atlantic crash upon the shore. It is rather colder here than further east along the Algarve coast and there is little protection from the westerly winds.

**Praia do Castelejo
Praia da Cordama
Praia da Barriga**

Torre de Aspa

Although a popular destination for walkers, the Torre de Aspa can also be reached by car (tracks lead there southwards from Vila do Bispo). The Torre de Aspa is an obelisk standing in the middle of the barren plateau and marking the highest point (156 m above sea level) on the south-western coast of the Algarve. A little further west steep cliffs drop down to the Atlantic from a height of at least 150 m.

Carrapateira

From Vila do Bispo the N 125 continues northwards through thinly populated countryside, with numerous small side roads branching off westwards down to lonely bays. On some of them the final stretch has to be negotiated on foot. 14 km along the N 125 lies the fishing village of Carrapateira where individual tourists can find simple accommodation.

Raposeira

The village of Raposeira, 2 km east of Vila do Bispo, has become famous because Henry the Navigator is said to have lived here in the Casa do Infante. There is also a small village church with a Manueline doorway.

★Ermida de Nossa Senhora de Guadalupe

Outside Raposeira to the east and north of the N 125, visible from the road, stands the chapel in which Henry the Navigator is said to have worshipped. The oldest church in the Algarve, it was built in the 13th c. and has an early Gothic doorway and a simple rosette above the entrance. Particulary attractive are the capitals in the interior, which are decorated with human and animal heads. In spite of the proximity of the busy N 125 this place still has a special atmosphere all of its own.

**Praia de Ingrina
Praia do Zavial**

4 km to the south of Raposeira are the Ingrina and Zavial beaches. These small sandy bays are almost undiscovered by tourists.

Salema

Salema, 8 km east of Vila do Bispo, on the other hand, is gradually falling prey to tourism. In recent years some sizeable hotels and apartment blocks have been built around the village with its picturesque centre. However, a number of houses still offer individual accommodation. There is a small municipal beach, but it is more peaceful on the Praia da Figueira to the west (approached via the little hamlet of Figueira).

Burgau

Burgau, a little fishing village on the cliffs above a narrow bay 12 km east of Vila do Bispo, has been more successsful than Salema in retaining its originality. It is frequented mainly by individual tourists who are quite happy with basic accommodation. The village square near the beach can get crowded during the high season, mainly because of the many parked cars.

Near Barão de São João to the north of Burgau are some woods which are ideal for walks.

Vilamoura G 5

Administrative district: Loulé
Population: 50,000

The holiday resort of Vilamoura was developed in the 1970s and 1980s near a modern marina a few kilometres west of Quarteira and 10 km east of Albufeira. In contrast to its neighbour Quarteira, this "Moorish village" has the air of an exclusive resort with ample luxurious acommodation and a wide choice of leisure facilities. There are several golf courses near the town, numerous tennis courts, riding schools and of course many opportunities to indulge in water sports of all kinds. A number of bars and nightclubs and a casino provide evening entertainment.

Remains of the Roman settlement Cerro da Vila at Vilamoura ➤

Townscape

The houses in Vilamoura are spread over a wide landscaped area; there is nothing in the way of natural vegetation. Blocks of similar-looking apartments and high-rise buildings are not grouped together but stand in individual settings. There are wide streets laid out in semicircular or horseshoe shapes, with the result that it is very easy to get lost – frequent town plans help you find the way.

Sights

Porto

The marina at Vilamoura was built in the 1970s and is one of the largest, most luxurious and well appointed of its kind in Europe, with almost 1,000 berths for luxury yachts and small pleasure boats. Restaurants and cafés line the promenade.

Cerro da Vila
Estação
Arqueológica

It is possible that the Phoenicians discovered a good anchorage and harbour on this section of the coast. Remains of a Roman patrician's house have been unearthed a few hundred metres from the harbour, evidence of a Roman settlement here between the 1st and 5th c. AD. Apart from the excavated foundations there are some interesting 3rd c. AD mosaics. All the items that have been unearthed to date are on display in the little museum adjoining the site. Traces of later cultures have also been discovered, including the Visigoths from the 5th to the 8th c. and the Moors from the 8th to the 13th c. Museum open daily 9am–12.30pm.

Beach

Excellent bathing can be enjoyed on the Praia da Falésia (➤ Albufeira) to the west of Vilamoura.

Vila Real de Santo António   L 4

Capital of the administrative district of Vila Real de Santo António
Population: 14,000

Vila Real de Santo António is located in the extreme south-east of the Algarve on the right bank of the Guadiana, which forms the border between Portugal and Spain. The small border town is linked to the Spanish town of Ayamonte on the opposite bank by a regular ferry service. The ferry has declined in importance since a motorway bridge was built over the Guadiana a few kilometres to the north, but river trips from Vila Real de Santo António are still charming and popular. The town is also the terminus of the railway line from Lagos that serves the Algarve coast. As Vila Real de Santo António lies a little way inland it is not unduly affected by tourism. Nevertheless it is a vibrant place with plenty of shops in the town centre. Most visitors are day trippers – both Algarve holidaymakers and Spaniards, who find shopping cheaper here. Until the 1960s the town had several fish-canning factories, processing mainly sardines and tuna; now only two factories remain.

History

The town of Vila Real de Santo António is relatively new, having been built in 1774 in place of Santo António da Arenilha, which had been destroyed in a catastrophic flood in the early 17th c. Santo António da Arenilha had been a small fishing community that also helped to defend the region against invaders from North Africa, and some of the towers that formed part of its fortifications survived until the 19th c. Vila Real de Santo António, however, was a new town built under the supervision of the Marquês de Pombal (➤ Famous People), chief minister to José I, and not just a reconstruction of its predecessor. Some of its inhabitants were fishermen from Aveiro on the west coast of Portugal who had been forced to move after the town had been cut off from the sea following a storm. Other new residents came from various regions of the Algarve, including the nearby village of Monte Gordo, many as a result of government pressure to move. Within a short time official subsidies produced an upturn in fishing, shipbuilding, commerce and agriculture, and by 1777 Vila Real de Santo António had some 5,000 inhabitants.

The town centre by the river is marked by a uniform style of architecture. This regular layout is the work of the Marquês de Pombal who had previously overseen the rebuilding of Lisbon after it had been largely levelled in the 1755 earthquake. Like Lisbon, the centre of Vila Real de Santo António is laid out in a chessboard fashion, a principle used in Greece in the 5th c. BC. It was in accord with the philosophy of the Marquês de Pombal, who was the major advocate of absolutism in Portugal; clean lines and functional practicality were the basic principles. The historic town centre is also known as the Pombaline Centre, in memory of the Marquês. The major planners and architects involved were Reinaldo dos Santos, Ramão de Sousa and Carlos Mardel, the latter having also been involved with the Lisbon rebuilding.

Townscape

Sights

Praça do Marquês de Pombal forms the centre of Vila Real de Santo António. This magnificent square was paved with a radial mosaic design in 1879; the rays spread out from the obelisk in the centre, the top of which is adorned with a crown and an armillary sphere or skeleton globe. It was erected in 1775 for José I, during whose reign many reforms in education and agriculture were carried out. Surrounding the square are some relatively uniform houses. The severity of the square is softened by the beautiful orange trees – which exude a delightful scent across the square in spring – and a few street cafés. A building on the

★Praça do Marquês de Pombal

Praça do Marquês de Pombal in the centre of Vila Real de Santo António

143

eastern side houses the municipal library and the Manuel Cabanas Museum in which some woodcarvings of regional scenes are displayed.

Igreja Paroquial
The frontage of the houses along the northern side of the square is broken by the Igreja Paroquial (18th c., extensively restored in 1949). The tiled baptistry is very attractive.

Avenida da
República
The Avenida da República extends along the bank of the Guadiana in the centre of Vila Real de Santo António. Parts of the avenue are lined with pleasant parks where visitors can sit on the benches and enjoy the view across the river with Ayamonte in the distance.

Surroundings

Monte Gordo
Monte Gordo, the town neighbouring Vila Real de Santo António to the west, is the only really unappealing tourist centre east of Faro. Like so many places in the central part of the Algarve, huge hotel and apartment blocks have been built right by the seashore in this former fishing village. Near the town and for some kilometres either side there are some fine sandy beaches, and the tourist infrastructure is good, with plenty of shops, restaurants, pubs, discos and a casino.

Manta Rota
Manta Rota is a small village rather lacking tourist facilities, lying about 10 km west of Vila Real de Santo António. The lagoon system of the Ria Formosa ends here, with the result that Manta Rota lies directly by the open sea. It boasts superb, long beaches reaching as far as Monte Gordo in the east; the best-known section of beach is the Praia Verde, which is lined with small pine woods.

View of the coast from the church at Cacelha Velha

Charmingly located above the coastal strip a further 2 km to the west is the tiny hamlet of Cacelha Velha that was once a more-important village. Today it has only a few houses but blends in very well with its surroundings. It probably dates back to a Phoenician settlement. The church forecourt is extraordinarily beautiful and offers a view of the mud flats, the offshore islands and the open sea beyond. The 16th c. church has a Renaissance entrance and a Gothic side doorway. Tourism is not really catered for and there is only one restaurant in the village.

★**Cacelha Velha**

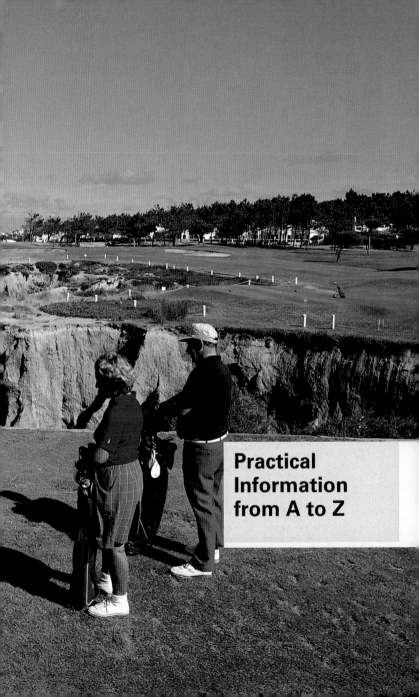

**Practical
Information
from A to Z**

Practical Information from A to Z

Accommodation

Camping   See entry

Hotels   See entry

Pensões   See Hotels

Pousadas   Pousadas are state-run hotels in converted castles, palaces and monasteries, or modern buildings located in places of outstanding natural beauty or historic interest. The interior, whether ancient or modern, is always attractive and furnished to a very high standard. As a rule the maximum stay is five days. Since the number of rooms tends to be very limited it is advisable to book well in advance. Room rates are relatively high, at between 18,000 and 30,000 Esc. for a double room, depending on the grading and season. Pousadas normally have their own restaurants with very good food and wine.

There are only two pousadas in the Algarve:

Pousada do Infante
Ponta da Atalaia
8650–385 Sagres; tel. (282) 624222, fax (282) 624225
Middle-ranking pousada with 39 rooms; lovely view over the rocky coast; the attractive amenities include a restaurant and a swimming pool.

Pousada de São Brás
8150–054 São Brás de Alportel; tel. (289) 842305/6, fax (289) 841726
Refurbished in 1998, this is a first-class pousada with 30 rooms in a quiet location above the city, with magnificent views; swimming pool, tennis court and restaurant.

Pousada in the southern Alentejo:

Pousada de Santa Clara
Santa-Clara-a-Velha; tel. (283) 98250, fax (283) 98402
This pousada on the Santa-Clara-a-Velha barrage has 19 rooms. Absolute peace and quiet, parkland with ancient trees and a terrace with wonderful views of the lake and mountain scenery.

Turismo de habitação

Portugal's *turismo de habitação* is a special kind of accommodation provided for visitors by the owners of some stately homes. Their spacious guest rooms are almost invariably tastefully furnished, often with antiques, and there are usually other leisure facilities in the vicinity. The historic homes in this scheme receive government subsidies,

◄ *One of the most-beautiful golf courses in the Algarve: Vale do Lobo*

are registered with the National Tourist Office, and must have the appropriate sign at the entrance. Other similar schemes include *turismo rural*, rural accommodation in country houses and wineries, and *agroturismo*, where it is possible to stay on farms and in farmhouses.

Information is available from travel agents and from TURIHAB (Associação de Turismo de Habitação), Praça da República, 4990 Ponte de Lima; tel. (258) 741672/742829, fax (258) 741444.

Casa Bela Moura (8 rooms) — Lagoa region
Alporchinhos, Apartado 323, 8365 Armacao de Pera; tel. (282) 313422, fax (282) 313025, email garcialius@net.sapo.pt

Quinta da Alfarrobeira (2 rooms, 1 apartment) — Lagos region
Estrada de Palmares, Odiáxere, 8600 Lagos; tel. (282) 798424, fax (282) 799630

Casa Belaventura (4 rooms) — Loulé region
Campina de Boliqueime, Alfontes, 8100 Loulé; tel. (289) 360633, fax (289) 366053

Quinta da Várzea (9 rooms)
Quinta da Várzea, Querenca, 8100 Loulé; tel. (289) 414443, fax (289) 422055

Quinta dos Rochas (6 rooms)
Fonte Coberta-Caixa Postal 600-A, Almansil, 8100 Loulé; tel. (289) 393165, fax (289) 399198, email quinta-dos-rochas@ip.pt

Casa Três Palmeiras (5 rooms) — Portimao region
Vau, Apartado 84, 8500 Portimao; tel. (282) 401275, fax (282) 401029, email casavaledelrei@mail.pt

Vila Rosa de Lima (4 rooms)
Estrada da Torre, Penina, 8500 Portimao; tel. (282) 411097

Quinta da Figueirinha (3 apartments) — Silves region
Quinta da Figueirinha, 8300 Silves; tel. (282) 440700, fax (282) 440709

Quinta da Fonte do Bispo (6 rooms) — Tavira region
Sitío da Fonte do Bispo, S. ta Catarina, 8800 Tavira; tel./fax (281) 971484

Quinta do Caracol (7 apartments)
Sao Pedro, 8800 Tavira; tel. (281) 322475, fax (281) 323175

Air Travel

Air Portugal (TAP), Rua D. Francisco Gomes 8, 8000 Faro; tel. (289) 817962 — Airlines
British Airways; tel. (289) 818476, fax (289) 818841
Portugália; tel./fax (289) 818535

Aeroporto Faro, the Algarve's international airport, is about 9 km east of Faro. It mainly takes charter flights and scheduled flights from the rest of Europe. TAP (Air Portugal) and Portugália also operate domestic flights to Lisbon and Oporto. — Faro airport
Information: tel. (289) 800800
Lost property: tel. (289) 818302

Buses run from the airport into Faro town centre, with stops at the railway station and central bus station, but they are relatively infrequent and not very reliable. — Airport buses and taxis

Water fun at an aquapark in the Algarve

A taxi to the centre of Faro costs about 1,000 Esc., plus extra for luggage.

Sightseeing
flights

Aero Clube do Algarve; tel. (282) 807199, fax (289) 823846
Aeródromo de Lagos; tel.fax (282) 762906
Aeródromo de Portimão; tel. (282) 495828, fax (282) 416784

Aquaparks

The Algarve has a number of aquaparks with giant flumes, high-diving shows and various other attractions.

Slide & Splash, east of Portimão at Lagoa on the N 125; tel. (282) 341685, fax (282) 341826
The Big One, east of Portimão at Porches on the N 125; tel. (282) 322827, fax (282) 322828
Atlantic Park, at Quarteira on the N 125; tel. (289) 397282, fax (289) 397757
Aqua Show, at Quarteira on the N 396; tel. (289) 388874, fax (289) 388233
Zoomarine, with dolphin, seal, sea lion and parrot shows on the N 125 at Guia/Albufeira; tel. (289) 560300, fax (289) 560309 (➤ Sights from A to Z, Albufeira)
Krazy World, amusement park with imaginative mini-golf course, animal enclosures and other attractions near Alvor; tel. (282) 574134, fax (282) 574898 (➤Sights from A to Z, Albufeira)

Beaches

The coast of the Algarve is famous for the beauty and variety of its beaches. In the rocky Algarve to the west they mostly take the form of small and often scenic sandy coves at the foot of tall cliffs. Here the Atlantic is still a force to be reckoned with, especially on stormy days in spring, autumn and winter. This western section of the coast is generally very good for diving. In the east, roughly from Quarteira onwards, there are fine flat sandy beaches stretching for many kilometres along the coast and often empty. The beaches listed below, running from west to east, are all good, long sandy beaches, or larger beaches in rocky coves. There are places to eat at all the tourist beaches; the remote bays on the west coast usually only have temporary eating places that are put up specially for the holiday season.

Some beaches have signs indicating whether they have lifeguards or not. *Area concessionada* means there are lifeguards on duty, while *Praia não vigilada* means the beach is unsupervised. Supervised beaches use flags to show when it is safe to go in the water. A red flag means it is forbidden to enter the sea, even close to the coast for paddling; a yellow flag means no swimming; and a green flag indicates that paddling and swimming are safe. A blue-and-white chequered flag means the beach is temporarily unsupervised.

Warning flags

Best beaches from west to east

Several breathtaking empty beaches at the foot of the cliffs south-west of Aljezur. These are often difficult to get to, and the Atlantic still pounds this coast with its full force, but sections of the Praia de Monte Clérigo are relatively safe. The beaches of Arrifana, Penedo, Vale de Figueiras and Bordeira are beautiful but not without hazards.

Aljezur

A few kilometres west of Vila do Bispo signs point the way down paths

Vila do Bispo

Evening light on the beach at Praia de Rocha near Portimão

Beaches

and sandy tracks to the beaches of Amado, Barriga, Cordama and Castelejo, beautiful sandy coves in the as yet relatively unspoiled rocky Costa Vicentina.

Sagres

Beliche, 5 km north-west of Sagres, has a 500 m stretch of beach reached by a path. Its location between steep cliffs is breathtaking. Access is from the parking place on the road between Sagres and Cabo S. Vicente via 156 steps. There is a small snack bar. Martinhal beach, east of Sagres, has 750 m of white sand and dunes, and is in the shelter of the harbour, making it a good beach for children. The beach at Zavial is much smaller, only about 200 m long but of fine sand, free of rocks and not crowded.

Salema

Salema has a pleasant sandy beach 750 m long surrounded by cliffs; good for surfing. There are rocky and sandy coves east and west of the town.

Burgau

Holidaymakers in Burgau have to content themselves with a relatively small beach 300 m long.

Luz

Lots of action at Praia da Luz, 200 m of sandy beach with rocks. Various water sports including scuba-diving; several restaurants. Suitable for children.

Lagos

Lagos itself only has quite small beaches, but nearby there are scenic bays amongst the steep rocks. Praia Dona Ana, south of Lagos, is one of those photogenic rocky coves of the Algarve. Praia Porto de Mós as well as Praia Caniaval are among the favourite beaches of the locals.

Meia Praia

East of Lagos marina there is one of the longest beaches of this part of the coast with good diving and surfing. Ideal also for those who just like to walk along the beach.

Alvor

Praia de Alvor and Praia dos Três Irmãos are the continuation of Meia Praia on the other side of the estuary and the jetties of Alvor – a very long flat sandy beach with some beautiful rocky coves near Prainha to the east.

Praia da Rocha

Broad sandy beach with some rocks; high-rise apartments line the clifftop road directly overlooking the beach; very popular in the holiday season. You will find the occasional sign indicating erosion and rock slides!

Ferragudo

Well-kept beach at the mouth of the Rio Arade, with a number of smaller rocky coves within walking distance, but rather spoiled by the skyline of Praia da Rocha on the other side. According to an EU report, the otherwise excellent water quality of the Algarve leaves a lot to be desired here.

Carvoeiro

Small sandy cove with rocks on both sides; packed in summer.

Armação de Pêra

Very long beach of golden sand stretching along the coast to the east, with a few fishing boats, and room to spare even in the peak holiday season, plus rocky coves to the west, including the extremely scenic Praia da Senhora da Rocha.

Albufeira

Albufeira's lovely town beach gets packed in the holiday season, but there is more chance of finding some space further east at Oura; there are also some very pretty coves west of the town such as Praia de São Rafael, Praia da Coelha and Praia do Castelo.

Praia da Falésia

The longest beach in the area although rather narrow. Suitable for children and surfers should have fun too.

A sandy bay near Armação de Pêra

Good sandy beach with safe swimming for children; high-rise apartments line the road overlooking the beach – very much a tourist resort, with plenty of sports facilities.

Quarteira

Flat beach of fine sand with rocks and cliffs; water sports, good surfing conditions.

Vale do Lobo

Long idyllic beach with dunes out in the lagoon, sometimes considered upmarket; pine woods towards the hinterland. Excellent water sports and good surfing.

Quinta do Lago

Praia de Faro beach, stretching for many kilometres, is on the sandspit that forms the lagoon and is accessible by car from near the airport. There are several other good beaches on the islands in the lagoon, such as Ilha da Barreta, accessible by boat. Quite crowded at the weekends (many weekend cottages).

Faro

Boats run regularly from Olhão to the islands of Farol, Culatra and Armona out in the lagoon; these have long flat sandy beaches with dunes and are ideal for children.

Olhão

Ilha de Tavira, which can be reached by boat from Tavira, or via a bridge from Santa Luzia further west, has extensive sandy beaches, dunes and a small wood. Ideal for children.

Tavira

Very good long, deserted beach on a spit can be reached by fishing boat or on foot at low tide. It is possible also to walk there from Manta Rota.

Cabanas/Cacela

Miles of golden sandy beaches and dunes extend along the coast either

Monte Gordo

side of Monte Gordo. Unfortunately there are high-rise apartment blocks near the small town itself.

Camping

Camping is usually not permitted by the roadside, in laybys or anywhere else that is not an official campsite.

Campsites

Portugal's public and private campsites are graded according to one to four stars. Besides a passport or identity card, campers may also need to produce a "camping carnet" – issued by the International Federation of Camping and Caravanning – if they want to use sites owned by clubs or the Portuguese Camping and Caravanning Federation.

Albufeira

✱✱✱✱Parque de Campismo de Albufeira, 8200 Albufeira; tel. (289) 589505, fax (289) 587633; 3 km from the station

Aljezur

✱✱✱Parque de Campismo do Serrão (at Aldeia Velha), 8670 Aljezur; tel/fax (282) 998612; 800 m from bus stop
✱✱✱Parque de Campismo Municipal de Aljezur (at Vale da Telha), 8670 Aljezur; tel. (282) 998444; 5 km from the bus stop
✱✱✱Parque de Campismo de Canelas, 8300 Silves; tel. (282) 312612, fax (282) 314718

Armação de Pêra

✱✱Parque de Campismo da Praia de Armação de Pêra, 8300 Silves; tel. (282) 312296, fax (282) 315379; 20 m from the bus stop, 4 km from the station

Lagos

✱Parque de Campismo da Trindade (at Praia de Dona Ana), 8600 Lagos; tel. (282) 763893; 800 m from the bus stop, 1 km from the station.
✱✱✱Parque de Campismo de Lagos (at Porto de Mós), 8600 Lagos; tel./fax (282) 760031; 50 m from the bus stop, 1.5 km from the station
✱✱✱Parque de Campismo de Valverde (at Luz), 8600 Lagos; tel. (282) 789211, fax (282) 789213; 50 m from the bus stop, 5 km from the station
✱✱Parque de Campismo de Espiche, 8600 Lagos; tel. (282) 789431; 5 km from the station

Olhão

✱✱✱Parque de Campismo do Sindicato dos Bancários do Sul e Ilhas, 8700 Olhão; tel. (289) 700300, fax (289) 700139; 400 m from the bus stop, 1.5 km from the station

Portimão

✱✱Parque de Campismo da Dourada (at Alvor), 8500 Portimão; tel. (282) 458002; 4 km from the station
✱✱Parque de Campismo de Ferragudo, 8400 Lagoa; tel. (282) 461121, fax (282) 461259; 100 m from the bus stop, 2.6 km from the station

Quarteira

✱✱✱Parque de Campismo de Quarteira/Orbitur, 8100 Loulé; tel. (289) 302821, fax (289) 302822; 30 m from the bus stop, 6 km from the station

Tavira

✱✱Parque de Campismo Municipal da Ilha de Tavira, 8800 Tavira; tel. (281) 324455, fax (281) 324752; 400 m from the bus stop, 2 km from the station

Vila do Bispo

✱✱Parque de Campismo Quinta dos Carriços, 8650 Vila do Bispo; tel. (282) 695201, fax (282) 695122; 100 m from the bus stop

Vila Real de Santo António

✱Parque de Campismoe Caravanismo do Caliço (at Vila Nova de Cacela), 8900 Vila Real de Santo António; tel. (281) 951195, fax (281) 956024; 500 m from the bus stop, 1.5 km from the station

✻Parque de Campismo Municipal de Monte Gordo, 8900 Vila Real de Santo António; tel. (281) 510970; 200 m from the bus stop, 1.3 km from the station

The Direcção-Geral do Turismo in Lisbon publishes an up-to-date and multi-lingual official guide to campsites (*Parques de campismo, guia oficial*), obtainable from: Direcção-Geral do Turismo, Av. António Augusto de Aguiar 86, 1004 Lisbon Codex; tel. (21) 3575086/3575145/3575015, fax (21) 3575220.

Camping guides

Casinos

The Algarve has casinos in Praia da Rocha, Vilamoura and Monte Gordo where French and American roulette, blackjack and baccarat are available plus the usual one-armed bandits. The casinos are normally open daily 3pm–3am, and there is usually an international floor show in the casino restaurant.

Children

The Algarve coast is a great place for family holidays for both younger and older children. Fine weather means that they can play on the beach even in spring and autumn, although remember that the Atlantic in the east of the Algarve is less rough and warmer than in the west, and that the east has long sandy beaches. The best beaches for children are at Martinhal, Luz, Vilamoura (Praia da Falésia, Praia da Marinha), Farol, Culatra, Armona, Monte Gordo and on Ilha de Tavor, plus the tourist resorts of Armação de Pêra and Quarteira. Many hotels and apartment blocks have their own swimming pool and children's paddling pool, and some have special child-care facilities. There are also plenty of sports on offer and organised programmes for older children and young people.

Suitable excursions for children are boat trips to the caves and coves of the west coast, from Portimão to Silves on the Rio Arade, along the Spanish border on the Guadiana, or by a little ferry to the islands in the lagoon on the east coast. Another option is to go on an organised ride and explore the hinterland on the back of a donkey (➤ Excursions).
    There are several aquaparks to delight young and old alike (➤ Aquaparks). You could happily spend a whole day at Zoomarine, for example, where the attractions include performing dolphins and a parrot show. Other interesting excursions include a trip to Europe's most south-westerly point (➤ Sights from A to Z, Sagres), a visit to the wildlife centre at Quinta de Marim (➤ Olhão) or a visit to the Costa Vicentina nature park (➤ Aljezur).

Excursions

Conversions

To convert metric to imperial multiply by the imperial factor; e.g. 100 km equals 62 mi. (100 × **0.62**).

Linear measure
1 metre   **3.28** feet, 1.09 yards
1 kilometre (1000 m)   **0.62** mile

Square measure
1 square metre   **1.2** square yards, 10.76 square feet
1 hectare   **2.47** acres

| 1 square kilometre (100 ha) | **0.39** square mile |

Capacity

1 litre (1000 ml)	**1.76** pints (**2.11** US pints)
1 kilogram (1000 grams)	**2.21** pounds
1 metric ton (1000 kg)	**0.98** ton

Temperature

°C	°F	°C	°F
−5	23	20	68
0	32	25	77
5	41	30	86
10	50	35	95
15	59	40	104

Currency

Currency

The Portuguese unit of currency is the escudo (Esc. or $), which, in theory, is sub-divided into 100 centavos. There are banknotes for 500, 1,000, 2,000, 5,000 and 10,000 Esc. and coins in denominations of 5, 10, 20, 50, 100 and 200 Esc. Coins for 1 escudo are hardly in use and the 2.5 Esc. coin has been invalid since 1998.

Euro

On 1 January 1999 the euro became the offical currency of Portugal, and the Portuguese escudo became a denomination of the euro. Portuguese escudo notes and coins continue to be legal tender during a transitional period. Euro bank notes and coins are likely to start to be introduced by January 202. 1 euro = 200 Esc.

Exchange rates

The escudo is subject to considerable fluctuations and, as is usually the case with countries that have a weak currency, it pays to change money before going to Portugal. When changing back Portuguese banknotes you usually lose from 11 to 30 per cent on the deal.

Currency import and export

Membership of the European Union means there are no restrictions on how much foreign currency a private individual can take into Portugal, although amounts in excess of 2.5 million Esc. should be declared on entry.

Credit cards

Banks, the larger hotels, established restaurants, car-rental firms and some shops accept most international credit cards. Visa and Eurocard are widely recognised, but the same does not always apply to American Express and Diner's Club. If a credit card is lost it should be reported immediately.

Customs Regulations

Allowances between EU countries

There is now no limit to the amount of goods that can be taken from one EU country to another provided they have been purchased tax paid in an EU country, are for personal use and not intended for resale. However, customs authorities have issued guidelines to decide whether your purchases are for personal use: 800 cigarettes; 400 cigarillos; 200 cigars; 1 kg of smoking tobacco; 10 litres of spirits; 20 litres of fortified wine (such as port or sherry); 90 litres of wine (of which not more than 60 litres can be sparkling wine); 110 litres of beer.

Entry from non-EU countries

For those coming from a country outside the EU or who have arrived from an EU country without having passed through custom control with all their baggage, the allowances for goods obtained anywhere outside

the EU for persons over the age of 16 are: 200 cigarettes or 100 cigarillos or 50 cigars or 250 grams of smoking tobacco; 1 litre of spirits or
2 litres of fortified wine and sparkling wine; 2 litres of still wine; 50 grams
of perfume; 0.25 litre of toilet water.

Electricity

The electricity supply is 220 AC, with continental two-pin plugs. Most
standard European plugs can be used in the big hotels, but American
flat-pin plugs require a transformer and an adaptor.

Embassies and Consulates

Embassy: Av. da Liberdade 110, 2nd floor, 1200 Lisbon; tel. (21)
3404666, fax (21) 3404575 — Australia

Embassy: Av. da Liberdade 144–156, 1250 Lisbon; tel. (21) 3474892,
fax (21) 3476466 — Canada

Embassy: Rua da Imprensa àl Estrela 1, 1200 Lisbon; tel. (21) 3961569,
fax (21) 3977363 — Eire

Embassy: Av. Luís Bivar 10/10a, 1050 Lisbon; tel. (21) 3535041,
fax (21) 3535713 — South Africa

Embassy: Rua S. Bernardo 33, 1200 Lisbon; tel. (21) 3924000,
fax (21) 3924188 — United Kingdom

Consulate: Largo Francisco A. Maurício 7, 1st floor, 8500 Portimão;
tel. (282) 417800, fax (282) 417806

Embassy: Av. das Forças Armadas 16, 1600 Lisbon; tel. (21) 7273300,
fax (21) 7269109 — United States

Emergency Calls

Throughout Portugal the freephone number for police, fire, medical and
rescue services is 112. — Emergency

There are free-standing orange emergency phones alongside the motorways. — Motorways

Breakdown assistance (24 hours) can be requested from the Portuguese
Automobile Club (ACP); tel. (21) 9429103. — Breakdown assistance

Events

Like the rest of Portugal, the Algarve has a full calendar of festivals and
ceremonial events, especially where local saints are concerned. Every
town and almost every village has its own patron saint and an annual
festival in his or her honour, which goes beyond purely religious observance to a day of free fun for the whole community. The festival usually
begins with a packed church for a full high Mass in the saint's honour.
This is often followed by a *romaria* when everyone proceeds through the

streets behind the image of their saint. Eventually the whole place is given over to the fun of the fair, with music and folk dancing. There are also a number of traditional seasonal events such as the almond blossom festival.

During the summer the Algarve also stages its share of concert series, film, folklore and dance festivals.

January

During the first 12 days of January, strolling musicians, or *charolas*, tour round all the villages in the Algarve, performing *janeiras*, songs to mark the new year – an age-old tradition in southern Portugal.

Vilamoura: celebration of the almond blossom festival in late January or early February.

February/March

Carnival, especially in Loulé, Moncarapacho and Portimão.

Loulé: Loulé is famous throughout Portugal for its carnival parade; it also celebrates the almond blossom festival at the same time.

Salir: Festa das Espigas, an Alpine-style festival as befits a pretty mountain village.

Alte: in neighbouring Alte, Festa dos Chouriços, sausage festival in honour of São Luís.

Easter

Good Friday and Easter Day processions in a number of places.

Loulé: Festa da Mãe Soberana, a famous *romaria* on the second Sunday after Easter when the Virgin is carried in procession up the rugged hillside to the chapel of Nossa Senhora da Piedade. This is followed by general festivities.

April

Celebrations, with rallies, song and dance, to mark Liberation Day, the public holiday commemorating the Carnation Revolution and an end to years of dictatorship on April 25th 1974.

May

Celebrations, similar to April 25th, with rallies and fairs, to mark May 1st.

Alte: Festa da Grande Fonte, early in May, when a grand picnic is held around the village spring; parades, music and dancing.

Many places show amateur films as part of the Algarve's international festival of low-budget films.

During the international music festival between April and June many places in the Algarve stage concerts and ballets starring prominent artists.

June

Festas dos Santos Populares take place throughout Portugal. These popular saints are particularly fêted in the places where they are the patron saints.

Faro: the feast of Santo António, patron saint of Faro, is celebrated on June 13th with a procession and a public festival. Saint Anthony is also the patron saint of the forgetful, of lovers and children.

Silves: Festival da Carveja, beer festival with music, folklore and dance.

July

Faro: Feira do Carmo, grand public festival in mid-July.

Fuzeta: Festa do Carmo is celebrated in Fuzeta, near Olhão, with a waterborne procession.

August

Olhão: Festival of the Sardines.

Castro Marim: São Bartolomeu is honoured on August 15th with a festival inside the castle walls.

September

Algarve folklore festivals in various place with dance performances and competition for the Algarve prize; finals in Praia da Rocha.

Albufeira: Festa do Beato São Vicente.

Vila Real de Santo António: Festa de Nossa Senhora da Encarnação.

Faro: people flock from all around to Faro's famous fair, the Feira de Santa Iria.
Monchique: October fair.

October

Various concerts before Christmas, the most important family festival of the year for the Portuguese.

December

Bullfighting in Portugal is different from its Spanish counterpart in that the bull leaves the arena alive, although it still gets slaughtered later (➤ Baedeker Special, p. 160).

Bullfighting

Excursions

There are plenty of opportunities to get around and explore the Algarve on excursions. The larger hotels normally offer trips to various Algarve destinations, and in all the main tourist centres trips by boat along the rocky coastline or sightseeing tours by coach can be booked.

Individual outings by car, train or bus can be made. Trains only go to the main towns and smaller places close to the coast, however. Some of the inland villages are accessible by bus, but there are very few bus services in the more isolated parts (➤ Public Transport). For more than one day's outing it is better to go by car (➤ Suggested Routes). Another option is to tour the hinterland by cycle (➤ Sport), but remember it can be quite hilly.

If you are holidaying in the east of the Algarve, it is possible to get to Seville relatively quickly by motorway. Mértola, in the south-east of the Alentejo, is another possibility for an excursion from this part of the Algarve.

Algarve Tours organise walks; tel. (282) 416190 or 490200

For the Parque Natural da Ria Formosa there are day-trips by boat from Faro, Olhão and Tavira out to the islands in the lagoon. You can also see something of the beautiful hinterland of the eastern Algarve by taking a river trip along the frontier up the Guadiana river. These are operated by Transguadiana from Vila Real de Santo António; tel. (281) 512997. Information is available from the tourist office in Monte Gordo.

Eastern Algarve

Turinfo in Sagres organises walks in the Costa Vicentina national park, as well as jeep, donkey and cycle safaris and boat trips around Cabo de São Vicente and along the Costa Vicentina; tel. (282) 624873.

Western Algarve

Fado

Fado, Portugal's own distinct form of folk music, is said to have originated in the backstreets of Lisbon and is essentially a ballad of the cities. Nowadays you may be lucky enough to hear authentic fado live in the bars of Lisbon or Coimbra, but you are unlikely to find a really good *fadista* in the Algarve. Here, it is mostly fado for tourists, but to get some idea of what this typically Portuguese music is like there are a few places that occasionally stage fado nights (*noites de fado*). In general they start with dinner (from 7.30 or 8pm), followed by the fado performance (at 9.30 or 10pm).

Armação de Pêra
Hotel Viking, Senhora da Rocha; tel. (282) 314876
Performances: Tuesdays.

Fado nights

Of Touros and Cavaleiros

Visitors to the Algarve may perhaps share the reservations voiced by the writer Felix Krull when invited to a Portuguese bullfight: "I'm rather squeamish, I said, and if I know me, not one for butchery in the guise of folklore. Take the horses, for instance — I'd heard that the bulls often slice them open so that their guts spill out; I wouldn't want to see that, let alone what happens to the bull, which I'd just feel sorry for. You could say that I ought to be able to put up with, if not exactly enjoy, a spectacle that even ladies can tolerate. But these ladies, these Iberians, are born and raised in this tough tradition, while I'm just a rather delicate foreigner ..."

And don't believe it if you are told that Portuguese bullfighting is bloodless compared with the Spanish version. The bull may not actually be killed in the ring, but death still awaits it in the wings.

Portugal's top *touradas*, as bullfights are called, take place in the Lisbon arena in front of around 8,000 spectators, and in the arenas of Santarém and Vila Franca de Xira, north-east of the capital. And throughout the country you will come across small local bull rings, or *corridas*, often no more than a few wooden slats nailed together. In the villages *touradas* are often simply put on in the market place or on a playing field on the edge of the village.

On the coast of the Algarve, however, you do not see the true classical bullfighting of the great Portuguese arenas. The heroism and costumes of the bullfighters often leave a lot to be desired, the events are only half as long as elsewhere in Portugal, and all

in all it is basically bullfighting for tourists.

The typical *tourada* always begins with a contest between the *touro*, the bull, and the *cavaleiro*, an elegantly costumed bullfighter on horseback. The *cavaleiro* first limbers up against a *tourinha*, an artificial bull consisting of horns mounted on a chassis. But then the whole affair gets going in deadly earnest.

The bull, which has been moving rather aimlessly round the perimeter, catches sight of the *cavaleiro* and his horse and gallops wildly at them, repeatedly charging them head on, diagonally and from the side. Horse and rider dexterously avoid the bull in a series of skilful manoeuvres or *sortes*. While this is going on the *cavaleiro* tries to plant a *farpa* or the shorter *ferros* in the snorting beast's neck. The onlookers howl their appreciation depending on how the *cavaleiro* performs — the bolder he is the better. Really daring *cavaleiros* hold their ground till the very last minute or, equally death defying, ride straight at the charging bull. Luckily for them, the horns of the Portuguese bulls are rendered virtually harmless by leather padding.

Once all the *farpas* and *ferros* have been planted in the bull, the referee, *O Intelligente*, decides whether *touro* and *cavaleiro* have had enough. Then follows the second part of the action, the *pega*, a no less tense encounter between man and beast. The *cavaleiro* withdraws and eight intrepid *forcados*, unarmed and on foot, advance one behind the other in teams of four to bring down the bull. The first hurls himself valiantly at the bull's horns and tries to hold onto its

A Portuguese bullfight in Albufeira

neck. The next grabs the bull's head, the third its shoulders or whatever comes to hand, and the last seizes it by the tail so that, using all their might and main, they bring it to a stop. This procedure is as dangerous as it looks and was banned in the 19th c. because of the number of *forcados* that were being killed. Accidents can still happen, and many injuries end up in hospital. It is hard to believe that, as unpaid amateurs, their heroic deeds go unrewarded except for what the spectators give them. The *cavaleiros*, on the other hand, are professionals and earn large fees for their appearances.

The bullfighting season is from Easter to October. They are usually held on Thursdays and Sundays, and last for about three hours. During this time six bulls will follow one another into the ring. As has been said, they are not killed until after the fight is over when, depending on how badly injured they are, they will either be despatched immediately or slaughtered the next day. The supposedly "bloodless" Portuguese *tourada* may appear to be easier on the bulls, but when the *touro* dies at the height of the bullfight it is at least spared several more hours of suffering.

Lagoa
Casa Velha, Rua Mouzinho de Albuquerque 60; tel. (282) 342800
Performances: Saturdays.

Porches
Restaurante Porches Velho; tel. (282) 381692
Performances: Fridays and Saturdays.

Portimão
Hotel Delfim, Praia dos Três Irmãos, Alvor; tel. (282) 458901, fax (282) 458970
Performances: Tuesdays.

Silves
Restaurante Quinta da Pomona; tel. (282) 442361
Performances: Wednesdays, Thursdays and Fridays.

Music

There are some very good fado recordings, available in Portuguese record stores (➤ Shopping).

Food and Drink

Eating out plays an important part in the life of the Portuguese. Many of them get their lunch (*almoço*) at a regular place close to where they work, and meet their friends in restaurants for dinner (*jantar*) in the evening. They like going out to eat on family occasions such as birthdays too, when they enjoy celebrating with a leisurely meal in their favourite restaurant.

Grilled sardines – a traditional Portuguese dish

Food

The Algarve has many restaurants catering solely for tourists and these have the advantage of providing menus in English, but they rarely offer genuine Portuguese cuisine. Good local dishes are usually unpretentious. Portuguese food is often simple and palatable, if somewhat lacking in variety. Lovers of fish and seafood will be in their element, but the same cannot be said for those who prefer vegetables and salads; these often have to be ordered separately. Sauces are few and far between – with fish, for example, you often just get potatoes and melted butter.

Local cuisine

Lunchtime is usually 12.30–2pm and dinner 8–10pm.

Meal times

Breakfast (*pequeno almoço*) is largely unimportant for the Portuguese, and they usually just have a coffee on the way to work. Hotels and pensions normally provide a continental-style breakfast of tea or coffee, and rolls plus jam, cheese or ham, while the larger hotels have self-service buffets. To get breakfast in a bar order a roll or a sandwich (*sanduíche*) with cheese (*com queijo*) or ham (*com fiambre*), buttered toast (*torrada*) or a ham and cheese toastie (*tosta mista*).

Breakfast

Lunch and dinner normally consist of three courses – starter, main course and dessert. A starter (*entrada*) is usually one of the excellent Portuguese soups. The main course will be a fish or meat dish with chips, potatoes or rice and occasionally vegetables and salad. Dessert (*sobremesa*) will be one of the delicious, often home-made sweets (*doces*), ice cream or fruit. There is always bread on the table and sometimes, before the starter, you will also get cheese and olives with it, or small plates of seafood. Just remember that every additional item probably costs extra, whether you ask for it or not. The Portuguese like to round off the meal with a small black coffe (*bica*) and a brandy (*aguardente*) or marc (*bagaço*).

Midday and evening meals

sopa do dia	soup of the day	Soups (*sopas*)
caldo verde	cabbage and potato soup with a slice of sausage	
sopa de legumes	vegetable soup	
sopa de feijão	bean soup	
sopa de peixe	fish soup	
creme de marisco	seafood bisque	
canja	chicken broth	
açorda à Alentejana	clear broth with bits of bread and a poached egg, seasoned with lots of garlic and coriander	
caldeirada	fish stew (Portuguese bouillabaisse)	
cataplana	stew with mussels, pork and vegetables	
feijoada	bean stew	
cozida à portuguesa	vegetable soup with pieces of meat	
bacalhau	dried cod (Portugal's national dish, once a "poor man's" food, now quite expensive but still prepared in many different ways)	Fish (*peixe*)
bacalhau cozido	dried cod, poached	
bacalhau na brasa	dried cod, grilled	
bacalhau à brás	dried cod fried with egg, potatoes and onions	
sardinhas assadas	grilled sardines	
cherne, robalo	perch	
lulas grelhadas	grilled baby octopus	
polvo	octopus	
peixe espada	swordfish	

Food and Drink

	atum	tuna
	truta	trout
	salmão	salmon
	linguado	sole
	enguia	eel
Seafood (*mariscos*)	camarões	shrimp
	gambas	scampi
	sapateira	crab
	lagosta	spiny lobster
	amêijoas	clams
	arroz de marisco	seafood risotto
Meat (*carne*)	bife (com ovo)	steak (with fried egg)
	costeleta	cutlet
	carne de porco	pork
	carne de porco à Alentejana	pork with clams
	leitão assado	roast suckling pig
	lombo de porco	roast leg of pork
	carne de vaca	beef
	borrego	lamb
	cabrito assado	roast kid
	espetada de carne	meat kebab
	frango assado	spit-roast chicken
	frango com piri-piri	barbecued chicken with hot little Angolan peppers (Algarve speciality)
	peru	turkey
Eggs (*ovos*)	ovos mexidos	scrambled egg
	ovos estrelados	fried egg
	omeleta	omelette
Vegetables (*legumes*)	cogumelos	mushrooms
	cenouras	carrots
	alho francês	leeks
	pimentos	peppers
	feijões	beans
	ervilhas	peas
	cebola	onions
	alface	lettuce
	salada de tomate	tomato salad
	salada mista	mixed salad
Fruit (*frutas*)	salada de fruta	fruit salad
	maçã	apple
	pêra	pear
	melão	melon
	melancia	water melon
	morangos	strawberries
	pêssego	peach
	uvas	grapes
	laranja	orange
Desserts (*sobremesa*)	gelado, sorvete	ice cream
	arroz doce	rice pudding
	pudim molotov	"floating islands"
	pudim flan	crème caramel
	leite creme	baked custard
	toucinho do céu	sweet made of sugar, eggs and ground almonds
Snacks (*salgados*)	tarte de amêndoa	almond tart

bolo de chocolate	chocolate cake
pastéis de bacalhau	small potato, parsley and dried-cod fishcakes
rissois de camarão	small shrimp patties
chamuça	small spicy minced-meat patties
prego no pão	hamburger

Drink (*bebidas*)

All the usual international soft drinks, plus mineral water (*agua mineral*), both still (*sem gás*) and carbonated (*com gás*), and good fruit juices (usually bottled rather than freshly pressed) are available. Soft drinks

Beer (*cerveja*) is very popular with the Portuguese. The best-known brand is Sagres, brewed near Lisbon; Superbock is somewhat sweeter. If you ask for a *cerveja* you get a bottled beer. *Imperial* will get you a small draught beer, *caneca* a large one. Beer

Wine served with food is normally either a *vinho da mesa* (table wine) or a *vinho da casa* (house wine). *Vinho tinto* is red wine and *vinho branco* is white wine. The most-popular wines are those from the Dão, Douro, and Ribatejo regions, from Colares, north-west of Lisbon, and, more recently, from Alentejo. *Vinho verde* (green wine) is a mildly sparkling youthful wine from northern Portugal, which accounts for about 20 per cent of the nation's wine output. Its name refers to its method of production: the grapes are harvested early and only fermented for a short time. Wine
    Portugal's most-famous wine is undoubtedly port, which gets its name from the northern town of Oporto. The grapes are chiefly grown on the upper slopes of the Douro on the slaty soils that give it a flavour all of its own. The partly fermented red wine is fortified with brandy and then stored for several years in casks or bottles. Dry port is mostly drunk as an aperitif, while sweet port is traditionally served at the end of a meal.

A favourite fruit brandy in the Algarve is *medronho*, a fiery spirit distilled from the fruit of the arbutus or strawberry tree that grows particularly well in southern Portugal. Other popular spirits include *bagaço*, made from grape residue like a French marc, and *aguardente velha*, a form of old brandy. *Ginjinha* is a cherry liqueur that can be ordered with (*com*) or without (*sem*) cherries. Spirits

Coffee comes as *café* or *bica*, a small cup of espresso, or you can order *galão*, white coffee in a glass. If you ask for *café com leite* you normally get white coffee in a cup. *Meia de leite* means a cup of coffee too but with less milk, while *meia de leite à máquina* is a cappuccino. Coffee

Getting to the Algarve

The Algarve's international airport is the Aeroporto de Faro. There are scheduled flights to the airport at Faro from Britain by Air Portugal (TAP) and British Airways, and from the United States by Transworld Airlines (TWA) and TAP, mostly via Lisbon. There are also charter flights to Faro from Britain and elsewhere in Europe. These are often particularly inexpensive off-season, and there are some very good package deals available, including flight and accommodation in one of the main holiday resorts. Flight time from Britain is approximately 2 hours 15 minutes. By air

Faro airport is about 9 km from the town centre. There are buses from there into town, but they are few and far between and run at irregular times. Taxis at the airport take you to anywhere in the Algarve at fixed rates (further details at the tourist information desk). At the time of publication the taxi fare from the airport to Albufeira was 6,000 Esc. International and local car-rental firms have desks in the arrival hall (➤ Motoring).

From Faro there are adequate bus services to all larger towns in the Algarve and a train link serving the rest of the Algarve coast (➤ Public Transport).

By car

Travelling from Britain to the Algarve by car there is a choice of cross-Channel car ferries to France, or the Channel Tunnel. Faro is approximately 2,170 km from the French Channel ports. The recommended western route is Paris to Bordeaux–Biarritz–Burgos–Madrid, then Badajoz–Setúbal–Algarve, or Mérida–Seville–Algarve. The eastern route is Paris to Lyons–Perpignan–le Perthus/La Junquera–Barcelona–Madrid, etc. When calculating the cost remember to include a substantial amount for motorway tolls. Another option is motorail from Paris to Lisbon: information from French Railways/Rail Europe Ltd, 179 Piccadilly, London W1V 0BA; tel. (0870) 5848848.

Another alternative from Britain is to take the car ferry from Plymouth to Santander in Spain – this takes 24 hours – and pick up the route via Burgos from there; it is about 1,300 km from Santander to Faro. Information from Brittany Ferries, Millbay Docks, Plymouth PL1 3EW; reservations tel. (0870) 5360360.

By coach

There are regular coach services between London and Lisbon, Oporto, Coimbra, Lagos and Faro. Tickets and information are available from any National Express or Eurolines agent.

By rail

A daily service runs between London and Lisbon via Paris and Hendaye or Madrid. From Paris this takes 23 or 26 hours respectively. Information from main railway stations. In Lisbon you have to change from Santa Apolónia station to Estação Sul e Sueste on the Praça do Comércio. The train from there to Faro takes between 4½ and 7 hours. For anyone with an InterRail pass this is a relatively inexpensive way to travel and can cost as little as a bargain charter flight.

Health

Emergency

Throughout Portugal the number to call for any emergency service, including medical assistance and ambulance, is 112 (free of charge). For vehicle accidents on the IP 1 call the emergency service from one of the free-standing orange emergency phones.

Emergency medical care

Most hospitals (*hospitais*) have a 24-hour emergency service. In urgent cases visitors can go straight to the casualty department (*urgência*) of the nearest hospital. Many of the smaller places have health centres (*centro de saúde*) that are open during the day. Telephone numbers of hospitals and health centres can be found on the first page of the local telephone directory. The central telephone numbers for hospital emergency services are: Faro, tel. (289) 803427; Portimão, tel. (282) 415115; Lagos, tel. (282) 763034.

Doctors/dentists

Names and addresses of doctors and dentists who speak English are available from tourist offices.

Treatment costs

Members of EU countries are entitled to obtain medical care under the Portuguese heath service, but it is necessary to have obtained a signed E111 form before leaving home. Without this form you will have to pay treatment costs yourself. Ask for a detailed bill in case you are able to claim costs back from your private medical insurance. It is advisable, however, even for EU nationals, to take out some form of additional short-term health insurance. Nationals of non-EU countries should certainly have insurance cover.

The sign for a chemist (*farmácia*) is a green cross. Chemists are usually open Mon.–Fri. 9am–1pm, 3–7pm, Sat. 9am–1pm. Besides medicines manufactured in Portugal they also carry well-known brands from elsewhere and these can often be less expensive here than in their country of origin. The addresses of chemists on duty at night and on Sundays (*farmácias de serviço*) are posted up in all chemist's shops, listed in the local press, and obtainable by calling 118.

Chemists

Hotels

Hotels are officially graded from five star (de luxe) to one star, but the quality within a single category varies considerably. The grading of motels and aparthotels is more or less equivalent to that of hotels.

Grading

The Portuguese form of guest house (*pensão*) is found almost everywhere in Portugal. A *pensão* in one of the lower categories can be more inexpensive but just as well-equipped as a hotel of an equivalent grade. A *residencial* is a small guest house or hotel which is comparable with a *pensão* in terms of comfort and price and is usually family run. *Albergarias* correspond to top-ranking *pensões*.

Pensões

Pousadas (➤ Accomodation) are top-of-the-range, state-run hotels that are usually located in historic buildings or at sites of special interest.

Pousadas

Turismo de habitação is a similar kind of special accommodation. In this case it takes the form of stately homes, ranging from castles and palaces to country houses, which are still privately owned but part of a state-controlled scheme (➤ Accommodation).

Turismo de habitação

The cheapest option is probably bed and (usually) breakfast on a private basis, and this is easy to find in the main tourist resorts along the Algarve coast. The rooms (*quartos*) are clean but simply furnished and breakfast is usually included.

Private rooms

Prices for hotels and *pensões* can vary considerably according to the season. A double room in a pensão will cost between 4,000 and 15,000 Esc. The rates given below are guidelines for a night in a well-appointed hotel room for two people. The price of a single room, both in *pensões* and hotels, is about 30 per cent less than a double room.

Prices

Grade	Double room
*****	35,000—55,000 Esc.
****	20,000—40,000 Esc.
***	15,000—25,000 Esc.
**	9,000—17,000 Esc.
*	6,000—12,000 Esc.

*****Sheraton Algarve** (215 rooms)
Pinhal do Concelho, Apartado 644, Praia da Falésia, 8200 Albufeira; tel. (289) 500100, fax (289) 501950
This clifftop Sheraton is one of the Algarve's finest hotels. All rooms and suites in this luxurious low-rise hotel complex are very spacious; there is a lift down to the beach.

Albufeira

****Alfa Mar Resort** (264 rooms)
Apartado 2159, Praia da Falésia, 8200 Albufeira; tel. (289) 501351, fax (289) 501069
Resort with hotel, apartments and bungalows, between Albufeira and Quarteira on the Falésia beach. The bungalows and apartments are particularly well suited for family holiday. A wide range of sports facilities are available at extra cost.

****Hotel Boa Vista** (93 rooms)
Rua Samora Barros 20, 8200 Albufeira; tel. (289) 589175, fax (289) 589180
Built into the cliff with a wonderful view of the sea, but not close to the beach; charming stylish interior, swimming pool but no sports facilities or organised activities.

***Hotel Apartomento Auramar** (287 rooms)
Praia dos Aveiros – Areias do São João, 8200 Albufeira; tel. (289) 587607, fax (289) 513327
Very good value; friendly atmosphere, solid comfort without lots of extras.

Aljezur

Hotel Vale da Telha (26 rooms)
Vale da Telha, Apartado 101, 8670 Aljezur; tel. (282) 998180, fax (282) 998176
Out of town and not too far from the beach, this is one of the few places to stay in these parts and is worth it if only for the beautiful, isolated beaches.

Alte

***Hotel Alte** (25 rooms)
Montinho, 8100 Alte; tel. (289) 685234, fax (289) 68646
The only hotel in the picturesque Alte in the hinterland of the Algarve.

Hotel Almansor near Carvoeiro

✳✳✳✳✳**Hotel Alvor Praia** (217 rooms)
Praia dos Três Irmãos, 8500 Portimão; tel. (282) 458900, fax (282) 458999
Located on a lovely beach between Alvor and Portimão. High-rise luxury
hotel with a wide range of organised activities and entertainment. Well-
appointed rooms.

Alvor

✳✳✳✳✳**Vila Vita Parc** (194 rooms)
8365 Armação de Pêra Alporchinhos; tel. (282) 315310, fax (282) 315333
Luxurious resort outside Armação de Pêra with plenty to offer, particularly popular with German holidaymakers; a good place to get away
from it all – an entire holiday could be spent in the Vila Vita complex.

Armação de Pêra

✳✳✳✳**Hotel Garbe** (140 rooms)
Av. Marginal, 8365 Armação de Pêra; tel. (282) 315187, fax (282) 315087
Popular hotel with a swimming pool and direct access to the beach, on
a busy road at the entrance to the village. The rooms with a sea view are
very quiet and highly recommended.

Albergaria do Lageado (19 rooms)
8550 Caldas de Monchique; tel. (282) 912616, fax (282) 911310
Comfortable long-established *pensão* in the idyllic village centre.

Caldas de
Monchique

✳✳✳✳**Apartamentos Turísticos Rocha Brava** (215 rooms)
Alfazina, Apartado 1047, Carvoeiro, 8400 Lagoa; tel. (282) 358775, fax
(282) 358542
Large and imposing resort high above the rocky coast, with well-
furnished apartments and its own good infrastructure. Because of its
location it is convenient to have the use of a car.

Carvoeiro

✳✳✳✳**Hotel Almansor** (293 rooms)
Vale de Covo, Apartado 1299, Praia do Carvoeiro, 8400 Lagoa; tel. (282)
358026, fax (282) 358770
Almost every room in this comfortable hotel has a sea view. Several
restaurants and bars, swimming pool, sauna, two tennis courts and
other sports facilities form part of the amenities. Suitable for confer-
ences of up to 900 people.

✳✳✳✳**Estalagem Monte do Casal** (12 rooms)
Cerro do Lobo, 8000 Faro; tel. (289) 991503, fax (289) 991341
Small elegant country house with rooms and suites, between Estói and
Moncarapacho; its restaurant has a very good reputation.

Estói

✳✳✳**Hotel Eva** (146 rooms)
Avenida da República 1, 8000 Faro; tel. (289) 803354, fax (289) 802304
Large modern hotel with attractive rooms right on the harbour; central
location and easy to get to.

Faro

2nd cat. **Pensão São Filipe** (10 rooms)
Rua Infante D. Henrique 53, 8000 Faro; tel. (289) 824182
Simple and inexpensive *pensão*, central but quiet location.

✳✳✳✳**Hotel Casabela** (53 rooms)
Vale de Areia, 8400 Lagoa; tel. (282) 461580, fax (282) 461581
Grand villa-like hotel outside the town close to the beach; few organised
activities and sports facilities but good for anyone in search of peace and
quiet.

Ferragudo

✳✳✳**Apartmentos Turísticos Meia Praia Beach Club** (77 apartments)
Casal dos Rochinhas, Estrada de Meia Praia 8600 Lagos; tel. (282)
769980, fax (282) 769989
Outside Lagos on a beach with dunes, relatively inexpensive; good standard
of service and fittings; would suit families (but no child care).

Lagos

Hotels

✳✳✳Hotel São Cristovão (76 rooms)
Av. dos Descobrimentos, 8600 Lagos; tel. (282) 763051, fax (282) 763054
Modern, well-run establishment on the edge of town.

1st cat. **Pensão Sol e Praia/Residencial** (103 rooms)
Praia Dona Ana, Apartado 33, 8600 Lagos; tel. (282) 762026, fax (282) 760247
Quiet *pensão* on the beach, which gets crowded in summer.

Loulé   **✳✳✳Hotel Loulé Jardim/Residencial** (52 rooms)
Praça Manuel de Arriaga, 8100 Loulé; tel. (089) 413094, fax (089) 463177
In an old mansion by a small park.

2nd cat. **Pensão Dom Payo/Residencial** (26 rooms)
Rua Dr. F. Sá Carneiro, 8100 Loulé; tel. (289) 414422, fax (289) 416453
Pleasant *pensão* with modern facilities.

Monchique   **✳✳✳✳Estalagem Abrigo da Montanha** (6 rooms)
Estrada de Fóia/Corte Pereiro, 8550 Monchique; tel. (282) 912131, fax (282) 913660
Just outside Monchique on the road up to the highest point in the Serra de Monchique.

Monte Gordo   **✳✳✳✳Hotel Casablanca** (42 rooms)
Rua Sete, 8900 Monte Gordo; tel. (281) 511444, fax (281) 511999
Stylish little hotel in the centre of Monte Gordo, away from the promenade, surrounded by a terrace. Few rooms with a sea view; very pleasant service and decor – peaceful relaxation guaranteed.

Built in the Moorish style: Hotel Apartamento Oriental in Praia da Rocha

**Hotel Ria Sol/Residencial (52 rooms) Olhão
Rua General Humberto Delgado 37, 8700 Olhão; tel. (289) 705267, fax
(289) 705268
Relatively central but quiet little hotel, the only one in the town.

3rd cat. **Pensão Bela Vista/Residencial** (9 rooms)
Rua Teófilo Braga 65, 8700 Olhão; tel. (289) 702538
Very simple *pensão* in the old town centre.

***Hotel Globo (66 rooms) Portimão
Rua 5 de Outubro 26, Apartado 151, 8500 Portimão; tel. (282) 416350, fax
(282) 483142
Good, unobtrusive service; central location, so rather noisy.

2nd cat. **Pensão do Rio/Residencial** (11 rooms)
Largo do Dique 20, 8500 Portimão; tel. (282) 423041, fax (282) 411895
In a busy square on the bank of the Rio Arade in the centre of Portimão.

*****Hotel Algarve Casino (209 rooms) Praia da Rocha
Av. Tomás Cabreira, 8500 Portimão; tel. (282) 415001, fax (282) 415999
Established luxury hotel on the promenade facing the beach. Well-appointed,
excellent service; children's pool and supervised play area; casino.

****Hotel Bela Vista/Residencial (14 rooms)
Av. Tomás Cabreira, 8500 Portimão; tel. (282) 424055, fax (282) 415369
A hotel with one of the richest traditions in the Algarve. The beautifully
restored old house on the promenade radiates a pleasant atmosphere; a
high standard of service and comfort.

****Hotel Apartamentos Oriental (85 apartments)
Av. Tomás Cabreira, 8500 Portimão; tel. (282) 413000, fax (282) 415413
Popular modern hotel in a green setting. Most rooms have a sea view,
with air-conditioning, phone, radio and satellite TV.

***Hotel Atis (80 rooms) Quarteira
Av. Dr. Francisco Sá Carneiro 145, 8125 Quarteira; tel. (289) 389771, fax
(289) 389774
Located on the main road through the town – not always quiet!

*****Hotel Quinta do Lago (141 rooms) Quinta do Lago
Quinta do Lago, 8135 Almansil; tel. (289) 396666, fax (289) 396393
The smartest place on the Algarve coast, out-and-out luxury, very attractive, surrounded by lawns and greenery; quiet but with plenty of sports
facilities.

***Hotel da Baleeira (108 rooms) Sagres
Baleeira, 8650 Sagres; tel. (282) 624212, fax (282) 624425
Relatively central, functional decor, few extras.

****Hotel Apartamentos La Réserve (20 apartments) Santa Bárbara de
Sítio da Igreja, 8000 Santa Bárbara de Nexe; tel. (289) 999494, fax (289) Nexe
999402
Exclusive small luxury hotel in lovely scenery and – although away from
the crowds – quite a good location.

****Albergaria Solar da Moura (22 rooms) Silves
Quinta do Pocinho, 8300 Silves; tel. (282) 443106/07,
fax (282) 443108
Very well-run small hotel with garden and children's play area.

***Aldeamento Turístico Pedras d'el Rei (273 apartments and villas) Tavira
Santa Luzia, 8800 Tavira; tel. (281) 325352, fax (281) 324020

Pleasant, green holiday complex particularly suitable for a family holiday; simple decor, no extras. The bridge to Ilha de Tavira can be crossed on foot or by island train to get to the long sandy beach.

2nd cat. **Pensão Horizonte Mar/Residencial** (20 rooms)
Rua Almirante Cândido dos Reis, 8800 Tavira; tel. (281) 325035, fax (281) 325037
Small *pensão* in the eastern part of town.

Vale do Lobo   ✶✶✶✶✶**Hotel Meridien Dona Filipa** (136 rooms)
Vale do Lobo, 8135 Almansil; tel. (289) 394141, fax (289) 394288
Luxury hotel on a grand scale in extensive grounds; very good infrastructure including various sports facilities.

Vilamoura   ✶✶✶✶**Hotel Dom Pedro Marina** (155 rooms)
Vilamoura, Rua Tivoli, Lote H 4, 8125 Quarteira; tel. (289) 389802, fax (289) 313270
Particularly popular with the Portuguese, with a welcoming atmosphere; relatively inexpensive, pleasantly furnished rooms, close to the beach.

Vila Real de Santo António   ✶✶✶✶**Estalagem da Cegonha** (9 rooms)
Vilamoura, 8125 Quarteira; tel. (289) 302577, fax (289) 322675
Individual accommodation in an idyllic location in the unspoiled countryside east of Vilamoura; for guests who demand something beyond the norm.

✶✶**Hotel Apolo/Residencial** (42 rooms)
Av. dos Bombeiros Portugueses, 8900 Vila Real de Santo António; tel. (281) 512448, fax (281) 512450
Simple but well-kept hotel.

Information

Internet   www.rtalgarve.pt
Home page of the Portuguese Trade and Tourism Board

www.nexus-pt.com/algarve
Detailed information from the Internet provider Nexus, with many useful links (including weather forecast)

ICEP

Overseas addresses of ICEP (Investimentos, Comércio e Turismo de Portugal – Portuguese Trade and Tourism Board):

Canada   Suite 1005, 60 Bloor Street West, Toronto, Ontario M4W 3B8; tel. (416) 9217376, fax (416) 9211353

Ireland   54 Dawson Street, Dublin 2; tel. (01) 6709133/4, fax (01) 6709141, email info@icep.pt

United Kingdom   22–25A Sackville Street, London W1X 2LY; tel. (020) 74941875, fax (020) 74941868, email iceplondt@aol.com

United States   4th Floor, 590 Fifth Avenue, New York, NY 10036; tel. (212) 3544403, fax (212) 7646137, email tourism@portugal.org, website www.portugal.org

Suite 310, 1900 L Street NW, Washington, DC 20036; tel. (202) 3318222, fax (202) 3318236, email mgarcia@portugal.org

Suite 1770, 88 Kearny Street, San Francisco, CA 94108; tel. (415) 3917080, fax (415) 3917147, email jfdias@portugal.org

There is a tourist office (*turismo*) in every place of any size in the Algarve, with English-speaking staff. T*urismos* are usually open Mon.–Fri. 10am–1pm, 3–5pm. In tourist resorts some stay open longer during the week and open for a couple of hours at the weekend. Algarve

Albufeira: Rua 5 de Outubro; tel. (289) 585279
Alcoutim: Praça da República; tel. (281) 546179
Aljezur: Largo do Mercado; tel. (282) 998229
Armação de Pêra: Av. Marginal; tel. (282) 312145
Carvoeiro: Praia do Carvoeiro; tel. (282) 357728
Castro Marim: Praça 1° de Maio 2–4; tel. (281) 531232
Faro: Rua da Misericórdia 8–12; tel. (289) 803604
Lagos: Rua Vasco da Gama (S. João); tel. (282) 763031
Loulé: Edifício do Castelo; tel. (289) 463900
Monte Gordo: Av. Marginal; tel. (281) 544495
Olhão: Largo Sebastião Martins Mestre 6A; tel. (289) 713936
Portimão: Av. Zeca Afonso; tel. (282) 419131
Praia da Rocha: Avenida Tomás Cabreira; tel. (282) 419132/457650
Quarteira: Praça do Mar; tel. (289) 389209
Sagres: Rua Comandante Matoso; tel. (282) 624873
São Brás de Alportel: Rua Dr. Evaristo Sousa Gago 1; tel. (289) 842211
Silves: Rua 25 de Abril; tel. (282) 442255
Tavira: Rua da Galeria 9; tel. (281) 322511

Language

The foreign languages most commonly spoken in Portugal are Spanish, English and French, and there are now also numbers of returned guest workers who have learned some German while working in Germany. In any event, however, it is well worth having at least a smattering of Portuguese.

On first hearing Portuguese spoken a visitor may not quite know what to make of it because it can sound rather like a Slav language (such as Polish). The written form of the language, however, can at once be recognised as a Romance language, and some knowledge of Latin or Spanish will be a great help in understanding it. Portuguese

Portuguese grammar is notable for the rich tense system of the verbs, in particular for the preservation of the Latin pluperfect (e.g. *fora*, I had been). A further peculiarity is the inflected personal infinitive: *entramos na loja para comprarmos pão* (we go into the shop to buy bread). Grammar
The plural is formed by the addition of "s", in some cases with the modification of the preceding vowel or consonant:

Singular	*Plural*
o animal	os animais
o hotel	os hotéis
a região	as regiões

The definite article is "o" (masculine) or "a" (feminine) in the singular, "os" or "as" in the plural. The declension of nouns and adjectives is simple. The nominative and accusative are the same; the genitive is indicated by "de" (of), the dative by "a" (to). The prepositions "de" and "a" combine with the definite article as follows:

de + o = do   de + a = da
de + os = dos   de + as = das

$$a + o = ao \qquad a + os = aos$$
$$a + a = à \qquad a + as = às$$

The Portuguese spoken in Portugal seems lacking in resonance, but is soft and melodious, without the hard accumulations of consonants and the rough gutturals of Castilian Spanish. It is notable for its frequent sibilants and for the nasalisation of vowels, diphthongs and triphthongs. Unstressed vowels and intervocalic consonants are much attenuated or disappear altogether. The stressed syllable of a word so dominates the rest that the vowels of the other syllables are radically altered in tone quality and not infrequently are reduced to a mere whisper. In the spoken language the boundaries between words are so blurred (in the phenomenon know as *sandhi*) that the individual word within a group largely loses its independence: thus the phrase *os outros amigos* (the other friends) is run together into a single phonetic unit and pronounced something like "usótrushamígush".

The nine vocalic phonemes used in Portuguese are represented by the five vowels a, e, i, o and u together with three diacritic signs or accents (í,ì,î), two of which (í and î) also indicate the stress. Nasalisation is indicated by the tilde (Portuguese *o til*: ĩ) or by the consonant "m" or "n".

The stress is normally on the penultimate syllable of a word ending in a vowel or in "m" or "s" and on the last syllable of a word ending in a consonant other than "m" or "s". Exceptions to this rule are marked by the use of an accent. It should be noted that "ia", "io" and "iu" are not treated as diphthongs as in Spanish but as combinations of separate vowels. Thus the word *agrário*, for example, with the stress on the second "a", requires an accent to indicate this in Portuguese but not in Spanish where it is *agrario* without an accent.

Some peculiarities of Portuguese pronunciation

a	unstressed, like a whispered e
à	long "ah"
c	k before a, o and u; s before e and i
ç	s
ch	sh
e	unstressed, like a whispered i; in initial position before s, practically disappears (*escudo* pronounced "shkúdo"; Estoril pronounced "Shturíl")
ê	closed e
é	open e
g	hard g (as in "go") before a, o and u; zh (like s in "pleasure") before e and i
gu	hard g
h	mute
i	nasalised after u (*muito* pronounced "muínto")
j	zh
l	in final position as in English or, in Brazil, like a weak u (*animal* pronounced "animáu")
lh ly	(with consonantal y): cf. Spanish ll
m, n	in final position nasalise the preceding vowel
nh ny	(with consonantal y): cf. Spanish ñ
o	unstressed, like u
ô	closed o
ó	open o
qu	k
r	trilled
rr	strongly rolled
s	s before vowels; z between vowels; sh before hard consonants and in final position; zh before soft consonants
v	v
x	sh
z	in final position sh; otherwise z

The Brazilian pronunciation of Portuguese is markedly different from the Portuguese mainland. In particular final "s" and "z" are pronounced "s" and not "sh", and initial "r" sounds almost like "h".

Numbers

0	zero	Cardinals
1	um, uma	
2	dois, duas	
3	três	
4	quatro	
5	cinco	
6	seis	
7	sete	
8	oito	
9	nove	
10	dez	
11	onze	
12	doze	
13	treze	
14	catorze	
15	quinze	
16	dezasseis	
17	dezassete	
18	dezoito	
19	dezanove	
20	vinte	
21	vinte-e-um (uma)	
22	vinte-e-dois (duas)	
30	trinta	
31	trinta-e-em (uma)	
40	quarenta	
50	cinquenta	
60	sessenta	
70	setenta	
80	oitenta	
90	noventa	
100	cem, cento	
101	cento-e-um (uma)	
200	duzentos, -as	
300	trezentos, -as	
400	quatrocentos, -as	
500	quinhentos, -as	
600	seiscentos, -as	
700	setecentos, -as	
800	oitocentos, -as	
900	novecentos, -as	
1000	mil	
2000	dois (duas) mil	
1 million	um milhão de	
1st	primeiro, -a	Ordinals
2nd	segundo, -a	
3rd	terceiro, -a	
4th	quarto, -a	
5th	quinto, -a	
6th	sexto, -a	
7th	sétimo, -a	
8th	oitavo, -a	
9th	nono, -a	
10th	décimo, -a	

11th	undécimo, -a; décimo primeiro
12th	duodécimo, -a; décimo segundo
13th	décimo terceiro
20th	vigésimo, -a
21st	vigésimo primeiro, -a
30th	trigésimo, -a
40th	quadragésimo, -a
50th	quinquagésimo, -a
60th	sexuagésimo, -a
100th	centésimo, -a

Fractions

½	meio, meia
⅓	um terço, uma terça parte
¼	um quarto
¾	três quartos, três quartas partes

Idioms and Vocabulary

Forms of address

Men are usually addressed as *Senhor*, women as *minha Senhora*. If you know a man's name you should address him by his name with the prefix *Senhor*; ladies are addressed as *Senhora Dona* and their Christian name, if this is known. "You" in direct address is *o Senhor*, *a Senhora* or *Você*, in the plural *os Senhores*, *as Senhoras* or *Vocês*.

In Portuguese names, which are frequently very long, the maternal surname usually comes first.

Idioms

Good morning, good day	Bom dia
Good afternoon	Boa tarde
Good evening, good night	Boa noite
Goodbye	Adeus, Até à vista
Yes, no (Sir)	Sim, não (Senhor)
Excuse me (apologising)	Desculpe, Perdão
Excuse me (e.g. when passing in front of someone)	Com licença
After you (e.g. offering something)	A vontade!
Please (asking for something)	Faz favor
Thank you (very much)	(Muito) obrigado
Not at all (You're welcome)	De nada, Não tem de què
Do you speak English?	O senhor fala inglês?
A little, not much	Um pouco, não muito
I do not understand	Não compreendo (nada)
What is the Portuguese for …?	Como se diz em português …?
What is the name of this church?	Como chama-se esta igreja?
Have you any rooms?	Tem um quarto livre?
I should like …	Queria …
A room with private bath	Um quarto com banho
With full board	Com pensão completa
What does it cost?	Quanto custa?
Everything included	Tudo incluído
That is very dear	É muito caro
Bill, please!	Faz favor, a conta!
Where is … Street?	Onde fica a rua …?
the road to?	a estrada para …?
a doctor?	um médico?
a dentist?	um dentista?
Right, left	À direita, esquerda
Straight ahead	Sempre a direito
Above, below	Em cima, em baixo
When is it open?	A que horas está aberto?
How far?	Que distância?
Wake me at six	Chamé-me às seis

Alfândega	Customs	Road signs
Alto!	Stop	
Atenção!	Caution	
Auto-estrada	Motorway	
Bifurcação	Road fork	
Cuidado!	Caution	
Curva perigosa	Dangerous curve	
Dê passagem!	Give way/yield	
Desvio	Diversion	
Devagar!	Slow	
Direcção única; Sentido único	One-way street	
Estacionamento proibido	Parking prohibited	
Ir a passo!	Dead slow	
Ir pela direita, esquerda	Keep right, left	
Nevoeiro	Mist, fog	
Obras na estrada	Road works	
Parque de estacionamento	Car park, parking place	
Passagem proibida	No entry	
Peões	Pedestrians	
Perigo!	Danger!	
Portagem	Toll	
Praia	Beach	
Proibido ultrapassar	No overtaking	
Rebanhos	Beware of livestock	
Serviço de reboque	Towing service	

accelerator	o acelerador	Vehicle terms
automobile	o auto, o carro	
axle	o eixo	
battery	a bateria	
bearing	a chumaceira	
bolt	o parafuso	
bonnet/hood	o capot	
brake	o travão	
breakdown	a avaria	
bulb	a lâmpada eléctrica	
bumper	o pára-choque	
bus	a camioneta (de passageiros)	
car	o auto, o carro	
carburettor/carburetor	o carburador	
Change ... (oil, tyre/tire, etc.)	Mudar ...	
Charge ... (battery)	Carregar ...	
check	verificar	
clutch	a embraiagem	
contact	o contacto	
cylinder	o cilindro	
damaged	avariado, avariada	
diesel engine	o motor Diesel	
direction indicator	o indicador de direcção	
distributor	o distribuidor	
driver	o motorista, o condutor	
driving licence	a carta de condutor	
dynamo	o dínamo	
engine	o motor	
exhaust	o escape	
fan belt	a correia da ventoinha	
fault	a avaria	
float	o flutuador	
fuse	o fusível	
garage	a garage, a garagem	
gas/petrol	a gasolina	
gas/petrol pump	a bomba de gasolina	

gas/petrol station	o posto de gasolina
gas/petrol tank	o depósito de gasolina
gasket	o empanque
gear	a velocidade, a mudança
gearbox	o câmbio de velocidades
grease (verb)	lubrificar
headlamp	o farol
hood/bonnet	o capot
horn	a buzina
ignition	a ignição
inflate	dar à bomba
inner tube	a câmara-de-ar
jack	o macaco
jet	o gicleur
lorry/truck	o camião
magneto	o magneto
make (of car)	a marca
map	o mapa das estradas
maximum speed	a velocidade máxima
mixture	a mistura
motorcycle	a motocicleta
number-plate	a placa, a matrícula
nut	a porca
oil	o óleo
oil pump	a bomba de óleo
park (verb)	estacionar
parking lot, car park	o estacionamento
petrol/gas	a gasolina
petrol/gas pump	a bomba de gasolina
petrol/gas station	o posto de gasolina
petrol/gas tank	o depósito de gasolina
piston	o postão
piston ring	o segmento de pistão
pump	a bomba
radiator	o radiador
rear light	a luz traseira
repair	reparar
repair garage	a oficina de reparação
road map	o mapa das estradas
scooter	o scooter
shock absorber	o amortecedor
snow chain	a cadeia antideslizante
spanner	a chave inglesa
spare part	a peça de sobresselente
sparking plug	a vela
speedometer	o velocimetro
spring	a mola
starter	o arranque
steering	a direcção
steering wheel	o volante
tow away	levar a reboque
transmission	a condução
truck/lorry	o camião
two-stroke engine	o motor do dois tempos
tyre/tire	o pneu
tyre/tire pressure	a pressão dos pneus
valve	a válvula
wash	lavar
water pump	a bomba de água
wheel	a roda
windscreen/windshield	o párabrisas
windscreen/windshield wiper	o limpa-pára-brisas
wing	o guarda-lama

aircraft	aeroplano, avião	Travelling
airport	aeroporto	
All aboard!	Partida!	
All change!	Mudar!	
arrival	chegada	
baggage	bagagem	
baggage check	guia, senha	
bus	autocarro, camioneta	
conductor (ticket collector)	revisor	
couchette car	furgoneta	
departure	partida	
fare	preço	
flight	vôo	
information	informação	
line (railway)	via férrea	
luggage	bagagem	
luggage ticket	guia, senha	
no smoking (carriage)	não fumadores	
platform	plataforma, gare	
porter	moço de fretes	
railroad/railway station	estação	
restaurant car	carruagem restaurante	
sleeping car	carruagem-cama	
smoking (carriage)	fumadores	
steward	comissário de bordo	
stewardess	hospedeira (do ar)	
stop	paragem	
ticket	bilhete	
ticket collector (conductor)	revisor	
ticket office	bilheteria, guichet	
timetable	horário	
toilet	lavatório	
train	combóio	
waiting room	sala de espera	

January	janeiro	Months
February	fevereiro	
March	março	
April	abril	
May	maio	
June	junho	
July	julho	
August	agosto	
September	setembro	
October	outubro	
November	novembro	
December	dezembro	
month	mês	
year	ano	

Monday	segunda-feira	Days of the week
Tuesday	terça-feira	
Wednesday	quarta-feira	
Thursday	quinta-feira	
Friday	sexta-feira	
Saturday	sábado	
Sunday	domingo	
day	dia	
holiday, feast day	dia de festa, dia feriado	

New Year's Day	Ano-Novo	Holidays and Religious Festivals
Easter	Páscoa	
Ascension	Ascensão	

Whitsun	Espírito Santo, Pentecostes
Corpus Christi	Festa do Corpo de Deus
All Saints	Todos os Santos
Christmas	Natal
New Year's Eve	Véspera do Ano-Novo, Noite de São Silvestre

Post office		
	address	endereço
	airmail	correio aéreo
	by airmail	por avião
	express letter	carta urgente
	fax	fax
	letter	carta
	letter box, postbox	marco postal
	packet	embrulho
	parcel	pacote
	postage	porte
	postcard	postal
	poste restante	posta restante
	postman	carteiro
	post office	correio
	registered letter	carta registrada
	stamp	selo, estampilha
	telegram	telegrama
	telephone	telephone

Language Schools

A number of tour operators offer special language packages to Portugal. There are also various schools where you can follow language courses. These generally last between two and four weeks.

Faro
CIAL – Centro de Línguas
Rua Almeida Garrett 44, 8000 Faro; tel. (289) 807611

Lagos
Centro de Línguas de Lagos
Rua Dr. Joaquim Tello 32, 8600 Lagos; tel. (282) 761070

Loulé
Escola de Línguas Europa Algarve
Rua José Fernandez Guerreiro 66, 8100 Loulé; tel. (289) 414128

Portimão
CLCC – Centro de Línguas, Cultura e Comunicação
Rua D. Maria Luísa 122 Largo Gil Eanes, 8500 Portimão; tel. (282) 416469

Markets

Since almost every small town in the Algarve has its own regular market, only a selection can be given here.

Albufeira
First and third Tuesday in the month. This oriental bazaar of a market has stalls selling household wares and clothing – and souvenirs of course – as well as fresh fruit and vegetables.

Alcoutim
A pottery market forms part of the May Day celebrations.

Estói
Second Sunday in the month. Country market selling just about anything: household good, clothes, ceramics and even chickens and sheep.

Typical weekly markets held in many small towns in the Algarve

First Friday and Saturday in the month. Large colourful market, particularly famous for its many flower stalls. — Faro

Every Saturday. The bus station is the place to find shoes and leather goods at bargain prices, plus some fine ceramics. — Lagos

Every Saturday. Stalls in the covered market and surrounding streets sell ceramics, wickerwork, wooden and leather goods as well as fruit and vegetables. — Loulé

First Sunday in the month. People flock here from throughout the district to stock up with everything from boots and clothes to seeds and even donkeys and sheep. — Moncarapacho

October 26th–28th. A typical Algarve market, with people coming from far and near to buy wares of all sorts including livestock and crafts. — Monchique

Every Saturday. CDs and tapes, wickerwork, clothes and household goods are on sale between and around the two covered markets. — Olhão

Fourth Sunday in the month. Country market, selling pottery, rugs, shoes and clothes. — Pereiro

Every Wednesday. Food and just about everything else for the home. — Quarteira

Every Saturday. Cheap-and-cheerful domestic wares, clothes, china and woodcarvings. — São Brás de Alportel

Media

Radio

Portuguese radio (RDP) broadcasts a short daily programme in the summer for tourists in English, French and German. Times vary, but it is usually transmitted between 8 and 10.30am. Solar Radio puts out English news bulletins at 8.30am on 90.5 FM, and it is possible to get the BBC World Service, Voice of America, and Radio Canada International on short wave.

Television

There are four channels on Portuguese television: the two state-run channels (RTP 1 and 2) as well as TVI and SIC. Foreign films are usually shown in the original language with subtitles. Satellite TV is available in hotels and many *pensões* and cafés.

Newspapers, magazines

English and American newspapers and magazines are on sale in all the main towns and tourist resorts. Local publications in English include a fortnightly newspaper, the *Algarve News*, a monthly magazine, the *Algarve Gazette*, and a weekly magazine, the *Algarve Resident. Discover*, the free monthly "what's on" magazine, can be obtained from tourist offices. The Portuguese daily papers are *Diário de Notícias* and *Público* where you can also find information on entertainment. Weekly papers are the *Independente, Expresso* and *Visão*.

Motoring

The best way of getting to know the Algarve is by car, if only because of the poor public transport away from the coast. There is a good road network, mainly well surfaced, but minor roads are sometimes rather rough. Some of the more remote areas have hard-surface sand tracks, but driving on them is not a problem. In the Algarve high speed is to be expected, in particular on the N 125 but also on smaller roads, and motorists should beware of drivers racing and overtaking dangerously, especially on winding mountain roads. At night be on the alert for vehicles with poor lights, or no lights at all – even on main roads.

Main routes

The main road along the south coast is the N 125, which can have very heavy traffic, especially between Lagos and Faro. The E 01 or IP 1 (Via do Infante de Sagres) is a new motorway that runs parallel to the N 125 from Albufeira to Ayamonte in Spain. Although toll-free it is little used as yet, making it a very attractive route to take. The connecting road from Albufeira to Alcantarilha has been opened for traffic in 2000.

Breakdowns

There are orange emergency phones at regular intervals on the motorways. On other roads telephone the Portuguese Automobile Club (tel. (01) 9429103) for help.

Portuguese Automobile Club

The Portuguese Automobile Club (ACP) has its main office in Lisbon: Rua Rosa Araújo 24–26, 1200 Lisbon; tel. (21) 3563931, fax (21) 3574732.

Fuel and filling stations

Filling stations are concentrated in the towns and on the N 125. To get fuel in the hinterland can occasionally be difficult. Most filling stations are open between 7am and 8pm, but they stay open longer on the N 125. All filling stations have unleaded petrol (*gasolina sem chumbo*; 95 octane) and unleaded super (*Super sem chumbo*; 98 octane).

Traffic regulations

Portugal's traffic regulations are similar to other European countries: drive on the right, overtake on the left and give way to traffic from the right. Road signs and markings are of the usual international type.
  Drivers who have held a licence for less than a year may not drive

faster than 90 kph and must display a yellow disc with "90" on it. This is obtainable from the Portuguese Automobile Club (ACP). A green (insurance) card must be produced in the event of an accident. Visitors driving a vehicle that is not their own must have authorisation from the owner. Vehicle and speed checks are relatively frequent.

The speed limit for cars and motorcycles is 50 kph in built-up areas, 90 kph elsewhere, and 100 kph on dual carriageways and 120 kph on motorways. For lorries, coaches and cars with trailers, speed limits are 70 kph outside built-up areas, and 80 kph on motorways. The minimum speed on motorways is 40 kph.

Speed limits

Traffic on the main road – which is indicated by a yellow rectangle edged with black and white – has priority, but at junctions or intersections of roads of equal importance you must give way to traffic coming from the right. Motor vehicles always have right of way over non-motorised traffic.

Priority

The legal limit for alcohol in the blood is 0.5 per millilitre. If you are caught with a higher level, expect to pay a hefty fine.

Alcohol limit

The wearing of seat belts is compulsory.

Seat belts

To hire a car in Portugal the driver must be 21 or over and have held a driving licence for at least a year. Expect to pay about £17–20 per day for a car of the lowest category. Weekly rates are often less inexpensive. Local car-rental firms are often considerably less expensive than international car hire companies.

Car rental

Faro
Airport; tel. (289) 818625, fax (289) 818540

Avis

Lagos
Largo das Portas de Portugal 11; tel. (282) 763691

Also agents in Albufeira and Praia da Rocha

Faro
Airport; tel. (289) 817907, fax (289) 818382

Budget

Also agents in Albufeira and Praia da Rocha

Faro
Av. da República 2; tel. (289) 823778 fax (289) 805051
Airport; tel. (289) 818726, fax (289) 817322

Europcar

Lagos
Estrada Nacional 120, Lote 1; tel. (282) 763173, fax (282) 767567

Also agents in Albufeira, Monte Gordo, Praia da Rocha and Vilamoura

Faro
Rua Infante D. Henrique 91a; tel. (289) 803956, fax (289) 803957
Airport; tel. (289) 818248, fax (289) 819194

Hertz

Lagos
Rossio São João, Edifício Panorama, Loja 3; tel. (282) 769809, fax (282) 760008

Also agents in Albufeira, Armação de Pêra, Praia da Rocha and Vilamoura

Nightlife

Most of the nightlife in the Algarve is in the bars and discos of the big hotels. Albufeira in particular is full of bars and pubs and, like other resorts in the middle part of the Algarve, has plenty of discos, but the fashionable places vary from year to year.

Popular evening entertainment includes fado nights (Fado) where you can dine to the accompaniment of Portugal's own distinctive folk ballads.

Opening Hours

Shops
: Most shops are open Mon.–Fri. 9am–1pm, 3–7pm, Sat. 9am–1pm. Many of the smaller shops stay open longer in the evening and at weekends. The big shopping centres are open 9am–midnight, even at weekends.

Chemists
: Opening hours for chemists are normally Mon.–Fri. 9am–1pm, 3–7pm, Sat. 9am–1pm. Lists of chemists on duty outside opening hours are posted in chemist shop windows.

Banks
: Banking hours are Mon.–Fri. 8.30am–3pm. Some banks close for lunch noon–1pm.

Post offices
: Post offices are generally open Mon.–Fri. 9am–noon, 2.30–6pm.

Filling stations
: Filling stations normally open 7am–8pm, but some are open 24 hours in larger places, tourist resorts and on the N 125.

Restaurants
: Restaurants open for lunch noon–3pm and from 6.30 or 7 in the evening. Orders will usually be taken up to 11pm.

Churches
: Most churches are closed during the day and only open for services on Sunday mornings or around 6pm during the week.

Post

Mail
: Ordinary letters and postcards to the rest of Europe usually take between three and seven days. Airmail (*correio aéreo*) will get there faster but is more expensive.

Postage
: The postage for ordinary letters (*cartas*) and postcards (*postais*) within Europe is 95 Esc., and the airmail rate is 350 Esc. for letters up to 20 grams. Stamps (*selos*) can be bought in post offices (*correios*) and in shops with the sign CTT Selos.

Letter boxes
: Letter boxes for ordinary mail are red and can be either pillar boxes or mailboxes on walls, while the mailboxes for *correio aéreo* are blue.

Poste restante
: *Poste restante* mail should be marked *posta restante* and sent to the appropriate post office. A passport or other form of personal identification is necessary when collecting mail.

Public Holidays

January 1st   New Year
February   Mardi Gras/Carnival

March/April	Good Friday
April 25th	Liberation Day (national holiday commemorating the Carnation Revolution on April 25th 1974)
May 1st	Labour Day
May/June	Corpus Christi Day
June 10th	Portugal Day (national holiday on anniversary of the death of poet Luís de Camões on June 10th 1580)
August 15th	Assumption Day
October 5th	Republic Day (national holiday commemorating the fall of the monarchy on October 5th 1910)
November 1st	All Saints Day
December 1st	Restoration Day (national holiday commemorating the restoration of Portugal's independence from Spain on December 1st 1640)
December 8th	Immaculate Conception
December 25th	Christmas

Public Transport

The Algarve has good bus links between the larger towns, with several buses a day. These often include express services (*expressos*) and are mostly operated by EVA-Transportes. The Linha Litoral runs along the coast between Lagos and Ayamonte in Spain, linking all the main resorts. The smaller towns and villages further inland can also be reached by bus, but buses run less frequently. The bus station (*estacão rodoviária*) is usually right in the centre of town. There are also *expressos* to Lisbon and the rest of Portugal.

Bus

Albufeira: Av. da Liberdade; tel. (289) 589755
Armação de Pêra: Av. da Liberdade; tel. (282) 315781
Faro: Av. da República; tel. (289) 899700
Lagos: Rossio S. João; tel. (282) 762944
Olhão: Av. General Humberto Delgado; tel. (289) 702157
Portimão: Largo do Dique; tel. (282) 418120
Quarteira: Av. Project. Apart. Golfo Mar; tel. (289) 389143
Tavira: Praça da República; tel. (281) 322546
Vilamoura: Aldeia do Mar; tel. (289) 302962
Vila Real de Santo António: Av. da República; tel. (281) 511807

Bus stations

In the south of the Algarve a railway line runs almost parallel to the coast connecting all the towns, large and small, between Vila Real de Santo António and Lagos. The trains are infrequent and very slow, but railway enthusiasts will find it a trip worth making, especially given the beautiful scenery along parts of the track. There are good, fast rail connections to Lisbon and further north.

Train

Apart from sightseeing boats the only regular public transport by boat is the ferry over the Guadiana between Vila Real de Santo António in Portugal and Ayamonte in Spain (daily 9am–7.30pm). This is less important than it was, however, now that the bridge over the Guadiana carrying the IP 1 has been built.

Boat

Restaurants

Although the Algarve is well supplied with restaurants, a mix of Portuguese and European cuisine or some form of international fare is found in the tourist resorts. For good, typical Portuguese meals look for somewhere quite plain and simple since, as a rule, in the smaller,

A popular snack between meals – grilled sardines

more homely places the food is very fresh and extremely palatable. Simple meals can be found in the *tascas*.

Mealtimes

Most Portuguese restaurants open for lunch noon–3pm, and again from 6.30 or 7pm, when they then carry on serving until at least 11pm. There are also restaurants, usually of a better category, that are open noon–11pm. It is advisable to book a table in advance.

Albufeira

Vila Joya
6.5 km out of town on the Praia da Galé road; tel. (289) 591795
Outstanding creative cuisine with prices to match, five-course menu every day; up-market dining in a villa by the sea with a terrace.

Três Palmeiras
Areias de São João (about 2.5 km east of Albufeira); tel. (289) 515423
Popular with tourists and locals.

O Montinho
Montechoro; tel. (289) 541959
French cuisine, country hotel with terrace, lovely view.

Almansil

O Tradicional
Estrada do Vale de Lobo; tel. (289) 399093
Highly rated restaurant in an old *quinta* (farm).

Alvor

Restaurante Luis
Praia dos Três Irmãos; tel. (282) 459688
Directly on the beach between Alvor and Prainha; you can sit outside or inside and enjoy the sea view; friendly service (medium price range).

Armação de Pêra

Clipper
Av. Beira-Mar; tel. (282) 314108
Aimed at tourists; menu not large but good.

O Serol
Rua Portas do Mar 24; tel. (282) 312146
One of the best fish restaurants in the Algarve, almost always full.

A Roda   Cabanas
Av. 28 de Maio; tel. (281) 370239
Simple place with terrace alongside the road, but lovely sea view; large
portions at reasonable prices.

Costa   Cacela
Fábrica at Cacela, east of Tavira; tel. (281) 951467
Very pretty setting off the beaten track on the edge of the lagoon (closed
part of the year).

Rafaiol   Carvoreiro
Rua do Barranco; tel. (282) 357164
One of the best restaurants in Carvoreiro with typical Portuguese food;
the *cataplana*, a stew with mussels, pork and vegetables, is excellent
(medium price range).

Café Aliança   Faro
Praça D. Francisco Gomes 26; tel. (289) 801621
Café rich in tradition; sells coffee, cakes and snacks.

Dois Irmãos
Largo Terreiro do Bispo; tel. (289) 823337
Traditional restaurant (opened 1925) with a small courtyard; good
Portuguese food.

Cidade Velha
Rua Domingo Guieiro 19; tel. (289) 827145
Superior Portuguese cuisine; intimate stylish restaurant in the historic
centre of Faro.

Camané
Av. Nascente (Praia de Faro, left of the bridge); tel. (289) 817539
Out of town on Faro beach, highly rated; specialises in fish and
seafood.

O Castelo   Lagos
Rua 25 de Abril 47; tel. (282) 760957
Elegant restaurant in the centre; quality worth paying for.

O Galeão
Rua da Laranjeira 1; tel. (282) 763909
Highly rated restaurant.

O Avenida   Loulé
Av. José C. Mealha 13; tel. (289) 411206
Friendly service, good Portuguese cuisine.

Bica Velha
Rua Martim Moniz 17; tel. (289) 463376
Highly rated; rustic decor.

Paraiso da Montanha   Monchique
2 km outside Monchique, Estrada de Fóia; tel. (282) 912150
Lovely dining on the terrace with a view of the mountains (medium price
range).

Taberna da Maré   Portimão
Travessa da Barca 9; tel. (282) 414614

Restaurants

Family-run restaurant, very small and simple but good plain Portuguese cuisine; specialises in *bacalhau* (dried cod) dishes.

Lúcio
Largo Francisco A. Maurício 2; tel. (282) 413962
Very good seafood; many Portuguese regulars.

Sambal
Rua de Santa Isabel 14; tel. (282) 422072
International cuisine.

Praia da Rocha **Falésia**
Avenida Tomás Cabreira; tel. (282) 423524
Restaurant with terrace (medium price range).

Safari
Rua António Feu 8; tel. (282) 423540
Seafood and African specialities.

Fortaleza de Santa Catarina
In the castle at the eastern end of the promenade; tel. (282) 422066
Fine opportunity to sit outside in the castle courtyard; you do not need to order a whole meal but can simply enjoy a cup of coffee.

Quarteira **Romeu**
Rua Gonçalo Velho 40; tel. (289) 313990
Fish specialities.

Quinta do Lago **Casa Velha**; tel. (289) 394983
First-class surroundings in an old mansion; good food.

Sagres **Fortaleza do Beliche**
On the road to Cabo de São Vicente; tel. (282) 624124
Elegant pousada restaurant in scenic setting overlooking the sea.

A Tasca
Praia do Baleeria; tel. (282) 624177
Popular with the Portuguese; excellent fish and seafood dishes.

Silves **O Rui**
Rua Comandante Vilharino; tel. (282) 442682
Fine place with good Portuguese cuisine; lovely view of the river and castle from the terrace.

Casa Velha de Silves
Rua 25 de Abril; tel. (282) 445491
Very good food and excellent service in the old town of Silves.

Tavira **Beira Rio**
Rua Borda de Água de Asseca; tel. (281) 323165
Good food at reasonable prices beside the river.

Vale do Lobo **São Gabriel**
On the road to Quinta do Lago; tel. (289) 394521
Smart, highly rated restaurant with a terrace.

O Favo
Tel. (289) 394653
Excellent wines.

Vilamoura **O Cesteiro**
Marina de Vilamoura; tel. (289) 312961
Fish and seafood specialities.

Edmundo
Av. da República 55; tel. (281) 544689
Unpretentious establishment beside the river.

Vila Real de Santo
António

Shopping

Good buys in Portugal include footwear, leather goods, and gold and silver items, although prices in the tourist resorts of the Algarve tend to be higher than elsewhere in the country. Lagos, Portimão and Faro are good places to shop. Sometimes items of clothing of fairly good quality can be found at bargain prices in the regular local markets (➤ Markets). Handiworks are very popular as souvenirs.

Azulejos – hand-painted tiles – make a lovely, typically Portuguese souvenir. New mass-produced *azulejos* are on sale everywhere in souvenir shops and markets, but tiles with traditional patterns are more likely to be found in antique shops.

Azulejos

In Portugal many craft products are still items of everyday use. This is particularly true of pottery and ceramics, which vary in form and style according to where they are made. The best known is the multi-hued Barcelos cockerel, originally from the North, which has come to symbolise Portugal as a whole. The Algarve specialises in miniature chimney pots modelled on the famous local chimneys.

Pottery

Beautiful embroidered tablecloths, hand-woven fabrics, wickerwork, and cork and wood carvings are sold in local markets and in specialist shops in the larger towns.

Other handicrafts

Fado CDs and tapes make a good souvenir of a holiday in the Algarve. They can be bought at bargain prices in the markets, but for really good fado it is better to go to record shops. Soloists whose recordings are worth recommending include the great Amália Rodrigues, best known of all the *fadistas* (some of her classic performances are now available on CD), Alfredo Marceneiro and Carlos Ramos. There are newer fado compositions by Carlos do Carmo and purely instrumental versions from Rão Kyão (flute and saxophone), Carlos Paredes and Pedro Caldeira Cabral. Elements of Portuguese folk music are featured in pieces by the Madredeus group, which has recently achieved international fame. Also very popular is the music of the legendary José Afonso.

Music

Port, from the Douro region in the north of the country, is a popular souvenir of Portugal, and comes in a whole range of prices and vintages. Other souvenir drinks include *ginjinha*, the local cherry brandy, *vinho verde*, and *medronho*, the fiery spirit distilled from the arbutus, which grows in the Algarve (➤ Food and Drink).

Drink

Spas

Of Portugal's 30 or so spas the only one in the Algarve is Caldas de Monchique (➤ Sights from A to Z, Monchique). It offers treatments for rheumatism as well as respiratory, liver, stomach and intestinal disorders.

Associação das Termas de Portugal (Association of Health Spas in Portugal) Avenida Miguel Bombarda 110, 2°Dt°, 1050 Lisbon; tel. (21) 7940574/7940602, fax (21) 7938233

Information

Direcção-Geral do Turismo
Avenida António Augusto de Aguiar 86, 1004 Lisbon Codex; tel. (21)
  3575086/3575145/3575015, fax (21) 3575220

Sport

Angling and sea fishing are favourite pastimes of the Algarvios. Boats
for deep-sea fishing can be chartered from the main centres of
Vilamoura, Portimão and Lagos, and no licence is needed provided you
are fishing on an amateur basis. The same applies to fishing from the
beach, but you will need a licence for lake and river angling. This is
obtainable from: Direcção-Geral das Florestas, Av. da República 72, Faro.

Angling

The best routes for cycling are the smaller country roads away from the
coast. These go through some lovely scenery, but remember that it can
be hilly. Near the coast the main roads are very busy, there are virtually
no cycle lanes and cyclists are given little or no consideration. Cycles –
and scooters – can be hired in Albufeira, Armação de Pêra, Carvoeiro,
Lagos, Praia da Rocha, Tavira, Vilamoura, Quarteira and Monte Gordo.
  Details of organised cycling tours are available from travel agents.

Cycling

Golf

Portugal is a paradise for golfers, and most of the golf courses are located
on the Algarve coast. At present there are 20 golf courses, with another 10
courses to be developed in the next few years. Golf has been played in
Portugal since the early 1930s when the British colony built a simple golf
course in Praia da Rocha. Penina, one of the first larger golf courses, was
built in the 1960s, designed by Sir Henry Cotton, the British golfing legend.

Pine Cliffs
Praia da Falésia, 9 holes; tel. (289) 500100, fax (289) 501950, email
sheraton_algarve@sheraton.com
One of Portugal's finest golf courses.

Albufeira

Salgados Golf Club
Apartado 2266, Vale do Rabelho, 18 holes; tel (289) 591111, fax (289)
591112, email salgados.golf@mail.telepac.pt
Many water obstacles; demanding course.

Pinheiros Altos
Quinta do Lago, 18 holes; tel. (289) 359900, fax (289) 398195

Almansil

San Lorenzo Golf Club Quinta do Lago, 18 holes; tel. (289) 396522, fax
(289) 396908

Quinta do Lago Course/Ria Formosa Course
Quinta do Lago, 18 holes each; tel. (289) 390700, fax (289) 394013, email
soc.golf@mail.telepac.pt

Ocean Course/Royal Golf Course
Vale do Lobo, 18 holes each; tel. (289) 353535, fax (289) 353003, email
golf@etudla.pt
Beautiful courses overlooking the sea (➤ picture, p. 146).

Pinta Course/Gramacho Course/ Pestana Golf & Resort,
Apartado 1011, 18 holes each; tel. (282) 340900, fax (282) 340901, email
np79ei@mail.telepac.pt

Carvoeiro

◄ *A display of ceramic ware outside a shop in Porches*

Vale de Milho Golf
Two 9-hole courses; tel. (282) 358502, fax (282) 358497, email gericonstroi@mail.telepac.pt

Lagos

Palmares Golf
Meia Praia, 18 holes; tel. (282) 762953/762961, fax (282) 762534, email golf@palmaresgolf.com

Parque da Floresta Golf and Leisure Resort
Vale do Poco, 16 km west of Lagos, 18 holes; tel. (282) 690055, fax (282) 695157, email golf@vigiása.com

Portimão

Alto Golf
Apartado 1, Alvor, 18 holes; tel. (282) 416913, fax (282) 401046, email golf@vigiása.com

Penina Golf & Resort Hotel
Apartado 146, Penina, 18 holes; tel. (282) 420200, fax (282) 420300, email mendienalg.sm@mail.telepac.pt

Quarteira

Vila Sol Beach, Golf & Country Club
Alto do Semino, 18 holes; tel. (289) 300505, fax (289) 300592, email vilasol@mail.telepac.pt

Vilamoura

Millennium Golf Course
18 holes; tel. (289) 310180, fax (289) 310183, email reservas_golf@lusotur.pt

Pinhal Golf Course
18 holes; tel. (289) 310180, fax (289) 310349, email reservas_golf@lusotur.pt

Laguna Golf Course
18 holes; tel. (289) 310180, fax (289) 310183, email reservas_golf@lusotur.pt

Horse Riding

The Algarve is ideal for anyone who wants a riding holiday or just likes to spend a few hours on horseback. It has about 20 riding centres (where you can also get tuition); those listed below are just a selection.

Albufeira region

Centro Hípico Vale Navio, Estrada da Branqueira; tel. (289) 542870

Aljezur region

Estância Equestre Herdade do Beiçudo, Valarinha, Carrapateira; tel. (282) 973123/96, fax (282) 973186

Lagoa region

Casa Agrícola Solear, Areias Porches; tel. (282) 381444

Lagos region

Centro Hípico Atalaia, Quinta da Atalaia, Odiáxere; tel. (282) 761921, fax (282) 798341

Loulé region

Centro Hípico Pinetrees Estrada do Ancão, do Meridien, Almansil, between Quinta do Lago and Vale do Lobo; tel. (289) 394369, fax (289) 393283

Portimão region

Centro Hípico Golf Penina, EN 125, Penina; tel. (282) 415415, fax (282) 415000

Silves region

Centro Hípico de Silves, Sítio da Cruz de Portugal, Silves; tel. (282) 444120

Tavira region

Centro de Equitacão Quinta das Oliveiras, EN 125; tel. (281) 322107

Sailing

The Algarve's finest marina, with the best facilities for boats and

The marina at Vilamoura

crews, is at Vilamoura, but there are a number of smaller harbours and anchorages all along the coast where sailing clubs offer boats for hire and sailing courses for beginners and advanced pupils. The best places to stay on a sailing holiday are Albufeira, Armação de Pêra, Alvor, Lagos, Monte Gordo, Portimão, Praia da Falésia, Praia da Oura, Praia da Rocha, Quinta do Lago, Tavira, Vale do Lobo and Vilamoura.

The rocky south-west of the Algarve coast is great for scuba-diving, and at depths of between 5 and 30 m you can find excellent and in some cases barely touched diving grounds. To hire equipment or get diving lessons try one of the numerous diving centres in Albufeira, Alvor, Lagos, Monte Gordo, Praia da Falésia and Vilamoura.

Scuba-diving

The surfing conditions are excellent along many different parts of the Algarve coastline. There are many places for learning how to surf and hiring surfboards (➤ Beaches).

Surfing

Almost all the Algarve's big hotels have their own tennis courts. There are also plenty of tennis clubs open to the general public. Among the best are Roger Taylor's Tennis Centre at Vale do Lobo.

Tennis

Walking and hiking in the Algarve are gaining in popularity, and a few tour operators offer walking holidays as a safe way of exploring the truly beautiful countryside, including the lovely hill country of the Serra de Monchique.

Walking

As roads and paths off the asphalt roads and beaten tracks are hardly signed, **guided walks** are worth recommending and include those offered by:

Tempo Passa
Kiosk Praça Teixeira Gomes, Portimão; tel. (282) 417110/471241

Turinfo
Tourist office, Sagres; tel. (282) 624873

Walks to the top of the Picota
A German couple, Ines and Uwe, lead regular individual and very informative daily walks in the Serra de Monchique (walking time is about 4–5 hours); tel. (282) 911041

Waterskiing

There are waterskiing facilities at all the Algarve's main tourist resorts where you can also hire equipment.

Taxis

The classic Portuguese taxi is black with a green roof, but white taxis are becoming more common. Almost all taxis have meters. Out of town there are set rates and up to 50 per cent extra is charged for night journeys and luggage. For longer one-way cross-country journeys the passenger may have to pay the full return fare. If using a taxi for an outing negotiate the price in advance. As a general rule Portuguese taxis are relatively inexpensive. The normal tip is 10–15 per cent.

Telephone

Local and international calls can be made from post offices and private telephone companies (e.g. Telecom) where it is possible to pay after making the call, and from public phone boxes. These take 10, 20, 50, 100 and 200 Esc. coins or a phonecard (*cartão para telefonar*); the card is available from post offices, Telecom Portugal shops and some kiosks and tobacconists. There are two different phonecard systems using different apparatus, so be sure to use the correct phone box.

There are cheap rates for international calls daily 8pm–8am as well as at weekends.

International calls

For international calls from Portugal via the operator dial 099 for Europe and 098 for elsewhere. For direct dialling, the country codes are as follows:

To Portugal
00 351, then dial the area code – eg. 281 (Tavira), 282 (Lagos, Portimão), 289 (Faro) – followed by the number.

From Portugal
Canada: 00 1
United Kingdom: 00 44
United States: 00 1

Time

Portugal is on Greenwich Mean Time or Western European Time (WET = Central European Time minus 1 hour). Summer time starts at the end of March and lasts until the end of October. Portugal is on the same time as the UK.

Tipping

In hotels and restaurants service is included, but waiters, chambermaids and porters normally expect a tip of about 10 per cent. An appropriate tip is also in order for tourist guides, hairdressers and taxi drivers, and it is customary to tip the person who shows you to your seat at concerts and the theatre as well.

Travel Documents

Visitors to Portugal from EU countries, including Ireland and the UK, and Australia, Canada, New Zealand and the United States require only a valid passport and can stay for up to 60 days without a visa. Children must either have their own passport or be entered in one of their parent's passports.

Personal
documents

Drivers of their own cars must have their national driving licence, the vehicle's registration documents, and a Green Card for their insurance. Visitors driving a car that is not their own must be able to produce proof that they are doing so with the owner's permission. In case of accidents and compensation claims, drivers from abroad need the International Green Card. Cars should display the country's registration plate if they do not yet have the new Euro plate.

Car documents

When To Go

At the height of summer visitors can expect packed roads, fully booked hotels and crowded beaches, and although temperatures from June to September are never too much to bear, it can get very hot. Hence the best time to visit the Algarve is either in spring (from mid-March to early June), or autumn (from early September to early November), when the temperatures are very pleasant; the weather in general is settled and swimming is still possible. Early spring has the added bonus of lush greenery and a host of flowers. Even in winter temperatures only briefly drop below 10°C and there are usually a few warm or at least mild days between December and March.

Water temperatures in the Atlantic are lower than in the Mediterranean, hardly getting above 20°C in summer and falling to 15°C in winter. Sea temperatures in the east of the Algarve are around two degrees higher than in the west.

Water
temperatures

Youth Hostels

The Algarve has four youth hostels (*pousadas de juventude*). Visitors must have an international youth hostelling permit obtainable from their own national YHA. Maximum stay is eight nights. Prices are between 1,200 and 3,000 Esc. per person per day (including sheets and breakfast).

Youth hostel places can be booked in advance at the central YHA office in Lisbon. In summer this is highly recommended:

Reservations

Associação Portuguesa de Pousada de Juventude
Avenida Duque de Ávila 137, 1000 Lisbon; tel. (21) 3559081, fax (21) 3528621

Youth Hostels

Pousada de Juventude de Alcoutim
8970 Alcoutim; tel./fax (281) 546004

Pousada de Juventude de Lagos
Rue de Lancerote de Freitas 50, 8600 Lagos; tel./fax (282) 761970

Pousada de Juventude de Portimão
Lugar do Coca Maravilhas, 8500 Portimão; tel./fax (282) 491804

Pousada de Juventude de Vila Real de Santo António
Rua Dr. Sousa Martins 40, 8900 Vila Real de Santo António;
tel./fax (281) 544565

Index

Source of Illustrations

Front cover: International Photobank
Back cover: AA Photo Library (P Wilson)

Archiv für Kunst und Geschichte: 30, 36
Bildagentur Schapowalow: 5, 146
Bildagentur Schuster: 7 (bottom left), 44, 107, 125
Borowski: 6 (x2), 12, 25, 26, 56, 59, 61, 72, 74, 77, 79, 81, 83, 85, 89 (left), 94, 106, 116, 118, 119, 129, 132, 138, 139, 144, 153, 189, 193
Fotoagentur Helga Lade: 8, 14 (top), 17, 23, 42, 135, 162, 170, 186
Friedrichsmeier: 112, 113
HB Verlag, Hamburg: 150, 161
Historia-Photo: 35, 37
IFA-Bilderteam: 6, 21, 50/1, 55, 98, 120, 121, 168
Missler: 3 (x2), 7 (top), 7 (bottom right), 16 (x2), 40, 67, 69, 86, 89 (right), 91, 93, 96, 103 (x2), 114, 130, 137, 141, 143, 181 (x2), 151

Imprint

87 photographs, 17 maps and plans, 1 large region map

German text: Dr Eva Missler

Editorial work: Baedeker-Redaktion (Birgit Borowski)
Consultation: Hans-Georg Becker

General direction: Rainer Eisenschmid, Baedeker Ostfildern

Cartography: Franz Huber, München; Mairs Geographischer Verlag
(large fold-out map)

Editorial work English edition: g-and-w PUBLISHING

English translation: Wendy Bell, David Cocking, Brenda Ferris

2nd English edition 2001
Reprinted 2002

© Baedeker Ostfildern
Original German edition 2000

© Automobile Association Developments Limited 2002
English language edition worldwide

Published by AA Publishing, a trading name of Automobile Association
Developments Limited, whose registered office is Millstream,
Maidenhead Road, Windsor, Berkshire SL4 5GD. Registered number
1878835.

Distributed in the United States and Canada by:
Fodor's Travel Publications, Inc
201 East 50th Street
New York, NY 10022

A CIP catalogue record of this book is available from the British Library.

Licensed user: Mairs Geographischer Verlag GmbH & Co., Ostfildern

Typeset by Fakenham Photosetting Limited, Fakenham, Norfolk, UK

Printed in Italy by G. Canale & C. S.p.A., Turin

ISBN 0 7495 2961 X

Principal Sights

★★
Carvoeiro: Algar Seco
Faro
Lagos
   Ponta da Piedade
Portimão: Ferragudo

★
Albufeira
   Praia da Falésia
Alcoutim
Almansil
   Igreja de São Lourenço
   Quinta do Lago
   Vale do Lobo
Alte
   Salir
   Rocha da Pena
Armação de Pêra
   Ermida de N. S. da Rocha
Castro Marim
Estói
Faro
   Praia de Faro
Lagos

★★
Sagres
   Cabo de São Vicente
Serra de Monchique
   Fóia
Silves

★
Loulé
Monchique
   Caldas de Monchique
Olhão
   Quinta de Marim/
   Parque Natural da
   Ria Formosa
   Farol, Culatra, Armona
Praia da Rocha
Sagres
Tavira
   Ilha de Tavira
Vila do Bispo
   Ermida de N.S. de
   Guadelupe
Vila Real de Santo António
   Cacela Velha

The places listed above are merely a selection of the principal places of interest in themselves, or for attractions in the surrounding area. There are many other places worth visiting, to which attention is drawn by one or two stars.

Tavira. Destination Portugal. Vila Gale. 4☆

Twin £25 pppn.   Own web site twin 82€ prpn.

Notes

Notes